TELL ABOUT NIGHT FLOWERS

Tell about Night Flowers

Eudora Welty's Gardening Letters, 1940–1949

For Susan Klaus

Selected and edited by Julia Eichelberger

Enjoy!

J. Eichelberger

UNIVERSITY PRESS OF MISSISSIPPI   JACKSON

www.upress.state.ms.us

The University Press of Mississippi is a member
of the Association of American University Presses.

Images and letters from the Eudora Welty Collection housed in
the Mississippi Department of Archives and History reprinted
by the permission of Eudora Welty, LLC, copyright © 1940–1949
Eudora Welty.

Letters from Diarmuid Russell to Eudora Welty reprinted by permission of Pamela Russell Jessup, copyright © Diarmuid Russell.
Letters from John Robinson to Eudora Welty reprinted by
permission of Michael Robinson, copyright © John Fraiser
Robinson.

First printing 2013 ∞

Library of Congress Cataloging-in-Publication Data
Welty, Eudora, 1909–2001.
  [Correspondence. Selections]
  Tell about night flowers : Eudora Welty's gardening letters, 1940–
1949 / selected and edited by Julia Eichelberger.
     pages cm
  Includes bibliographical references and index.
  ISBN 978-1-61703-187-8 (cloth : alk. paper) — ISBN 978-1-61703-
188-5 (ebook) 1. Welty, Eudora, 1909–2001—Knowledge—Gar-
dening. 2. Welty, Eudora, 1909–2001—Correspondence. 3. Au-
thors, American—20th century—Correspondence. 4. Russell,
Diarmuid, d. 1973—Correspondence. 5. Robinson, John, 1909–
1989—Correspondence. I. Eichelberger, Julia, 1959– editor of
compilation. II. Title.
  PS3545.E6Z48 2013
   816'.52—dc23   2012044738
British Library Cataloging-in-Publication Data available

In memoriam:
Hugh L. Eichelberger, Jr. 1934–2007
Elizabeth Welty Thompson 1944–2012
Noel Polk 1943–2012

Now and then an image comes in my head, or maybe it is a dream, of some one bringing cupped hands together and holding something safely. She is just an intent figure in a blowing wind. Perhaps she holds the key to the joy and tenderness that people dream of giving or finding but cannot give, or simply some little flower. You might imagine her too.

—Eudora Welty to Diarmuid Russell, June 26, 1942

CONTENTS

CONTENTS

ACKNOWLEDGMENTS

This work would not have been possible without the support and generosity of Eudora Welty's nieces, Mary Alice Welty White and the late Elizabeth Welty Thompson. I am very grateful to them for trusting me with this project, and I thank Mary Alice for meeting with me and sharing family photographs. I regret very much that the book was not finished in time for Liz to see it. I'm also grateful to Pamela Russell Jessup for permission to quote from her father's letters, and to John Robinson's nephew, Michael Robinson—first for his assistance in preserving and returning to Welty the letters he found in a trunk under the Robinson home, and then for sharing his memories of his uncle and granting permission to quote from his letters.

I am also particularly indebted to Suzanne Marrs. She has shared her expertise on Welty's life and the Eudora Welty Collection, not only through her books, but also in person on many occasions, and has provided encouragement and advice whenever I asked, at every stage of this project. I gratefully acknowledge the many kinds of help I have received from Tim Seldes, Joy Azmitia, and others at Russell & Volkening. I'm also grateful for the professionalism and expertise of Forrest Galey and the staff at the Mississippi Department of Archives and History; of Leila Salisbury, Valerie Jones, Anne Stascavage, Carol Cox, John Langston, and the University Press of Mississippi; of Karen Redhead, Katie Hamm, and the staff at the Eudora Welty House; to Peggy Prenshaw and Noel Polk for their reviews of the manuscript; and to Patti Carr Black for talking with me about Welty and her letters. For information on Welty's life and career, I am also indebted to the published work of Michael Kreyling, Harriet Pollack, Peggy Prenshaw, and Patti Carr Black; likewise, I would have been lost without the bibliographical work done by Bethany Swearingen, Suzanne Marrs, and Noel Polk. I also wish to thank the members of the Eudora Welty Society for their ongoing interest in this project and for all that they have taught me about Welty. Of course, any errors in this book are mine alone.

The College of Charleston has provided much support as I worked on this book. I appreciate the efforts of our library in securing inter-library loan requests, and I thank the Faculty Research and Development Committee and the School of Humanities and Social Sciences for the grants they have awarded this project. I also wish to thank the Graduate School of the College of Charleston for supporting three very helpful graduate research assistants, Maggie McMenamin, Will Murray, and Dana Woodcock, who worked with me during several semesters. Thanks to grants from the College of Charleston's Office of Undergraduate Research and Creative Activities, two undergraduates were able to speed my progress in Charleston and at the archive in Mississippi. Rachel Reinke worked with me on a trip to Jackson in a very cold week in January, and Crystal Frost assisted me ably during an unbelievably hot week in August. Rachel's research skills contributed to conference papers that advanced my progress on this book, and Crystal's diligence, acuity, and wit were indispensable during the summer she and I worked together, deciding which letters to include, proofing transcriptions, and researching hundreds of factual questions. The Department of English has helped to fund my travel, and my colleagues have provided much advice and encouragement. I've been fortunate to be able to discuss the project with Trish Ward, Susan Farrell, and Joe Kelly; I've received valuable feedback on work in progress from Mike Duvall and from Scott Peeples, who was of particular help as I was revising the introduction.

I also wish to thank my mother, Priscilla Eichelberger, and my husband, Roy Hutchinson, for accompanying me on some of my Mississippi trips and for helping me proof transcriptions. I thank our children, Ben and Sara Hutchinson, for their help with transcription and research, and Robert and Lucy Phillips for their hospitality during Mississippi visits. My friend and former colleague Carolyn Russell has been especially generous in transcribing many letters, reading a draft of the entire manuscript, and helping me to verify dates for the appendix. For all those who have remained enthusiastic about this project and cheered me on as months turned into years, I am more than grateful.

Gardener, Friend, and Artist

Eudora Welty (1909–2001) is an acknowledged master of the short story form. For over fifty years, such Welty stories as "Why I Live at the P.O.," "A Worn Path," "Petrified Man," and "Livvie" have appeared in anthologies and textbooks treating short fiction, literature by women, American literature, and literature of the U.S. South. Welty's novels, memoir, and essays are also widely acclaimed. In 1999 she became the first living writer to be published in the Library of America series, alongside Hawthorne, Melville, Faulkner, and other giants of American fiction. Welty is admired for her detailed and affectionate portraits of Mississippi families and communities, and is also recognized as an astute social critic and superb stylist. Her prose eloquently reveals the inner lives of individual characters, allowing readers to glimpse the private disappointments, passions, and dreams that other characters may never perceive. Each of Welty's works was an occasion for artistic innovation, for a new approach to point of view, narrative structure, setting, or genre.

Like her published writing, Welty's remarkable letters are vivid and multilayered, sometimes humorous and sometimes poignant, rich and evocative as poetry. For this book I have selected and excerpted letters that allow readers to glimpse Welty's life as a gardener and as a friend to Diarmuid Russell and John Robinson, fellow gardeners who were also her first readers in the 1940s. These letters' discussions of planting and pruning, changing seasons, and natural scenery are delightful in themselves, and are also metaphoric expressions of Welty's affection for her friends and her anxieties and ambitions for her art. Taken together, they form a story of their own, that of Welty's artistic development in the 1940s.

During this decade, when Welty went from being a relatively unknown writer to an acclaimed author of five books, Russell and Robinson were two of the most important people in her life. Diarmuid Russell

(1902–1973) was Welty's literary agent and a lifelong friend; on her trips to New York, Welty frequently stayed with the Russell family. A tireless and effective advocate for Welty's writing in the literary marketplace, Russell also provided Welty with advice on the fiction she was writing, encouraging her as she began to create longer, more ambitious texts. Another reader Welty relied upon, John Robinson (1909–1989), had been part of Welty's circle of friends since high school, and by the 1940s, their friendship had become a romantic one. Just as Welty's writing career was gaining momentum in the early forties, Robinson was drafted; the couple wrote often while he was overseas. After the war, when Robinson moved away from Jackson, they were often in touch by letter as well. Welty encouraged Robinson's own writing career, and he published a few stories in the late forties, one dedicated to Welty. Their romance eventually ended, although the friendship endured; in the 1950s, Robinson moved to Italy, spending the rest of his life with an Italian man, Enzo Rocchigiani. Welty's connection to Robinson in the forties inspired several of her best-known works, especially those set in the region Robinson's family came from, the Mississippi Delta.

Because almost all of Welty's letters to Russell and Robinson contain some mention of gardening or a related subject, they provide a wealth of information on Welty's gardening practices during the forties, when her family's garden was in its heyday. At 1119 Pinehurst Street in Jackson, Welty and her mother, Chestina, cultivated flowers, shrubs, and some fruits and vegetables. Welty loved bulbs and enjoyed searching for new varieties in commercial catalogues and in the *Mississippi Market Bulletin*, where Mississippi residents advertised bulbs to sell or trade from their rural gardens. In the Weltys' suburban neighborhood, mice, insects, neighboring children, and birds sometimes thwarted the gardeners' efforts, as Welty reported to Robinson in April 1944: "All around the rose beds we have strawberries and have daily races and fights with the birds to see who gets each berry. Mother indignantly ate a little half-bowl for bkfst this morning" (4.17.44).[1] Winters in Mississippi could alternate between mild days and sudden freezes that threatened the tender buds of Welty's beloved camellias. In an early 1942 letter, she described a freeze to Russell, writing, "If you could see the camellia bushes in the yards your heart would go out to them for the indignities they are suffering—just as they were prepared to shine forth all in bloom people have run out and covered them from top to bottom—just in anything—stakes are driven round them and then carpeting, dish pans, curtains, flowered cretonne, blankets and old sheets are put on them" (1.7.42). Welty's letters also document her struggle with the poor soil of their Belhaven neighborhood; she told Russell that, during a period of drought, "all we do is against the concrete earth—it makes spading and digging real labor, no matter how we water and try to soften the clayey ground" (12.4.42).

The horticultural information in her letters is enhanced, of course, by Welty's superb descriptions. She provides vivid detail about plants, as in this letter to Robinson: "Today a big beautiful amaryllis opened many flowers—the white kind with pale pink lines, and rose stamens with gold hoods on them, and the most delicious fragrance, like a cool magical something you could drink—" (9.1.43). As lyrically as she does in her fiction, Welty conveys her impressions of the weather and atmosphere: "it was like a spell, silver to look at, rain in every breath of the atmosphere, on every leaf and blade of grass, but not falling—when you took a walk it was quiet and still, the tree trunks seemed luminous, and violets were cool and filled with weight in their heads when you picked them—" (12.12.41).

Welty's descriptions often suggest that for her, the natural world was both a physical and a spiritual phenomenon. As she told Russell in a 1941 letter, the garden held more than the plants she tended; it connected her to some vast, transcendent reality. "Every evening when the sun is going down and it is cool enough to water the garden," she wrote Russell, "and it is all quiet except for the locusts in great waves of sound, and I stand still in one place for a long time putting water on the plants, I feel something new—that is all I can say—as if my will went out of me, as if I had a stubbornness and it was melting." Many gardeners can identify with the mystical feeling Welty described:

> when I feel without ceasing every change in the garden itself, the changes of light as the atmosphere grows darker, and the springing up of a wind, and the rhythm of the locusts, and the colors of certain flowers that become very moving—they all seem to be a part of some happiness or unhappiness, an unhappiness that something is lost or left unknown or undone perhaps—and no longer simple in their own beautiful but *outward* way. (8.28.41)

In another letter, Welty told Russell, "I was born with the feeling that if time and hurry were forgotten, something quiet and wonderful would happen in their place. Maybe because on summer nights in deep content and quiet, lying on the grass, unhurried and so in deepest waiting, that is when you see the shooting stars, and the touch is almost made between the sky and the earth" (6.26.42). For Welty, gardens and other natural settings were particularly conducive to this posture of supreme attention, of "deepest waiting."

Welty characterized her experiences with literature in similarly mystical terms. In another 1941 letter to Russell, Welty describes herself as a college student, encountering the works of the Irish poet A.E. (George Russell, who was Diarmuid Russell's father). Her description sounds much like her account, a month earlier, of watering her garden—an intimate, even sensual encounter. Reading A.E.'s poetry, she told Russell, was

> a little like first waiting on a shore and then being enveloped in a sea, not being struck violently by a wave, never a shock—and it was the same every day, a tender and firm and passionate experience that I felt in all my ignorance but with a kind of understanding. I would read every afternoon, hurry to read, it was the thing the day led to. What you look for in the world is not simply for what you want to know, but for more than you want to know, and more than you can know, better than you had wished for, and sometimes something draws you to a discovery and there is no other happiness quite the same. (9.30.41)

This was the kind of joy and communion Welty hoped her own fiction would produce; as she had told Russell a year earlier, "to communicate is the hope and purpose and the impulse and the result and the test and value of all that is written and done at all, and if that little spark does not come, and with a little sheltering, flash back and forth, then it's the same as being left confined within ourselves just when we wished most to reach out and touch the surrounding life that seemed so wonderful in some way" (11.5.40). Her mystical experiences in the garden were another version of this narrative, another story of a mind extending beyond its own subjectivity and connecting with something much greater. Friendship and art, for Welty, were like her garden in that both could reveal a similarly transcendent reality.

Through these letters' discussions of gardens and Nature, we can better understand how Welty's rich literary texts came to be. During this period, her fiction evolved from shorter, more straightforward stories with numerous external incidents, like "Why I Live at the P.O." or "A Worn Path," to longer, more meditative texts with multiple points of view, in which the most important "events" were interior. In her letters about gardening, Welty was also discussing her literary work in progress: innovative forms that she developed slowly, in a process similar to the cultivation of a garden. Welty wrote Russell in 1941, "I planted 4 seeds the other day, and in 4 or 5 years I can see what I've got—they never run true to seed and may be any kind of marvelous new thing" (9.30.41). Welty could have said the same thing about her stories and novels, for they gradually revealed their true identity to her as they were being written, much as a plant slowly reveals its appearance while the gardener helps it reach its full growth.

Welty was sometimes anxious that a new literary work might not succeed, and her discussions of gardening and Nature seem to have provided her with a coded reassurance. Her letters often mentioned troublesome stories alongside her discussions of strange or delicate plants that she hoped would succeed in her garden. In the winter of 1941, for example, after referring to a story she had sent to Russell that he felt needed more revision, she then mentioned the health of a gardenia she had sent him earlier. "I feel that I have let you down, both in my story and in the little gardenia which will not bloom. I asked the old man that runs the greenhouse here what to do about gardenias and he said 'Wait! Wait'—I knew that, but it was supposed to bloom in winter. It may yet" (1.18.41). At other times, Welty's sense of increasing possibilities for her fiction coincided with her excitement about her gardening. She wrote Russell in early 1942:

> After some more stories accumulate we can see how they do and what combination would be the best for a book. So far no one-act plays or anything have entered to throw things off but something may at any time, for I feel the way you feel always in spring, as if it might be possible to go in some place that is different, by a different way, and as if it would be easy to be far away and doing something spacious and free. People from the country are in the markets selling their jonquils and hyacinths, that are blooming before ours, and I long to speak out and ask them things. (2.9.42)

While she was writing these letters, Welty was probably not always conscious of connections between gardening and writing; they simply unfolded as she composed. "Is that sale of the book good?" she asked Russell in November of 1942, surprised by the success of *The Robber Bridegroom*. Two sentences later, Welty was talking about something different. Or perhaps she wasn't.

> It [the sales figure] seems more than I imagined, but my imagining was vague. I just cleaned out montbretia bulbs from a bed, and used to think spider lilies multiplied fast. Ha—from a space 4 ft. long I took up by count (it's a long Sunday) 986 montbretia bulbs, not counting those I didn't get. If things can be said to petrify, what this dirt did was to bulbify. Each one sends out long rays of root like a star, and each star end becomes a bulb, and then sends out its own rays, a whole universe down there. (11.22.42)

By the end of the passage, Welty's wry account of a gardening chore has attained mythic proportions, its apparent offhandedness making it all the more intriguing.

As a letter writer, Welty often changed the subject, moving from gardening to other topics and back again. Part of her letters' charm is their spontaneous, miscellaneous character. It's not unusual for the gardening talk to recur several times during a letter, surprising the reader and perhaps the writer with its ability to link disparate aspects of Welty's experience. Occasionally, a letter seems to begin shaping itself very early, forming a lovely essay in miniature (for example, April 5, 1942, or September 1, 1943). Others begin as a random collection of news and queries, then seem to come into focus just as Welty is signing off, often with some kind of botanical reference, weather report, or description of a natural horizon. Particularly evocative sentences sometimes appear near the end, requiring Welty to use the margin or a PS to complete them. In a 1945 letter to Robinson, Welty had already filled the page with a report on her visit to the Delta, but she managed to write more in the left and top margins: "The water very high—bayous on both sides of the road full and only a blue heron and two owls plus little pigs did I see. From Yazoo where the afternoon sun fell behind on the Delta I looked back and saw it blue like the sea, far as could be seen" (2.13.45). Reaching the end of her space on the page, Welty managed to include a vivid glimpse of a seemingly unending stretch of blue.

Welty's encounters with Nature, which she portrays as mysteriously limitless, are also a figurative account of her own artistic development. The book's title, *Tell about Night Flowers*, comes from a 1942 letter in which Welty tells Russell about watching a flower unfold. Welty had seen "the Calypso daylily opening—it is a night daylily—palest pure yellow, long slender curved petals, the color of the new moon," and she mused on this plant's seemingly magical transformation.

> To see it actually open, the petals letting go, is wonderful, and its night fragrance comes to you all at once like a breath. What makes it open at night—what does it open to? in the same progression as others close, moment by moment. Tell about night flowers. (6.12.42)

Welty was struck by the way the flower bloomed almost secretly, inscrutably, in response to some invisible force. Her description can also be read as an account of the creative process of an artist responding to the "night flowers" of the unconscious mind. The writer's task is to "tell about" these revelations, to translate them into art. In this passage, which Welty wrote as she was running out of space on the page, it seems as if the gardener is offering the artist a whisper of encouragement and urgency: *Tell about night flowers.*

Some of the flowers in Welty's letters were those she saw in dreams, and these plants seem to have been emblems of the beauty Welty wished to create in her fiction. She wrote Russell about an iris she dreamed about that "set people to paint or to dance or to plan structures and systems or to follow after some romantic thing [. . .] . I had the feeling that it could go on giving off images like a fountain, for as long as I could dream it" (4.5.42). The flower, it seemed, could radiate creative power "as long as [she] could dream it"—as long as the artist remained connected to the wellspring of unconscious imagination.

The gardens in Welty's letters also seemed to be the antithesis of war, a refuge from all that war threatened to destroy—new life, stillness, and sheltered realms where living things may flourish.

> My friend John Robinson, of New Orleans, is in the Air Force now and what can I do but think about his life, which is dear to me and close to mine. I know it is the same story everywhere. Six yellow rain lilies opened this morning—they never did bloom in their lives before and while I was weeding they opened right under my

eyes—lovely, clear, and fragrant with a cool fragrance—I took them as a sign. I feel as if I could just *turn into* something that would keep people safe, if I knew how. (8.31.42)

Throughout the war years, Welty associated gardens and growing things with everything that was precious to her, including the life she hoped to share with Robinson on his return. Writing to him in October 1944, Welty described a moment of intense awareness in her garden, coalescing into a wish for him to experience the moment with her: "John—take care—you *have* to be all right—That's all I know but I wish you were here, on this day—so hard—Smelling the sweet air right here in deep breaths—and your eyes on the camellias doing so well—and hear the water running over their roots, the Leila and the Herme—the way it is now—" (10.18.44). The yearning in this letter, filled with dashes and unfinished phrases, seems to reach beyond Robinson to encompass the entire world, "the way it is now."

As the war continued, even Welty's dreams contained plants that expressed her hope for an end to the war and her sadness at the destruction it had wrought. In the spring of 1945, while awaiting the announcement of an end to the war in Europe, she wrote to Robinson:

Yesterday when I was writing to you in the park a vast jimson weed
in the grass was so shining and tall and green and blowing there in
the wind, dancing—it looked beautiful to me—and tears came in
my eyes—and last night I dreamed it was on your hill where you
could see it (I didn't dream you did, just hope still), only many, it was
repeated all along the hill, blowing and bending freely the same, the
same beautiful thing, again and again. (5.1.45)

Now all Welty's hopes were intertwined—hopes for the end of the war, for her own creativity, and for her relationship with Robinson: not simply marriage but a wholehearted emotional connection, with each sharing fully in the life of the other. After Robinson's return, Welty's letters continued to associate the garden with the couple's future, as in early 1946 when she told Russell that she and Robinson had succeeded in grafting new camellias onto the trunks of older shrubs. The human relationship was apparently less successful. In late April Welty told Russell that she had dreamed of a different kind of gardening scene—an animated version of the painting *The Gleaners*, in which the gleaners could not escape from the picture. A month later she was writing Robinson, who had left Jackson, "Sometimes I feel part of something I don't know all of—or its destination—sometimes left, no part. It is all right the not knowing, but not the not being. So fresh and moist early this morning—sometimes the suspense of life rests like a flying bird not pumping its wings. I felt if we could just ride somewhere, not far, but this morning" (5.21.46).

Distressed by Robinson's unease and lack of direction, Welty urged him to seek out a life that made him happy, even if this took him away from her. Writing, she believed, could bring fulfillment to him, and therefore to her. She told Robinson that writing can transform and heal, enabling the writer to "feel things highly and even more than you knew you might, and they reveal themselves to you in a way that gives some pain too, but in the work something is resolved, and let go" (8.17.46). Robinson's artistic ability and ambition, however, were insufficient for this transformation. At some level Welty must have sensed this, for her letters to Robinson seemed at times to be diminishing her own gifts in order to make his seem greater. She wrote of being "so pleased over it when you approve that it's just as if the *story* got better [. . .] when you like it I have the feeling that what I *meant* to do came through—you supply the rest in the reading" (10.28.46). Welty sometimes closed her letters to Robinson with scenes of misty gardens or tranquil fields, as she had done during the years they were separated by war. Now attempting to span an emotional as well as physical distance, Welty's scenes evoked a transcendent realm in which she felt joined to Robinson, as in this 1948 letter:

> I rode out in the country—it had been a cold damp day—about 5 o'clock the light broke out all over the fields. The gravel roads out Old Canton Road Way—they were a bit muddy, made a little sound riding over—the hills in deep flowers and pink grass, and then the haystacks—bitterweed and goldenrod and coreopsis, the willow trees turning, a persimmon tree hanging full—a fresh wild scent coming out of everything. The fields brighter than the sky, all lovely and slanting and the near trees hanging drops and bright.
>
> Love, and goodnight to you—thanks for reading my story with all your goodness and knowing—and the undeserved praise too I cherish—Who else has you to see, always has? How else could I?
> Yours,
> E (9.30.48)

In her tender and poetic letters to Robinson, Welty seems to have been describing the relationship she hoped for, rather than the one she had. She was aware that all was not well, that her encouragement was not enough to cure Robinson's discontent. Respectful of Robinson's apparent need for solitude, she often traveled with other friends in the late forties, and planned a 1949 trip to Europe on her own. But the possibility, however vague, of some kind of romantic connection with him remained until the early fifties, when Welty became aware that Robinson was romantically involved with Enzo Rocchigiani, an Italian man in his early twenties. Robinson soon relocated to Europe, where he spent the rest of his career working for the army's continuing education program, remaining with Rocchigiani the rest of his life.

Readers who are saddened by the way Welty's romance ended may feel unsure what to make of the loving letters she sent to Robinson. Her letters to Diarmuid Russell clearly conveyed Welty's delight in their friendship; her reports from the garden, much like the actual flowers and plants she sometimes sent, affirmed Welty's trust in Russell as her friend, first reader, and advocate for her art. But what was she affirming when she described gardens and sunsets for Robinson, a man who could not fully return her love, whom she thanked for his "undeserved praise"? Because Welty's apparent self-doubt seems unfounded, it is tempting to regard her relationship with Robinson as a hindrance to her artistic development. However, Welty also expressed such anxieties to Russell, with whom she enjoyed a feeling of complete trust and security. A year into their friendship, after Russell had already sold her first collection, Welty expressed dissatisfaction with her new stories, writing, "I have been in a misery lately, for the desire to make a story do something it cannot do, or at least mine cannot, and the great care I felt simply laid a heavy burden on me, it weighted down my heart and I couldn't do anything, I wanted so to write these exact, perfect, magic stories I could just see" (5.41). Confiding in a friend she trusted completely, telling him what she hoped to accomplish in her art, Welty expressed doubts, but also considerable ambition. She told Russell in June 1942, "Maybe some day I will write a story of the imagination that will really do what I hope, really be an incantation to make what I feel or have delight in come alive." In this letter, describing her own preference for "magic things" over "clever things," she was both modest and hopeful, saying, "I am not magic but my heart lives in that country" (6.8.42). Welty's desire to perform "magic" was similar to her desire to protect loved ones from the war—a wish, as she had written to Russell, to "just *turn into* something that would keep people safe, if I knew how."

The gardening scenes and natural landscapes that marked Welty's letters to Robinson can also be seen as "incantations," Welty's attempts to create a portal to their ultimate union. These moments that Welty shared with Robinson, scenes of an expansive horizon or a moonlit garden, evoke the feeling that she had described to Russell earlier, of "melting" into an intense awareness of the garden's colors, movement, and sound, until "the identity of the garden itself is lost." In 1946 she wrote Robinson:

> The most beautiful night sky—full moon and racing clouds—the clouds pure white and long and traveling fast, north from the southwest—brilliant dark-blue sky in between—the planets bright and full-looking too, in and out—The air fresh, leaves on the trees stirring, flying—shadows in all kinds of agitation—all bright everywhere— makes you *look back* at it—the world, to come in a house—Those moments when you are without the name of where you are—just on the surface of the world—under that star [. . .] . (11.10.46)

These descriptions did not connect Welty with Robinson as she hoped; instead, they would eventually acquire a different meaning and power. They forecast friendships that were still to come; they were fragments of stories she had yet to write.

Over the course of this decade, Welty's gardening language and gardener's worldview had collaborated with the artist, bringing details to her attention, reminding her of the long process necessary for a work to be completed, and surprising her with unexpected new growth. For all the uncertainty Welty felt about her work throughout the 1940s, in hindsight it's clear that her fiction had evolved in exciting ways during this decade. Each book contained new surprises—the wild spirit of *The Robber Bridegroom*, the slower-paced, ambitious explorations of characters in *The Wide Net*, the "Delta story" that could not be told fully until it became a novel, and finally, the network of connections in *The Golden Apples*, which continued to surprise and please the writer over the three years she spent writing and revising the story cycle. By 1949 Welty was far from incapable of the art she hoped for; she was at the height of her powers. *The Golden Apples* turned out to be more ambitious than Welty would have predicted, with interrelations that revealed themselves to her as she wrote. As Welty explained years later, she did not invent, but discovered them, the way a gardener might learn what kind of bulb she has planted. "From story to story, connections between the characters' lives, through their motives or actions, sometimes their dreams, already existed: there to be found," she wrote.[2]

The characters Welty created in *The Golden Apples* are confined by the expectations of their small community, Morgana, which "only hoped to place them, in their hour or their street or the name of their mothers' people. Then Morgana could hold them, and at last they were this and they were that" (394). Morgana's expectations and traditions range from family and community norms to larger historical forces, even myth and legend, and they extend and intertwine across seven stories and beyond Mississippi, following characters for generations. In a few delightful moments in Welty's cycle, some characters—often children, such as Loch, Virgie, and the grandchildren of King MacLain—resist these imprisoning conditions through small transgressions, but Morgana's and Mississippi's social structures seem as firmly established when the cycle ends, in the 1940s, as they were in 1904 when it began. With the recent disappearance of much of Morgan's Woods to logging companies, the outward conditions of Morgana seem increasingly deadening at the end of the cycle.

Yet the stories also reveal another realm of existence, in scenes that are much like the moments of ecstatic communion that Welty had described to Russell and tried to evoke for Robinson. "Sir Rabbit" ends with Mattie Will seeing "the drift of it all, the stretched land below the little hills, and the Big Black, clear to MacLain's Courthouse, almost, the Stark place plain and the fields, and their farm, everybody's house above trees [. . .] . And Morgana all in rays, like a giant sunflower in the dust of Saturday" (411). In "The Wanderers," Virgie recalls how, as a teenager, coming back home to Morgana in apparent disgrace, she experienced a moment of joy so powerful that it has returned to her years later:

> For that journey, it was ripe afternoon, and all about her was that
> light in which the earth seems to come into its own, as if there would
> be no more days, only this day—when fields glow like deep pools and
> the expanding trees at their edges seem almost to open, like lilies,
> golden or dark. She had always loved that time of day, but now, alone,
> untouched now, she felt like dancing; knowing herself not really, in

her essence, yet hurt; and thus happy. The chorus of crickets was as unprogressing and out of time as the twinkling of a star. (546)

Through these scenes, the *Golden Apples* stories resolve the conflict they have depicted, not through the events of the plot, but through a visionary moment that suggests a realm apart from Morgana's status quo.

In these scenes in Welty's letters, then, we can recognize nascent versions of scenes she had not yet planned to write. Just as Welty's stories in the late forties turned out to be about characters different from those she began writing about, her letters to Robinson, expressing her hopes for their continued life together, proved to be part of a different story. The kind of happiness Welty had once imagined sharing with Robinson—"those moments when you are without the name of where you are"—now appeared in her fiction.

[Virgie] knew that now at the river, where she had been before on moonlit nights in autumn, drunken and sleepless, mist lay on the water and filled the trees, and from the eyes to the moon would be a cone, a long silent horn, of white light. It was a connection visible as the hair is in air, between the self and the moon, to make the self feel the child, a daughter far, far back. Then the water, warmer than the night air or the self that might be suddenly cold, like any other arms, took the body under too, running without visibility into the mouth. As she would drift in the river, too alert, too insolent in her heart in those days, the mist might thin momentarily and brilliant jewel eyes would look out from the water-line and the bank. Sometimes in the weeds a lightning bug would lighten, on and off, on and off, for as long in the night as she was there to see. (547–48)

Scenes such as these contain all the fulfillment suggested in the natural scenes from Welty's earlier letters. Nature and the subjective consciousness become one, bringing a contentment that is both spiritual and sensual, a connection that is flickering and endlessly flowing. Welty's letters to Robinson, intended to deepen his connection with her, were rehearsals for another kind of joy—for the fulfillment Welty could celebrate and foster in her art. In her fiction, characters unite wholly with the present moment, no longer imprisoned by their past. Virgie experiences this liberation during her swim in the Big Black River, as she feels the river sand

and the grasses "touch her and leave her, like suggestions of some bondage that might have been dear, now dismembering and losing itself." Like Welty who, in 1941, felt that "my will went out of me" while standing in her garden, Virgie is "aware but only of the nebulous edges of her feeling and the vanishing opacity of her will" (530–31).

Welty's 1940s letters, read alongside these splendid moments in her fiction, show us how well the gardener's sensibility served the ambitions of the artist. Just as a flower's beauty depends partly on its transient nature, Welty's fiction celebrates that which is inherently impermanent. The "magic" of her art is in the way it makes that which is fleeting more real to us as we read about it—the writer restores to the reader something we have already lost, showing us how to love it more. This was what she spoke of in her early letters to Russell, just after the United States entered the war: "I don't know what I will write next, but I wish it would be something that could make an individual and tender life when seen alone seem sacred and inviolate from all beastliness and violence that besets it" (12.23.41). As she told Robinson in 1944, what was most important would continue to be "the little, personal, everyday things—a personal matter, individual—I cherish that still and always—*Moments* will count, still, then—and be magical and colored, good and bad, as some little thing makes it—War and peace do not change that, do they? Not any sheltered thing will seem to have been lost—that is my hope—" (7.13.44). Thus the artist's modest and ambitious wish: to preserve forever "some little thing" which cannot last.

Welty's earlier anxieties over her lack of "magical" artistic powers seem to have dissolved by late 1949. Her next work of fiction, "Circe" (originally titled "Put Me in the Sky!"), was told from the point of view of the goddess who could transform men into whatever she wished them to be. But in this version of the myth, the goddess looks with envy upon mortals. "I know they keep something from me, asleep and awake," Circe muses. "There exists a mortal mystery, that, if I knew where it was, I could crush like an island grape. Only frailty, it seems, can divine it—and I was not endowed with that property" (641–42). Welty's goddess senses that her divine powers bar her from another sort of agency, whose value she cannot dismiss. Circe says of the human beings she can control so easily:

They live by frailty! By the moment! I tell myself that it is only a mystery, and mystery is only uncertainty. (There is no mystery in magic!

Men are swine; let it be said, and no sooner said than done.) Yet mortals alone can divine where it lies in each other, can find it and prick it in all its peril, with an instrument made of air. I swear that only to possess that one, trifling secret, I would willingly turn myself into a harmless dove for the rest of eternity! (642)

Human art—particularly speech and language, "an instrument made of air"—can "divine" this transient glory, something the immortal Circe will never do.

In the last letter included in this book, Welty recorded her enjoyment of her first transatlantic voyage. Writing to Russell as she crossed the ocean, Welty reported, "I like the people, but have all the peace and privacy I want [. . .] . It's warm here up on deck—Love to all, Eudora" (10.21.49). Like the solitary Virgie Rainey, who ended *The Golden Apples* by taking leave of Morgana, Welty was savoring a seemingly limitless horizon and looking forward to more transformations. After landing in Italy in the fall of 1949, she took a tour of Europe that lasted over eight months, meeting up with old friends and making new ones along the way. In 1950 Welty and other friends from the States explored Italy with Robinson, who had received a Fulbright fellowship to study in Florence. As enjoyable as these travels were, Welty's relationship with Robinson had already become less important to her than it had once been. She was delighted to be traveling so freely; in 1948 she had told Russell that she hated "a plan ahead that ties me down. [. . .] Why can't people, friends, move freely and meet by delightful surprise and chance, and not make plans?" (4.12.48).

Welty's career continued to flourish after the 1940s. In the next decade she published numerous essays, a short novel, *The Ponder Heart* (1954), and a collection of stories, several of them inspired by her European travels (*The Bride of the Innisfallen*, 1955). She had become so acclaimed that her Jackson friend Charlotte Capers asked her to begin donating her papers to the Mississippi Department of Archives and History, where Capers was director. Welty's writing pace slowed in the late fifties and sixties, when more of her energies went toward caring for family members and less to her own work. Her brother Walter died in 1959, leaving a wife and two young daughters to whom Welty was devoted. By 1960 Welty's mother needed constant care; Welty had little time to complete the long novel she had been working on since the 1950s. In 1966 her mother and then her remaining brother, Edward, died within a few days of each other. In the wake of these losses, Welty began a story based partly on her mother's life, which became *The Optimist's Daughter* (1972); an earlier version of that book had filled an entire issue of the *New Yorker* in 1969. Her long novel, *Losing Battles*, was finally published in 1970. Other publications included her *Collected Stories* in 1980, her 1984 memoir, *One Writer's Beginnings*, which was a best seller, and several books of her photographs. By the time of her death in 2001, Welty had received dozens of awards and honorary degrees.

Welty's personal life had been extraordinarily rich in friendships, many of them sustained by letters. In addition to Diarmuid Russell, Welty kept up an extensive lifelong correspondence with Frank Lyell, Mary Lou Aswell, and two friends she made in the 1950s, William Maxwell and Reynolds Price; these are only a handful among the hundreds of people to whom Welty wrote.[3] Her correspondence with Robinson decreased after the early 1950s, but they continued to write and visit each other periodically, remaining friends until Robinson's death in 1989. Most of Welty's correspondence with Russell was preserved in the files of the Russell & Volkening agency, then returned to Welty when Russell retired. Robinson managed to preserve a huge number of Welty's letters to him, even though he was traveling and moving frequently in the 1940s. In 1983, a trunk containing these letters was found in a storage area under the Robinson family home in Jackson. Robinson, who had been living abroad for more than thirty years, made sure the letters were returned to Welty. His nephew, Michael Robinson, recalls that he "put them in a garbage bag and took them to Eudora. There must have been hundreds of them."[4]

The 1940s letters Robinson wrote to Welty, however, are gone. Sometime after this decade, Welty destroyed them, except for two—one 1943 letter about the invasion of Sicily, and another from 1948 that may have been simply misplaced. Welty probably had several reasons for keeping Russell's letters and getting rid of Robinson's. She talked to a friend, Patti Black, about destroying the Robinson letters after the fact and did not disclose her reasons. Perhaps Welty had felt Robinson's homosexuality would become more public if his 1940s romantic relationship to Welty became more widely known. Black believes Welty wanted to protect Robinson's privacy, even though Robinson probably had not asked to be protected.[5] Not only did Robinson's letters record a romance that had ended; more importantly, Welty did not want anyone except the intended recipient to read *any* of her private letters. Personal exposure of any kind, even revelations that would be flattering to the people involved, seemed abhorrent to her. For a time Welty did not want her correspondence with Russell preserved. Her letters to him, along with many carbons of his letters to her, were returned to her in 1973, not long before Russell died. By this time, she may have already destroyed Robinson's letters to her. After Russell gave her their correspondence, Welty told friends that she had wanted to destroy these letters; she said that the idea of other people reading them was "something I shy off from too much to think about."[6]

Fortunately, Welty's friends, including Reynolds Price and another writer, Kenneth Millar, encouraged her to preserve her correspondence. Millar, who wrote mysteries under the name of Ross Macdonald, had become friends with Welty through an exchange of letters motivated by the writers' mutual admiration. They then met by chance when both were visiting New York. Millar was married, although somewhat unhappily, and Welty seems to have respected his wish not to leave his wife; the relationship was carried out primarily through their letters. With Millar, Welty experienced much of the fulfillment that, thirty years earlier, she had been seeking in a partnership with Robinson. She had written Robinson in the 1940s, "I know some things, like some people, or one person, can show us the whole intent of our lives by their rarity that could light up everything that the rest had kept dark—we come under their magnitude and we *know*—and the most passionate hope was not too much" (2.8.44). Such was the bond that she was to form decades later with Kenneth Millar. In 1971, he wrote Welty with similar passion and awe, telling her, "When I got your letter today, something went through me like a vibration of light, as if I had had a responsive echo from a distant star. As if a half-imagined relationship to the great past had come real in my life before my life ended." Even after Millar's Alzheimer's disease made it impossible for him to write her, Welty cherished their connection. "Dear Ken, I have all your letters to keep me company," she wrote in 1982. "Every day of my life I think of you with love."[7]

In her 1984 memoir, *One Writer's Beginnings*, Welty reflected on experiences that had contributed to her fiction. "In writing, as in life," she wrote, "the connections of all sorts of relationships and kinds lie in wait of discovery, and give out their signals to the Geiger counter of the charged imagination" (944). We can now glimpse this charged imagination at work, often when Welty herself was unaware of it, in these letters to Russell and Robinson. Created for her friends alone, they would also become part of another story; they were rehearsals, impromptu preludes, for fiction she had not yet planned to write. Essentially unrevised and unrevisited, preserved almost by accident, they now document a creative imagination working as an advance guard for the conscious mind. As Welty once wrote to Robinson, "We feel so far ahead of what we know" (8.44). She did not know then whether she would achieve what she longed to create in her art, "an incantation to make what I feel or have delight in come alive." In another letter to Russell, one recounting a dream in which she had discovered the plant from which all camellias originated, Welty had concluded, "I would never in my waking moments consider starting back so far" (12.23.41). The art she would create in the future surpassed these conscious expectations. Welty's night flowers helped the gardener's dreams to lodge in the artist's imagination.

EDITORIAL NOTE

The letters in this book come from the Eudora Welty Collection in the Mississippi Department of Archives and History in Jackson, Mississippi. In addition to letters Welty wrote, this collection holds hundreds of letters Diarmuid Russell and John Robinson sent to Welty, and I have quoted from these letters throughout the book; I hope this adds to readers' understanding of these friendships, while also clarifying particular references Welty makes in her letters. The archive houses over 750 letters from Welty to Russell and Robinson written between May 1940 and October 1949. (By my count, there are over 381 letters from this period to Robinson and 376 to Russell.) I have quoted in full or excerpted fewer than half of these letters, and therefore many wonderful letters or portions of letters were omitted in an attempt to create a more readable book. By focusing on Welty's interest in gardening and the natural world, I have tried to highlight the interconnections that exist between this subject, Welty's friendships, and her artistic development.

Although most of the letters in this book are presented without addresses, I identify the correspondents' locations whenever it is not self-evident. Almost all Welty's letters to Russell went to his office in New York City. Her letters to Robinson went to an APO address during the war, and afterwards, to the various places he lived and visited in the late 1940s; I have noted the city if that information was available.

I have silently corrected obvious typographical errors or missing words in these letters, except when the writer commented on the error. An ellipsis surrounded by brackets indicates that part of a letter has been omitted. I have attempted to reproduce Welty's choices regarding paragraph breaks, but for greater readability, I have indented her paragraphs more consistently than she did, have transcribed "&" and "+" uniformly as "and," and have regularized the formatting of her salutations and closings, since Welty's variations often seemed to have been caused by the amount of space remaining on the page.

I have supplied as complete a date as I was able to determine for each letter. I have used a consistent format (month, date, year), unlike Welty, who did not always write a complete date or even the day of the week on her letters. Scholars interested in more detail on each letter quoted, excerpted, or cited in this book should see my appendix. In this chronological listing, I indicate the letter's length, whether it is typed or handwritten, and whether the date I have given comes from the letter or from other evidence.

This book's chapters are preceded by quotations from Welty's "A Curtain of Green" (first published in 1938), "The Wide Net" (1942), "The Winds" (1942), "Some Notes on River Country" (1944), *Delta Wedding* (1946), and "The Wanderers" (first published as "The Hummingbirds," 1949). Chapter five is followed by quotations from "Circe" (first published in 1949 as "Put Me in the Sky!") and "Going to Naples" (1952). All these texts were later revised when Welty published them in book form. My quotations are taken from Welty's revised versions of these works, as published in the Library of America editions of her *Stories, Essays, and Memoir* and *Complete Novels*. Elsewhere in the book, all references to Welty's published works come from these editions unless otherwise noted.

TELL ABOUT NIGHT FLOWERS

It might seem that the extreme fertility of her garden formed at once a preoccupation and a challenge to Mrs. Larkin. Only by ceaseless activity could she cope with the rich blackness of this soil. Only by cutting, separating, thinning, and tying back in the clumps of flowers and bushes and vines could she have kept them from overreaching their boundaries and multiplying out of all reason. The daily summer rains could only increase her vigilance and her already excessive energy. And yet, Mrs. Larkin rarely cut, separated, tied back. . . . To a certain extent, she seemed not to seek for order, but to allow an over-flowering, as if she consciously ventured forever a little farther, a little deeper, into her life in the garden.

She planted every kind of flower that she could find or order from a catalogue—planted thickly and hastily, without stopping to think, without any regard for the ideas that her neighbors might elect in their club as to what constituted an appropriate vista, or an effect of restfulness, or even harmony of color. Just to what end Mrs. Larkin worked so strenuously in her garden, her neighbors could not see.

—"A Curtain of Green," 1938

CHAPTER ONE

May 1940–December 1941

When Welty wrote her first letter to Diarmuid Russell in May of 1940, at the age of thirty-one, she was not famous, but her fiction had been successful enough to attract Russell's attention as he sought clients for his new literary agency. A native of Jackson, Welty had graduated from the University of Wisconsin in 1929 and began studying advertising at Columbia University in 1930. The Depression and her father's 1931 death brought Welty back to her family's home in Jackson, where she found part-time work writing scripts for a local radio station and society columns for the *Memphis Commercial Appeal.* She later worked as a publicity agent for the Works Progress Administration in Mississippi, covering WPA projects throughout the state and bringing her camera along to take unofficial photos of people she met. In 1936 Welty's photographs were exhibited in a small New York gallery, and she began publishing stories in "little magazines." By 1940, her fiction had appeared for three years in a row in the annual *Best Short Stories,* and the editors of the *Southern Review* and other writers had nominated her for awards and tried to help her find a book publisher. Editors from half a dozen major publishing houses had corresponded with Welty by 1940,[1] but they all indicated that authors needed to publish a novel before publishers would consider bringing out a collection of short stories. One of these editors gave Welty's name to Diarmuid Russell, who was starting up a new literary agency. Russell then wrote Welty offering to become her agent, explaining that he had experience with literature both as an editor and as the son of an Irish author, A.E. (George William Russell), a poet Welty greatly admired. Welty replied that it "seemed inevitable" that Russell should become her agent; he soon became her friend as well.

Welty and Russell quickly discovered their mutual love of gardening, and she was soon sending him homegrown gifts—preserves, cut flowers, and live plants and bulbs she wanted him to try in his garden in Katonah, New York—in addition to her work in progress. In the summer and fall of 1940, while Russell tried without success to place her stories in national magazines, he gave Welty his assessment of the stories she sent him, advice that was "something so new to me and of such value," as Welty wrote, "a way to know a few bearings. Is this what was in our contract? I didn't understand it would be so much" (11.5.40). By January 1941 Russell had sold a story to a national magazine and had found a publisher for her first book. Welty's discussions of gardening in this period resonate with her experiences as a friend and as an artist. Writing to Russell about the changing seasons, the plants she and Russell were tending, and her occasional dreams of flowers, Welty was also expressing her gratitude for his friendship and her anxieties and hopes for the fiction she was writing.

1119 Pinehurst St.
Jackson, Mississippi
May 31, 1940

Mr. Diarmuid Russell
Russell & Volkening, Inc.
522 Fifth Avenue
New York City

Dear Mr. Russell,

Thanks for your letter. Yes—be my agent. Just as the letter was given to me, I finished a story, and holding one in each hand, it seemed inevitable. [. . .]² What you think of this one and its chances will interest me very much, and I hope to hear from you soon.

Sincerely yours,
Eudora Welty

Early June 1940³
Dear Mr. Russell,

[. . .] Thanks for telling me what you think of the story.⁴ [. . .] Now I have something hard for you to do. I have a collection—a collection of short stories by an unknown writer who doesn't ever want to write a novel first. They are things I've written in the past year or so, and one trouble you will have is I don't know where they have been. They will throw you out and say "I've already seen these things once!" Ford Madox Ford, at the instigation of Katherine Anne Porter, had almost this same collection.[5] [. . .] Mr. Ford was a very kind person and for all I can be sure he may have shown them to every publisher in New York and that will be the end of it.

Please do not tell me that I will have to write a novel. I do not see why if you enjoy writing short stories and cannot even think in the form of a novel you should be driven away from it and made to slave at something you do not like and do badly. Of course I know nothing about publishing. One publisher wrote me that if he could just get me in a restaurant he could persuade me. What is this?

It is the rainy season now and I shall try to write more stories, as having an agent makes me feel guilty. It looks impossible, getting back stories already sent out. I think they use them for table-napkins, at least for eating Hersheybars.

Sincerely yours,
Eudora Welty

In August of 1940, Welty attended the Bread Loaf Writer's Conference in Vermont. She stopped en route in New York, a city she visited whenever she had the chance, to meet the Russell & Volkening agents in person. Russell and his colleagues Henry Volkening and John Slocum entertained Welty in town, and Welty also met Russell's wife, Rose, and their young daughter, Pamela, at their home in Katonah, New York. By the time Welty returned to Jackson, Russell had written her that someone at Dodd, Mead had expressed some interest in a collection of stories set in Mississippi (9.6.40).

Early September 1940
Dear Diarmuid,

I was so glad to get your other letter, which came on down on the train with me and followed me out to the house at last—and I did feel just a little sad when the train let me off at Jackson that dawn—it had been very splendid, the whole trip—I felt so proud and lucky all the time that you were my agents, and as for having faith in the future of this, it is you who should wonder about that—the stories will be coming to you—because yes, I am inspired now, didn't I tell you—I wonder what the people at Dodd Mead are thinking—All kinds of things and ideas kept coming into my head—I rather hope you will make them let me do it—There are some things about a state that nobody could even know about who has not lived there a long time, and those things should determine the whole approach, don't you think? [. . .] I do wish you could see Mississippi, because I think you might like the things I do about it, the folk quality to the little adventures and stories and the directness and simplicity, really the dignity, in the way they find and hold their beliefs, and the feeling of the legendary and the endurance of something rather wonderful in a way of life, that you get when you see some of the ruins and haunted houses. [. . .] I wonder if Johnny Appleseed came this way— if he did somebody came along behind him, because there aren't any apples—and yet I've heard of him, around—maybe it was a play, written by the Carolina Playmakers? He sounds enchanting and it is good that you are getting him into a book.[6] Such characters are like fountains or spring-water, and should never be allowed to die away and be forgotten—who knows, he might be Apollo or one of them come down to us that way. Did you really bring home some plants from Maine? The only thing I dug up was the Indian Pipe, I thought of sending it to you and remembered you were gone, and then I saw lots more, not rare in the least. It was growing on the very top of a mountain, with a view of Lake Champlain in the distance, there seemed something a little exclusive about it somehow, and I took it. There is something very choosy about digging up plants—you have to have a certain one, absolutely—Do you like those very small jonquils, the true kind, single, round, golden, very delicious to smell—have you got any—I don't believe they are ever sold by nurseries, all I have I've gotten away from old ladies in gardens out in the country—I do like the single, true, original flowers and they keep wanting to sell you extra-large double giant new hybrids—we just had a circular from Robert Wayman[7] of some poppies, "Glamour Girls of the Modern Perennial Border"—Anything that you might think of between now and spring that you might want from here, tell me and I will watch for it—I will remember the bird's-foot violets—All the way across Mississippi through the swamps I had been thinking that first of all I must make some muscadine preserves to send up to you—that is a wild grape that grows in the swamps, a wonderful wild taste—you can't get muscadines except by waiting for somebody to come around to your back door—some little nondescript fellow who whispers, "muscadines?"—but this year they never got over the hard winter—even the little fellows too might have been frozen away—someday I will send you some—it is a sad deprivation, no muscadines—I do like putting up preserves—we make little expeditions to pick wild plums and the like, and so nearly every jar has its little history you see—I'm going to send you all some in the office, but just now I'm in the middle of some watermelon-rind preserves and I'll wait on them—it takes four days—one of those old-fashioned recipes with lots of setting things out in the sun, that made me think of Edward Lear's[8] recipe for Gosky Patties, do you remember, did you ever make any—you put a pig on the roof and visit him and give him a beating every day for 8 days, and if at the end of that time he has not turned into Gosky Patties, then he never will, and you might as well let him go. When they come, the figs are for you—they really are rare and precious this year. You all can have tea some afternoon [. . .]—I wanted to send you something you could have in the house for winter, but I just can't think—I wish you could have one of these little mimosa trees that are coming up—in the house, in a tub, but I'm afraid it's impracti-cal—even if it would ever live for you in a house, it would be the devil to send—so sensitive you know—and a long long taproot, God knows you would hesitate to claim it at the window—it would of course have to be marked SENSITIVE, on all four sides—

Well, I did write a long letter—I hope to send Powerhouse soon, Cleanth Brooks has been sent a little memo,[9] to find it, I bet it's lost—Write to me when you can or when anything happens—

yours

Eudora

Russell told Welty in a September 10 letter that he was sorry he had no good news to report. "Occasionally when I get home I go into a little daydream and send you a cheque for a couple of thousand dollars or so as pin money coming from some story." To Welty's offer to send him a plant, he replied, "The mimosa sounds rather too delicate but I will tell you what I do want and that is a little gardenia bush. Even a cutting will do. I never knew anybody in the South before who would send flowers and if you could get a cutting from a gardenia it would be fine" (9.10.40).

September 13, 1940
Friday
Dear Diarmuid,

The little gardenia is the very thing, I don't know why I couldn't think of that—I got the florist down the street to ship it under his label so it won't be tied up at every stateline for the inspection—You'd better put it in a larger pot, and I do hope it will live and those little buds will come out—I have one that's a good deal bigger in bloom outside—I hope you won't expect these little gardenia bushes ever to grow big and have big blooms like our cape Jessamine, and be disappointed—It's cape jessamines we have in our gardens, but you know they won't live any further north—We used to have a hedge of them ten feet tall, but the cold came and killed them back to the ground last year—so we have these little gardenias to console us. I forgot to say I wrote Katonah on the label, so you wouldn't have to carry a bush out on the millionaire's special, and it ought to be at the express office Monday or Tuesday I should think—let me know if the poor little thing is still alive. If the white fly ever gets on it, spray with nicotine, (though it doesn't do any good, I say). The fringed gentian I would love to see, but I wouldn't have you send a plant down here, because it couldn't live, and it would take away from the place you know. I read in the Garden Encyclopedia about it, have you got that book?[10] It tells about a plan of seeding that you might not have tried—mix equal parts of pure sand and soil from beneath blooming plants, thus securing the fungus associated with the gentian's root system—Put 1 inch of broken crocks in a 12-inch pot, cover with an inch of fine gravel, then fill with above soil mixture—Gather seed as soon as ripe (in September) and sow on the surface of the soil, firming lightly—Water daily by setting pot in deep basin of water—Germination soon occurs and as soon as the 2nd leaves have formed, but before the long tap-root has started prick out the tiny plants into individual paper pots (heavens) which should be placed in a cold frame or in flats with moistened sphagnum between them. Before freezing weather, set the plants (in the pots) where they are to bloom, preferably in conditions like those of a damp meadow, and cover with light straw and leaves. The plants should winter well, grow vigorously in the Spring, and in Sept. send up blossoming stalks, thus, though they are really biennials, giving blossoms the first year. Now to get your place like a damp meadow!—It must be a wonderful sight in the Spring with daffodils everywhere. [. . .] I am not a real cook, they keep me out of the kitchen, but when they are away I seize my chance and make preserves. That peach pickle in the box you get was not made by me, I traded with a lady because we didn't have any, and I must say I was furious with her for sending over that outcast bottle. I made her feel as bad as I could by telling her when it was too late that it was for some New York men on Fifth Avenue and that I had pasted a piece of paper on the jar saying "Mrs Fox's Peach Pickle." "Oh," she said, "with that mashed one on the bottom, what will they think of me". You know—it was disgraceful.

[. . .] That was a very kingly daydream and thank you. I can use it in my nightly wishes over the record catalogues. [. . .]

Yours,

Eudora

Writing to Welty on September 23, 1940, Russell typed Welty's address, then began, "Mississippi is a wonderful word to write. When young and in Ireland I used to chuckle at [Mississippi] for the word seemed a joke and I imagine I must have felt that surely no place of that name could really exist." He had not yet had success in placing Welty's stories, but he was not giving up. He told Welty he planned to bring her story "Powerhouse" home with him for Pamela Travers, who was visiting them. Travers, the author of the Mary Poppins books, was a client of Russell's; in the 1920s she had published poetry in the Irish Statesman, the newspaper edited by Russell's father. Russell explained to Welty that he expected that Travers would show Welty's story to her publisher, Gene Reynal, and then "tell him off in no uncertain language for being dumb if he doesn't snap you up as an author straight away." Russell also reported on the good health of the gardenia, which he had begun fertilizing.

Late September 1940

Dear Diarmuid,

It is wonderful of you to sic Pamela Travers onto Reynal & Hitchcock—[. . .] I am glad the gardenia got there and is under your hand, and it had better bloom. If it gets to be ten feet high, send me a cutting—Just now I'm trying to root you something called the magnolia-fuscata, because we might as well try everything. It has the most wonderful, sweet, thimble-sized blooms like little bananas all over it, and it is the shrub we all grew up with here—We would all go to school every morning with a handful of magnolia-fuscatas, getting all hot and brown rapidly, and the people we liked we would hold out one to, and say "Here"—they were to put in your handkerchief and lie down on your desk with while the teacher was talking, and you could simply go off into another world smelling them—They were so wonderful they had to be smelled through a handkerchief, and then the teacher would be sure to call you by your whole name and say "Bring those magnolia-fuscatas to me, and get your book open"—They get to be 15 feet high—but you could trim it. All this, and it's not rooted yet.

It is hard to think that you were laughing in Ireland at the name of Mississippi, while I was here writing the Book of Kells on my Santa Claus list.[11] [. . .] It *is* a funny place, just like its name. It has its own look. The other day I was out in a boat in the swamp around Pearl River, not far away, and when I saw the way it looked, the dark, dark green still trees, with the red-violet of the gum trees, and the big arched roots of the cypresses like caves over the water, and the utterly quiet water like the darkest of mirrors, I thought that no matter who had been sitting there in that boat, if he were waked up out of a sound sleep of a hundred years and asked where he was, he would take one look and say "Mississippi"— especially if he looked up in the sky and saw a buzzard.

I've been writing like a demon, and you will soon get the result. How can I wait to know what you think of it—you will either like it, or throw it out the window. It is going to be necessary to be careful when I type the finished thing—as soon as I start writing on it, off it goes, with me holding on. Of course that's why I like it.

Please don't worry because you can't make editors buy my stories now. I am sorry to think of you working so hard and diligently when you could never make any money from what I send you. It makes me mad too. Just don't send me the 6-day notice—I don't speak of the future much, but someday I swear I will write something, I don't know what, that is so furiously and so carefully done (both) that with the push from you it will simply leap up over the boundary the publishers have set up to keep it out, and suddenly like magic turn into something both good and profit-making, and we will all be astonished and rich, and I couldn't say which the more—

Yours,

Eudora

In early October, Welty sent Russell a story that would eventually be called The Robber Bridegroom. *Russell was delighted with it, although he admitted that it was so original that it could be hard for him to sell. "I think you have extended the dream perfectly; it has that kind of chaotic and unreal reality that characterizes dreams. [. . .] It is as if you had spent many dreamy afternoons meditating on the romantic history of the South and on the fairy and folk tales of your youth" (10.8.40).*

October 10, 1940
Jackson Thursday night
Dear Diarmuid,

Thanks for the letter. I was so glad to get it, and to know that it was well received at the office. I could hardly believe it, for I had arrived at a lost feeling that you would think I had been impetuous with high things, and mixed them with a disregard and lightness that was unworthy, even though the tale had no pretenses. [. . .] I was reassured that you seemed to think my story was what I thought it was, something that came out of dreamy afternoons. It didn't trouble me at all until after I had finished it, but maybe because it meant something more to me than the others, I worried about it.

As for the commercial angle, I didn't know it had one. At least by itself—I was only hoping you could ease it into the collection by your persuasions [. . .].

I can tell you are being good to the gardenia. It never expected all those fine vitamins, I'm sure, and will probably come out all in double flowers. I know those are buds, I go by mine, which is about the same. I like to think it will bloom out there where I had such a good time, it seems so long ago. I wish you could see the Sasanqua camellia in bloom here now—the frailest of them all, and the only one in the fall—the most delicate and marvelous pale flower, white with a little pink on the edge.

I forgot to say, here is another story—I had to do something while waiting for you all to read that. [. . .]

Yours,

Eudora

The story Welty had just written was "A Worn Path," which would eventually become one of her best-known works. By the end of October, however, after sending Welty's work to several national magazines, Russell still had no good news to report. He wrote Welty that he had been "meditating" on why the stories were not being accepted; he suggested that they sometimes seemed obscure to the editors who read them. Russell did not want Welty to try to change the way she wrote, because he still liked the stories and thought that her future work would be even better. All Welty needed to do was "to write and sooner or later some of the dumb editors will wake up" (10.29.40).

November 5, 1940
Dear Diarmuid,

Thanks for the letter and the meditating you did on the stories, which is really of help. I have done a lot of wondering from this end, since I began to send stories out. The Southern Review people, while they were nice and friendly, and helped me greatly by starting me out and printing what I wrote, still never made any remarks or comments at all, and it was just like being kept in the dark. They stayed like that, after all they had done for me, up to the last story I sent, Powerhouse, which they returned without a word about it. Of course, their sending it back was a sort of sign—but were they bored, enraged, or what. They were a little sultanic, don't you think? An acceptance was equally baffling—they would just send me up a proof-sheet to correct. And I remember the day the Key came back, there was no letter at all attached, just the naked story—it may have been a mistake, but that was a blank feeling. Even with the good luck I had in finding them at the start, I wonder that I kept on writing. I would not say this elsewhere, and it does not mean that I'm not grateful for all they did. Anyway, in an isolation or not, I am one of those who believe that to communicate is the hope and purpose and the impulse and the result and the test and value of all that is written and done at all, and if that little spark does not come, and with a little sheltering, flash back and forth, then it's the same as being left confined within ourselves just when we wished most to reach out and touch the surrounding life that seemed so wonderful in some way. You can see that I have been burning to say this. If you keep telling me when what I write is clear and unobscured and when it is not, as it appears to you, then I will have something so new to me and of such value, a way to know a few bearings. Is this what was in our contract? I didn't understand it would be so much.

[. . .]

Yours

Eudora

November 12, 1940

Dear Diarmuid,

It was for your hard work I was feeling discouraged, and I couldn't help that, but for myself, that there are people like you and K.A.P.[12] in the world fills me with the most opposite feeling to discouragement. A fine security, and I am all settled and writing in it. Soon I will have something new to send, and there is always the chance that this time this will turn out to be the one. Anyway, I can wait and wait, for time does not seem to press very closely down here. It is just in the city that it prods and presses and holds up delays to you and acts important.

We had a little cyclone here the other night, that blew a lot of trees and roofs away, but it was the most wonderful storm—the wind sounds like voices very elated, and you wake up thinking something wonderful has happened, and the lightning does not flash or give a crude light at all, it moves on and off rapidly and soundlessly, with more light than darkness it is so constant, and is like a soft beating on the air—if you look out you see trees bending to the ground in this strange light. That cyclone was the way our winter came, and now it's cold and the chrysanthemums are very pert and spicey.

[. . .]

Yours

Eudora

On November 18, Russell reported that he had met with John Woodburn, the editor at Doubleday who had put him in touch with Welty earlier in the year. "I told him about my suggestion about stringing a series of stories on the necklace of the Natchez Trace. He thinks that would be a good idea and that if you wrote a letter to indicate that this was your next work and to sketch in some degree the outlines he may be able to persuade them to pay money for an option." He also report-

ed that the gardenia Welty had sent was now in his kitchen "to smell the odors of the cooking and maybe this wholesome smell will make it grow better than all the vitamins in the artificial fertilisers. [. . .] Good luck to your own gardening and good luck to the writing—you'll need it with such an agent."

November 23, 1940
Dear Diarmuid,

Such fine news has me terribly excited and I hope I wrote the proper letter. [. . .] If Doubleday doesn't want it, I still think I will do it, and then maybe you can sell it to somebody else. There's no use trying to sell something that wouldn't be good enough not to be written no matter what. That's such a bad sentence that I will stop. Good luck and let me hear. I am glad John Woodburn likes it and I hope he will get it if it turns out to be good. It is just like spring here and all the bulbs in the garden are up 12 inches. My gardenia is stubborn too. I don't see why all food wouldn't interchange all right, because the other night in a movie a lady was sitting next to a man who was coughing, and she took a little box out of her purse and said "Have a cough drop." He ate one, and stopped coughing. When she got home she found her cough-drop package intact, and the one that was opened contained vitamin B-1 tablets for plants. Of course he was a stranger, and she never heard whether he died, bloomed somewhere, or what, but one thing is sure, he never coughed a single time after, any more than a plant in a pot. Her doctor was very learned about it and said it would all be perfectly all right.

In the meanwhile I am going out to take a look at the Natchez Trace, and good luck up there.

Yours,
Eudora

Russell's efforts to place Welty in a respected national magazine were finally rewarded when the Atlantic *accepted "Powerhouse" and "A Worn Path" on December 4. Sending the news to Welty, Russell noted, "Thank heavens for some perspicuity somewhere" (12.4.40).*

Early December 1940

Dear Diarmuid,

[. . .] What I was about to buy for myself was some kind of little telescope—something wild must have showed in my letter. But I will put it off until the amount from the *Atlantic* is divulged. The stars are wonderful now, though. When I was little my father would try so patiently to show me the stars through a little telescope he had, but I could never look the right way, and finally I would have to say "Yes, I see it," just to please him, when I really couldn't. [. . .] The sale to the *Atlantic* created a lot of excitement here, people rush up and kiss me on the street, and one *stranger* said, "When they send you the check, I want to know how much you got." The grand old lady of Jackson said, "Well my dear, I would certainly write another one!" Is the snow over everything up there? Everything looks terrible here after the freeze. It is possible to pick only a handfull of violets and a pansy or two. My mother and I are in two different schools about covering up plants—she thinks they should learn to be Spartans, and I hold that nothing should be Spartans, and that one should not impose one's will over any thing, especially a helpless bush. Anyway, all our camellia buds are lying on the ground on the north. I got out some old pictures of the garden in spring to restore my faith. I will send you one—iris and hemerocallis, with some roses—April. Today is fine and the whole congregation of house plants is moved out into the sun, and I have just passed among them with the water and vitamins. In Natchez I acquired a few cuttings, since I carry around a pair of strong scissors in the car, and a hatfull of live-oak acorns, which are the most beautiful acorns you ever saw—long, slender, dark, polished ones with pale yellow tips. It is a problem where to plant them! I know somebody that did, and got a little hedge, before so very long, of pretty little live-oaks. All of you take care of yourselves in the ice and snow. I am still so excited about the great feat, and when people ask how it was done, I can only reply that it was mysterious.

Yours

Eudora

By mid-December Russell had reported the amount that the Atlantic *would pay for "Powerhouse"—two hundred dollars. Although other magazines like the* Saturday Evening Post *paid higher royalties, Russell was delighted to place Welty's story in the* Atlantic, *a prestigious venue for serious literature.*[13] *In the following letter Welty painted a cartoon angel in blue, yellow, and pink watercolor, typing the letter in the blank spaces left on the page.*

Mid-December 1940
Dear Diarmuid,

It is the most delectable sensation to be receiving all this good news and I think the money is a fortune. And all the Christmas lights seemed to be turned up another notch by having it coming so soon—how did you stir them to such promptness. I am not much of a Christmas letter decorator but I have no red at all in my typewriter. You will have to take this little creature. [. . .] After I got your letter I thought it was the time to go and buy the Christmas tree, and I paid my annual visit to Alphonse, a colored man in shell-rimmed glasses with a sort of Oriental splendor—this year he was feeling affluent too—he had a helper, and though he wasn't doing a thing when I came up, he lifted a finger and intoned to the helper, "Here is one of our most reliable customers approaching. Find her a tree that is 100%, one that will please all her friends, and stand it up for her." I do think it has a high percentage. I was thinking, the little gardenia may be waiting for the most timely and gracious moment to come out in flower, since they are very aristocratic, and I hope that maybe it is only choosing its proper season. I think this season would be Christmas, but of course, it may know better. I do wish it would bloom then. I can't tell whether mine will or not—I surround it with other things that are blooming, to see what would happen. I hope all kinds of good things come to you, and that all of you have a fine time. We are making fruitcakes this minute, I am cutting up the citron, they think. It would be hard to tell you how terribly pleased I am that all this is the way it is. Merry Christmas.

Yours,
Eudora

December 30, 1940
Dear Diarmuid,

[. . .] I would like to take all that money now and go where there is a hot sun. Aren't you afraid that winter is absolutely non-magical? At its best, it is only a time for ingrowing—the acceptance of imprisonment—I remember reading once in some art history how the long winter evenings must have set the German peoples to wood-carving—and that is how the intricate toilsome repetitive Gothic spirit (even in elation) got nurtured. Think how some early German engravings are nothing but accumulations, all vine-like—or little lost holy families in millions of veined leaves. Like puzzles. If it had been a little warmer and a little lighter, they might have thought of color. I never want anything in winter either, except spring. I think that our feelings must keep closer than we imagine to the parabola of the seasons, and as we have to wait for the spring we feel that much older (really ancient) in its opposite. O Persephone! Some flowering quince and spirea and forsythia are blooming here, entirely at their own risk. Happy New Year.

Yours,
Eudora

In early January, Russell was able to report that Welty's collection of stories was being read at Doubleday, Doran; Russell was lining up another publisher who had also expressed interest, in case Doubleday turned it down (1.2.41).

January 8, 1941
Dear Diarmuid,

I am so pleased and I think you are doing mighty deeds with the stories. Let me know all that happens. [. . .]

I'm sending you up a story this weekend. I can't tell about it yet, and maybe I should wait.

Good luck.

Yours
Eudora
P. S. I think my gardenia may be going to bloom because the buds are swelling and I can smell the flowers (I think!)—See if you can note these signs in yours—

January 9, 1941
Dear Diarmuid—

Here is the story I was talking about—it took my last sheet of paper. I hope you like it.

Today James Laughlin sent me a check for the story they took,[14] and it was for $9. I could make a graph showing improvement made with use of agent, and you could paste it up.

We have a mad iris blooming by the driveway and every time I come in in the car, it scares me. Of course it is not supposed to have come out. But it is just like spring.

Yours
Eudora

Welty's new story was an early draft of "First Love." Russell wrote that it seemed to have "too much obscurity and the full vision does not come through" as yet. "Don't think badly of me and don't feel badly yourself," he added (1.15.41).

January 18, 1941
Dear Diarmuid—

You know you have a standing warning to catch me if I fall, and so already I may have tried something too hard. Of course I don't think badly of you, your letter is a good thing and to me what you feel is a kind of advice. I did try terribly hard in this story, and it may be the fault was not that it is not clear in my own head, but that I have not been able to do what I attempted. I think that the only thing left to do is to give the story more time. You know when I wrote to you I said that maybe I should wait with this one. [. . .]

When anything happens about the collection let me know, and good luck, with your own story equally. I feel that I have let you down, both in my story and in the little gardenia which will not bloom. I asked the old man that runs the greenhouse here what to do about gardenias and he said "Wait! Wait"—I knew that, but it was supposed to bloom in winter. It may yet. All my critics here tell me that an even temperature is of the essence, but that is their only point of agreement. I just spent a great sum of my new gains on flower seed from Burpee's, and the telescope from Sears ought to arrive any day now, or night, it really should come at night. I think they ought to knock off something from the price because I have missed the comet. Did you see it?

Yours,
Eudora

*On January 21, Doubleday made an offer to publish Welty's first collection of stories. Reporting the good news, Russell's letter closed, "Dear Eudora, see how incoherent my sentences become when pleasure and delight overcome me" (1.21.41). On February 11 he wrote that the forthcoming book was boosting Welty's standing among publishers. The At-*lantic *had accepted "Why I Live at the P.O."* and Harper's Bazaar *had "asked that the stories they turned down before should be sent to them again—and this made me grin because it was what I promised myself they would do in my original fury at their having the ignorance to turn down so good stories. . . . I really feel so pleased I could jump and bambol," he added, correcting his mistyping of "gambol" by writing a "g" above the line and then adding "or is it better as bambol?" (2.11.41).*

February 14, 1941
Dear Diarmuid,

It's nice to be remembered on all the holidays, Christmas, Robert E. Lee's birthday, St. Valentine's etc. with a little contract or check or something. If you did a bambol I did a bambolina. [. . .] I really am so delighted—you really have no idea how hard it is to believe something like this in Jackson! Yesterday while sitting out in the car in front of a little bootlegger's house in the woods, with all the frogs tuning up around us, drinking a glass of beer, I wondered if this could happen, and it seemed more possible in the future than it does in the present.

[. . .] Maybe a title will come to you. I thought that maybe someday I would call some book "As the Seed Waits," from the song that William Blake wrote—"And as the seed waits eagerly watching for its flower and fruit, Anxiously its little soul looks out into the clear expanse To see if hungry winds are abroad with their invisible array . . ."[15] But that would be pretentious for the stories here. [. . .] I think the contract is beautiful, the news is all delightful and good, and I feel so favored by the gods, and you should add "Miracles Done" to your letterhead, and I must type now.

Yours enchanted
Eudora

February 21, 1941
Dear Diarmuid—

Thanks for the letters, for Clytie, and the check—I am now surrounded by mail, a delicious state (I type in bed, like an island). [. . .] I hate to think of everybody being up there in the snows still—I wish I could bring up some flowers—of course I could sell them in the subway—you see the mercenary spirit agents have developed in me. I do have a camellia cutting I have been growing for you for a long time, I thought for some occasion, and here you have a new baby,[16] so it is time, but I don't know if I should trust the mails to take it—it is so tender—it has done wonderfully and is putting out new leaves all the time now. I keep thinking I will come up and tote it! The stories ought to be all tidied up by tomorrow and they will be along right away [. . .] I hope you approve. In the front it says "To Diarmuid Russell." I have some cheese boxes planted with seeds on the back porch—this year I'm taking infinite pains with them—I even baked the dirt—[. . .]

Yours

Eudora

Russell advised Welty against dedicating her first book to him; he suggested that there were probably more important people whom Welty should thank publicly, whereas "we, after all, are just a commercial outfit whose business it is to recognize merit and grab 10% of it" (2.24.41). Welty was not dissuaded.

February 26, 1941

Dear Diarmuid,

[. . .] It is cold and miserable here, not sunny at all, and I do not do well in it. I think I ought to be transplanted further S. until the trees are in leaf. I would never send the camellia out into the cold, I am watching over it carefully. How would you say this photo of me would do, enlarged 20 times of course, wandering among the shrubbery in a fruit dish and caressing a pineapple, I think.[17] Or do you like it better *in* a tree? At last I have tracked down some pink violets—Rosina—there was one lady in a town nearby who had some, and would not give any away, and I was haunted by the worst thoughts, but now I am getting some honorably, Vaughn's is offering them under NEW (pooh),[18] but they are wrong about where to plant them—they like sandy sunny poor soil, such as our garden abounds in. Everything in the seed box is pushing up and looks simply dreamy, I can hardly wait.

Yours

Eudora

Russell's next letter commented on photographs that Welty had sent. "The photographs are along the right line but aren't they a little conventional? I favor one of you swimming the Mississippi [. . .] . You would be seen far out in a smother of foam holding up your two hands above your head joined in the traditional sign of sure victory." He also reported that a jar of Welty's jelly was now consumed. A recent guest had been so greedy in helping himself to the jelly that Russell had almost scolded him, "Look, this is no way to treat Eudora's royalties" (3.3.41).

March 8, 1941
Dear Diarmuid,

I was glad to get such a nice long letter. [. . .] It is the worst weather, and just as I have plants all waiting to be set out. Snow fell this morning—it is gone now, but we are still feeling the rebuff. I won't send your camellia yet awhile. Here is a little bulletin received this morning from Mobile, and after giving it study I am sending it on to you so that you may realize the profound and wonderful experience you are about to enter into by getting a camellia. Mr. Rubel[19] keeps us all in a constant nervous state, and the subject of camellias will last a whole roomful of people here for three hours of talk any time.

Yours,
Eudora

P.S. [. . .] Your Miss. River theory is nice but I am afraid to test it—A combination whirlpool and alligator would be sure to bite me at the moment of victory—

March 12, 1941
Dear Diarmuid—

Here is a new story ["The Winds"]—I am a little anxious about how it will sound to you—it is so long for me to write—I'm tired too—Maybe it will sound like an "effusion"—[. . .] I can't write more now for I am so anxious to get this in the mail—I hope the big blizzard did not harm your garden—

Yours
Eudora

P. S. I haven't forgotten the Natchez Trace stories but these just came up—

March 15, 1941
Dear Diarmuid,

This story was a bit of the out-reaching you mentioned for me—it may have failed. Those were little fragments out of my own life and what I sent you is the first story I've tried directly attempting to remember exact real sensations and the structure they might have built, and the structure may be all felt in myself and not communicated. Tell me how you feel about it. [. . .] Have we any unfinished business (besides camellias). [. . .] As you are probably aware, camellias are a very deep subject, embracing whole fierce schools of thought, battles of wit and the making and breaking of fortunes, and as it is very late I will just ask you, which would you rather have, a Pink Perfection, or a Chandlerii Elegans? Both being only little stems you know. Be careful how you answer that. Camellia growers attach all Chinese philosophy to making a choice. It is probably because camellias take so long to bloom and ask so much care, that the growers come to brooding and reading the old histories. I really want to know whether you like the formal, imbricated flowers, or the loose peony-like ones? I wish you could see them down here in a good year, hundreds and hundreds of different kinds. If only people would just grow them and not lie, steal, blacken people's names, and fall into such scorn and greed, and I am one, for I have stolen the flowers out of cemeteries and chased little children that took mine.

Yours
Eudora

Reporting on a plant that Welty had sent back in September, Russell wrote, "The Gardenia is acting very strangely in that the buds it has had all along seem to remain about the same while it has produced about four new buds that are growing rapidly. However the fact that it is alive and growing is satisfying and my perplexity as to its behaviour may be satisfied later" (3.17.41).

March 19, 1941
Dear Diarmuid,

[. . .] Gardenias are a little strange, inconsistent. If you let them get dry even once, they will stubbornly set their buds at that point and not go any further. Mine had a little spell with the plague and I had to give it baths in kitchen soap, leaf by leaf, but it is better now. I believe the camellia you might like is the Herme and I will send you the little cutting up today in the hope that it will get to Katonah still alive and green. Debates rage over it and its ancestry but I will not let it be troubled. Yes, there is danger that I will pour all my riches into camellias, I have just been waiting for the chance. If I can find a little picture of a Herme somewhere I'll put it in so you can know a little what your flowers may look like someday. They like to be cool and moist and at an even temperature, and I think always do best watered from the bottom. I have my cuttings in an unused room and give them a little sun and air every day. As soon as it is warm enough I'm going to bury the pots in the ground for the summer.

[. . .]

Yours

Eudora

March 19, 1941

Wednesday

Dear Diarmuid,

I forgot what day this is and that you probably wouldn't get a letter that wasn't airmail—so here's this to say watch out for the camellia. It ought to get to Katonah Friday or Saturday and I hope to heaven it is still with its right end in the dirt and its leaves shiny. Its name is Herme. It's spring here—is this a shamrock? A man on the Atlantic, Mr. Fitzpatrick, wrote me a note in handwriting, purple ink, that I must pass on, "Last night at my Club, Altrusa, my dinner partner spoke of your paper with such feeling that tears came to her eyes." I wrote you about the story—but there's no need to be tentative in judgment on it and if all of you feel an uncertainty there's no doubt reason, but since I have done all I could on it, positively, for now anyway, try it on an editor and see what he thinks. Cleanth Brooks might like it—can't tell. To tell the truth I am filled with the fevers of spring and might as well go out and be done with it, out of the world of editors. This may happen to you next.

Yours,

Eudora

Do not be alarmed by the way I packed up the camellia—when I am wrapping up a package I get so fired with it I am absolutely ruthless and will seize anything to hand that might go to help with the package. I couldn't bear for the little plant to be damaged.

March 31, 1941
Dear Diarmuid,

I'm glad the little plant got there—I'm pessimistic about sending things off, never think they will be seen or heard of again—but go to some little world of their own. [. . .]

Enclosed photos—me in a camellia shed, for Harper's Bazaar, as requested (but not advocated here),[20] and Henry Miller in a ruin and by a mosque in Mississippi. I didn't know why he should look me up—but he did not seem frightening after all—a little lonely-like.[21]

I did mean a feeling of cycles to move through the last story, and also an identification of some kind, of life and change with the revolving earth. It is a wonderful thing to find out when you grow up and read, that the way you felt in the naivete of childhood about yourself in the world is a literally true way—that every body exerts its influence and pull on every other body, no matter how far apart or how different they may be, stars on stars, or a falling flower on the motion of the universe—the pull is each upon the other, and it is only a difference in weight that keeps the rest of the universe from showing its disturbance and lets the flower float to the ground.

I wish you could see the yellow jessamine which is in garlands from tree to tree all the way to the coast, and all the fruit trees are in flower, little pink hollow squares around each negro cabin in the country. In New Orleans the trees are green, but here they have just that little cloud of color over violet branches and twigs that I love better. The skies are wet and changing and sunset over the Mississippi River is worth going many miles to see, and the smell of woodsmoke is everywhere. Along the Sunday roads the negroes walk to church in their white clothes, and by next Sunday they will have raised their umbrellas for shade.

I might be through there one of these days—Yaddo wrote and asked me what I would do if they were to invite me to come up and live free in May.[22] That's K. A. P. getting me put on the list. I wrote back that I was liable to accept, if they did. Isn't that grand—two springs, that's all.

Yours
Eudora

April 5, 1941
Dear Diarmuid,

[. . .] I too wish that you could come to the station of the South Wind (Herodotus influence) one of these days—I believe we must grow things a little like yours in Ireland, and that your white jessamine might be the same as Confederate jessamine. We do have a great big vine that I couldn't find the name of, that I have seen growing in the old river towns down the side of the bluffs down from the old gardens—and it might have been brought from Ireland, because that was where a good many of us down here originated. If they got over camellias from France and marble from Italy and silver from England, they might just as well have sent back to Ireland for a bit of vine to train round it all. I have some Confederate jessamine that turned out to be a left-handed vine; after I changed the direction of the string it went nicely up. My mother speaks out now and then from her meditations on the garden to state that this is going to be a good iris year. Do you agree? It ought to be something, to atone for its lateness in coming. Just today we have a Dainty Bess rose in bloom and a lot of common white iris down in the woods behind, and English daisies, pansies, violets, rain lilies, phlox, alyssum and such things. I have some botanical tulips blooming that I love—slender little Asiatic looking things. I've been working in the backyard so long and hard that when I finally shut my eyes at night I see certain kinds of leaves in my head—I see weeds the way Lady Macbeth saw spots, and next I will be going out somnambulistically to pull them up. Yesterday I set out lupins, pinks, canterbury bells, forgetmenots—against the grain I am trying to grow delphiniums, which are not for us, and they have already sent up flower spikes, being all hopped up on vitamins so they don't know what they're doing. I saw some grand manure the other day and thought of you. It was down by that old ruin on the river where I took Henry Miller's picture—and you didn't say, didn't you think the pictures were just right? small of course, but capable of being blown up to any size—you could make a mural for John Slocum's office while he is away at camp.[23] It was well rotted manure—practically antique. But I had no way to make off with it. I carry scissors, diggers, and hatchets, but no manure compartment in my car.

Yes, Yaddo might do strange things to me. The idea of hibernation is attractive, and I might try it, except that I fear peep-holes.[24] Maybe they have it fixed up to force writers, with warm moist rooms and sprinkling of vitamins on the soup, and we will all write exotic large-scale things that you will have to sell to strange little men in back rooms. Maybe I will send you in double-stories instead of single, all with double titles if not in double talk, giant, double-size, everblooming stories with which you cannot fail. [. . .] When Henry Miller came through I happened to be right in the middle of Herodotus on Egypt and was in the spirit to relate to him many things about our vanished civilization, since he too seemed very patient and credulous in a strange country, and maybe I did tell him a little too much about lost Indian cities and heroes, but I think nothing that was not true. I pointed him out some directions and left him to his own resources.

Yours

Eudora

P.S. [. . .] Don't worry, it will be spring soon. This letter probably makes no sense, because outdoors it is so grand—But you know how this is and can forgive.

April 18, 1941

Dear Diarmuid,

Here is a new little story, see how you like it ["Asphodel"]. It seems to have a little flute obligato.[25]

[. . .] I'm still waiting to be invited to Yaddo. It looks like a problem. Do you suppose it was a mistake for me to commit myself so, and that I should have replied more coyly, "Come and get me." It is summertime here and the sun is smiting everything and I have to get little paper hats over my new plants at break of day, to shade their brows. They may not like it, but if they go without they reel over on their noses.

Yours

Eudora

April 30, 1941

Dear Diarmuid,

[. . .] It's summertime and so beautiful and everything smells ambrosial. Under my window is a magnolia fuscata tree and I can smell it anytime by just drawing my breath. I'm sorry your Louisiana iris didn't rise up and bloom, we will have to try it again.[26] Why don't you make a little greenhouse or pit, and I could bring you everything under the sun.

Everything that smells good is in bloom now, irises, roses, honeysuckle, lilies, pinks, sweetpeas, and in the cool of the evening we ride down to negro town to inhale the celestial chinaberry trees. They're drifting with little lavender flowers now and the most fragrant spicy airy delicious soft scent in the world. White people don't have them—I don't know why. They used to. I guess they gave them to the negroes.

[. . .]

Yours

Eudora

Welty's invitation from Yaddo eventually arrived. In May, as Welty made her way to Yaddo in Saratoga Springs, she made stops in New York City, Katonah, and the Finger Lakes near Geneva, New York.

May 1941

Hotel Bristol, New York

Dear Diarmuid,

When you have time this week write and tell me what you think of this for a table of contents for the Natchez Trace book. [. . .] I have been in a misery lately, for the desire to make a story do something it cannot do, or at least mine cannot, and the great care I felt simply laid a heavy burden on me, it weighted down my heart and I couldn't do anything, I wanted so to write these exact, perfect, magic stories I could just see. Have you ever seen in your mind all the steps of some impossible thing? It is like understanding how to juggle, just not being able to do it. Anyway, I am about to write away on the Natchez stories. There is one that is going to be a little adventure, in those days—a search, a man alone and he has a lonely walk, which is a vision and a dream sustained with him— I see whenever I think about the Trace now a kind of wanderer and all the gloom he walks in and the flicker of poor little uncertain lights about him that give him hope and the stubborn radiance he lets rise inside him and all that he passes by or imagines is there in a sort of panorama. I want to keep it very simple and very clear, almost abstract, the way you see things when you are lonely and on a journey. But I will send it to you.

How is your garden. If I once see a garden I have to think of it then from day to day. I miss mine. I asked a waiter in the Rainbow room what the vines were they have growing under glass and he said "Fuscias." A poor excuse for a waiter.

I'm in the middle of packing. All night long up my street somebody practices on a horn the opening bars of "Afternoon of a Faun," straight through the tired midnight of a city.

Yours
Eudora

Late May 1941
Dear Diarmuid—

I came to the top of the building in Radio City and looked down on the sunset before leaving New York—So beautiful—the grand purple mountains in the distance showing—river shining—I think it is about a year ago now that you first happened to write me and it made a change in my life so I had a tender place in my heart for the day when it came around again—It has seemed like a magical year and whatever is ahead, that will keep—Today I've been studying over story notes, and I read all I could on Johnny Appleseed—Then I'll go float on the Finger Lakes hoping that in that nice calm way they will come to something I can do—I must have seemed flighty on this trip—it is all because of a kind of tantalization (is that a word?) over one thing and I am trying to get it straight in my head—Don't worry for fear the product will be impossible and wild, until you see it—Thanks for the good times—It was fine to see you and to go to Katonah and see everything coming up and looking that bright new-green—It made two springs. [. . .] Hope the next time you count you will have 711 gladiolas—and that all is well with you—

yours—
Eudora

Rochester, NY
June 7, 1941
Dear Diarmuid,

Thanks for the letter. The joy is in the doing, I believe that, but the joy has to be kept alive like any other, by letting it grow with the work growing—I know how good and patient you are not to press me— [. . .] There's really nothing to worry about, I am only beset by something in myself, not by circumstances—a concern with communication and feeling in themselves, that gets too complex now and then for one like me—[. . .]

This is a wild beautiful country—lots of waterfalls—some with rainbows—Have you ever had seeds from here? [. . .] It's not long till Yaddo and I am waiting for the day when you and K. A. P. and I can sit down and drink a planter's punch together—[. . .]

Yours
Eudora

Yaddo, Saratoga Springs, N. Y.
June 17, 1941
Dear Diarmuid,

Yaddo is delicious! It all turned out much more wonderfully than I expected. [. . .]

Oh God the worst thing—Carson McCullers[27] is here—we glare in the halls and speak, but that's all. I think she is cutting KAP dead. All to the good. She is here sort of on probation, KA says she broke her neck to get invited, and if she ever gets drunk and sinsults everybody (what a lovely word) she is a goner. Thank God I am not in the same house with her again. I won't be glad when she is dead, particularly, but I don't stop in my tracks and send up thanks ever that she is alive. I know you wouldn't like her if you only knew her! (she said eagerly). Everybody that comes along, she tells long horrible stories to (she says they are horrible) and then they give her their mother's rings. She flutters her eyes: it's just shyness. Once she said to me, "Am I responsible if I am an enfant terrible?" I said yes. Just to think of her here at my kitchen table makes me furious and I will start banging pots and pans in a minute.

I hope your garden does well and that some of our fine rain fell on it. A remarkable number of gladiolas.[28] My mother wrote me about the cape jessamines blooming and I wished that you could be having them by the dozens to fill your house instead of one poor little flower of a gardenia. She said the mimosa tree was all in flower. The delphiniums I planted in my ignorance have all bloomed like everything and are getting ready to bloom for the second time and Mother says the ladies of the garden club come over each day to worship and grit their teeth. [. . .]

Yours
Eudora

Yaddo, Saratoga Springs, N. Y.
June 26, 1941
Dear Diarmuid,

[. . .] There is a very funny sculptor here who speaks three languages very badly and all as one, and wears boy scout shorts, and is very concerned about his cat back home who have operation. He have kits. "$22—am I a millionaire?" and he looks cross-eyed for a comment. He told me he had been to New Orleans and brought back some Spanish moss which he put all around his room and it had lived for four months. I told him it was a parasite and was probably living off the furniture. He turned white and has dashed into New York today, probably to snatch off the moss, because I couldn't quiet him down at all.[29] [. . .]

To me it is a crazy kind of life, and I miss my own easy-going light-hearted people—we are all light-hearted down there—what a claim!—and my garden, and the interruptions, and all that is domestic. [. . .]

yours,
Eudora

Welty and Russell had been waiting for months for Katherine Anne Porter to finish writing an introduction to A Curtain of Green. *Porter had agreed to write the introduction in February, and Russell had sent her the manuscript in March, expecting her to finish by May. Welty's book had been scheduled for publication in early September, but was delayed because Porter did not finish writing the introduction until August.*

Yaddo, Saratoga Springs, NY
July 14, 1941
Dear Diarmuid,

[. . .] No, things aren't any better here, I can't tell you in a letter. I cling to the hope that one day K.A. will begin writing again and all will be solved, in the right way. The days and nights are beautiful here, and the hay is being cut in all the meadows around and smells nice. Good luck to you,

Yours,
Eudora

Drawing of wild lily: What wild lily is this? Drawn from life. (Sunday)

Life size. Saffron, lemon, or coral—Ought to be called "Turkish Slippers"—grows in bogs—[30]

Yaddo, Saratoga Springs, NY
July 23, 1941
Dear Diarmuid,

[...] I'm glad it's nice weather there. It was wonderful for transplanting here, cool and cloudy, and once I planted some seeds out at K.A.'s farm in a washtub, which is evidently the former site of the garden, on a post in the front yard—something I bought called "anchusas," so I went out and thinned the plants out yesterday. The gardens in Saratoga go with the architecture—round beds of red geraniums with a cast-iron rabbit in the middle. And at Yaddo they have acres of only Radiance roses, and the flower gardens have nothing but petunias, button zinnias, and ragged robins. I don't even look.

Yes, I am a member in bad standing of the J. L. [Junior League]—they won't give me professional membership ("We all have hobbies") or inactive ("Nothing but pregnancy counts") and I won't go to meetings, and I think it inane, but it is nice of the magazine to offer to fill a column with publicity. It is a terrible magazine, but I wouldn't want anything not good in it by me. I think the reprint idea is good if it works. Otherwise I believe I have a little thing at home I can send them—you wouldn't want it, it's called "Women!! Make Turbans in Own Homes!", about a little sewing adventure I had—I sent it to the New Yorker, I remember, and found it in the mailbox when I got home, they had shot it back out of a cannon. [...]

Love,
Eudora

Jackson, MS
August 11, 1941
Dear Diarmuid—

It was so nice being in New York and Mt. Kisko and Katonah—I had such a good time—I got home about dark Thursday and went out with a flashlight and lo the big pink insects were cutting away at my little camellias, and the closer I held the light and the more I said "ouch" the better they worked, just like surgeons. It was time I came back to them.

The heat is on here and I go out at 6 to water the garden a few hours so it will live through the day, then I myself fall under the butterfly-lillies and go into a trance. I got the "Who's Who" thing. What do you consider my greatest achievement? I just drew a little doodling. There were two copies of the Southern Review here so I sent one up—see that the Yeats number is announced for Winter. Did you read the correspondence between him and Dorothy Wellesley that ought not to have been published, that she published? No matter what kind of man you say he was, it was a sad hectic little flare-up to have for an end. A little parade of country people goes by the house yelling "Blackeyed peas and okra!" Do you want to try some vegetables from these parts next spring? Blackeyed peas should be grown everywhere, it is the dish you're supposed to eat on New Years Day and you will never go hungry—we always take out this insurance. Tell Rose not to look for new pictures—the lens of my camera disappeared the last morning at Yaddo, but I didn't know it till I had films developed. They said someone must have stolen it. All the good pictures I took at Katonah too, clicking away. Somebody may have taken it for a joke at the party when I left, not knowing its value. But now and then I was of a mind that R & V had better give me a bodyguard if I go off on any more summers to these strange wild places—

Good luck soon,

Yours,

Eudora

August 18, 1941

Dear Diarmuid—

[. . .] People may have been lenient with you about "The Key" but they have been writing to me asking me to please state what it means, and I hope H. Bz. hasn't got duplicates or they'll never take anything more.[31] I want to just send these people their 35¢ (or is it 50¢) back, a refund on the magazine, and then they have no right to question me. Parts of a new story are done, but I can't write with the usual energy because most of the time I have to stay in bed with malaria.[32] But I hope to leap up soon and finish it. I worry about the strange bugs eating my plants. They could be the Texas pink boll weevil, or some of those exotic, strong bugs from N.O.

You may not see the lilies for a while. Here they come up in September. First it has to rain. Then one morning they will all be standing on leafless stalks—I always expect to see them spinning up, like piano stools. Here the crepe-myrtles are blooming for the second blooming—their hour is just after the sun goes down and they turn the deepest flame color in the reflected light, the most glowing things anywhere, we seem to have a row of 7 incandescent trees just at dark. I've just communicated with W. Atlee Burpee, requesting mariposa tulips, dog's tooth violets, and mixed ixias—glad I didn't have to speak it. Do you like zephyranthes—I didn't see any there—delicate small low-growing pink lilies, you must know them of course. This reminds me of a dream I had—it is a kind I have now and then, of listening while someone reads me some long wonderful thing, really chants it—the dream is all words and seems to last all night long. Sometimes the one giving it has it written down and sometimes it is a chant, but always it is something before which I simply recline and marvel. (A grand kind of dream, nobody has to move.) Anyway this one was yours, it was read off from notes and augmented by something like oratory, it was very important and nothing was left out— the subject was flowers, and I think you should go on and write it. It took up all kinds, one by one, but there was more to it than just descriptions and cultivation—the structure and anatomy, very particular, and since I am unfamiliar with that it impressed me greatly, and the history going back to the beginning, like with the fleur-de-lis and the symbolic flowers, like the blue water-lily of the Nile and Solomon's Seal, and the lotus, and the category of flowers people have been changed into or out of—all including the cultivation and care, and the use of Vitamin B-1—in other words, complete. I can't tell you how far-reaching it was. All the real, legendary, decorative (like in illuminations), primal, symbolic, and imaginary flowers were there—a lot I had never heard of—I didn't know Solomon's Seal was a plant but I looked it up in the dictionary this morning. The name of the book was "Flowers of the World" and it was strictly alphabetical, and practical—a reference work. When it was over I had to ask one question, some trifling thing, which was quickly cleared up—I can almost remember it but not quite—or I would ask it now. [. . .]

Yours
Eudora

August 28, 1941
Dear Diarmuid—

[. . .] This is not sent air mail for any reason—only it would be bad to get such a letter the day after Labor Day when all New York is supposed to buzz with terrible enterprise, and you will probably be selling a hundred stories. I haven't anything for you to sell today. My story got stopped—sometimes they get cut in two like that, and I feel that when they are finally completed the little mended place is bound to show.

We have had terribly hot days, sensational sunsets, and beautiful nights. Every evening when the sun is going down and it is cool enough to water the garden, and it is all quiet except for the locusts in great waves of sound, and I stand still in one place for a long time putting water on the plants, I feel something new—that is all I can say—as if my will went out of me, as if I had a stubbornness and it was melting. I had not meant to shut out any feeling that wanted to enter.—It is a real shock, because I had no idea that there had been in my life any rigidity or refusal of anything so profound, but the sensation is one of letting in for the first time what I believed I had already felt—in fact suffered from—a sensitivity to all that was near or around. But this is different and frightening—no, not really frightening—because for instance when I feel without ceasing every change in the garden itself, the changes of light as the atmosphere grows darker, and the springing up of a wind, and the rhythm of the locusts, and the colors of certain flowers that become very moving—they all seem to be a part of some happiness or unhappiness, an unhappiness that something is lost or left unknown or undone perhaps—and no longer simple in their own beautiful but *outward* way. And the identity of the garden itself is lost. This probably sounds confused, and I am, but *it* is not. The intensity is very great, it is too much not to regard seriously, and to try to understand and even be glad for, but I can't remember it clearly enough to write it down here, although the feeling I could not forget. I can only recognize it, and know what moods or experiences somehow belong to it. It seems to have no relation yet to my mind, and when I begin to wonder, it all goes away—just as you wake up from a dream if you interfere with it. Today it has seemed so strange, that I felt I had to pick a time to write a letter when I *could*—or if I put forward myself, some little chain of thought will be broken, that is going along of its own impulse, too complex and too delicate to be broken, and I feel now that I have broken the threads before. Such an intensity of feeling is likely to go the way it came, but the influence will stay. It is a little like the sense of deep unknown feelings that used to come to me when I was a child, as they must come to all children—at the same time of day, just before dark, when we would all fall back in the grass and look up and wait for the first star to come out. I suppose there is a great deal of feeling in the world now and some of it is in my garden—but no, that gives a wrong idea, there has probably been a great deal more than this before. It has beauty of some kind.

Yours,

Eudora

September 20, 1941

Dear Diarmuid,

[. . .] Are big bombers flying all over New York and do they fly low, in under your desk? They do here, they fly under my bed at night, all those in the Louisiana manoeuvers go over Jackson when they make a curve, and really one went under the Vicksburg bridge over the Mississippi River the other day, too lazy to clear it. I feel as if my bones are being ground to pieces but I suppose I will get used to it if I stay here for Jackson is filled with air bases, air schools, air fields, and barracks and tents, a changed little place, loud and crazy. Then when it comes the quiet seems so quiet, which may be why I have those strange concentrations of feelings and dreams, I feel no identity with any of that other, and this identity or love for something else grows deeper still.

Yours

Eudora

September 30, 1941

Dear Diarmuid,

[. . .] This is not a business letter—just the opposite, for I just gave the Jr. League Magazine 3000 words free[33] and neither of us will get any money. Is that all right? [. . .]

The sweet smells of late summer are everywhere, with drifts of woodsmoke coming in from the country. I did find what in a small way I felt. "As I walked in the evening down the lanes scented by the honeysuckle my senses were expectant of some unveiling about to take place. . . . The tinted air glowed before me with intelligible significance like a face, a voice. The visible world became like a tapestry blown and stirred by winds behind it. If it would but raise for an instant I knew I would be in Paradise." Except that I could not say Paradise or be sure. I read The Candle of Vision[34] and the books I have again. I don't know what I apprehended from them when I read them first—it was not what I understand now or what I may understand later—but I suppose it was what I needed. It was the first crisis of a certain kind in my life, and I was frightened—it was when I was sent to the Middle West to school. I was very timid and shy, younger than the rest and those people up there seemed to me like sticks of flint, that lived in the icy world. I am afraid of flintiness—I had to penetrate that, but not through *their* hearts. I used to be in a kind of wandering daze, I would wander down to Chicago and through the stores, I could feel such a heavy heart inside me. It was more than the pangs of growing up, more more, I knew it then, it was some kind of desire to be shown that the human spirit was not like that shivery winter in Wisconsin, that the opposite to all this existed in full. It was just by chance, wandering in the stacks of the library, that I saw one of these books open on one of the little tables under a light. I can't tell you and it is not needed to, what it was like to me to read A.E. but it was a little like first waiting on a shore and then being enveloped in a sea, not being struck violently by a wave, never a shock—and it was the same every day, a tender and firm and passionate experience that I felt in all my ignorance but with a kind of understanding. I would read every afternoon, hurry to read, it was the thing the day led to, and at night what I had read would stay as my secret heart, for I did not let anybody there really know me. What you look for in the world is not simply for what you want to know, but for more than you want to know, and more than you can know, better than you had wished for, and sometimes something draws you to a discovery and there is no other happiness quite the same.

My Herme camellia like yours has flower buds, and I am going to try to keep it cool in the house this winter and see if ones that little can bloom. I planted 4 seeds the other day, and in 4 or 5 years I can see what I've got—they never run true to seed and may be any kind of marvelous new thing. I just bought a magnolia tree and two new camellias—sort of an orphanage, the air base is taking over land where a nursery grew and somebody had to buy the plants or the steam roller would get them. All in all now, counting our old ones, I have 26 camellias, ranging from 10 feet high to seeds, and I intend to cover them all this winter and have an enchantment of bloom.

Yours
Eudora

Welty was planning a trip to New York to celebrate the November publication of her book A Curtain of Green and Other Stories.

October 7, 1941

Dear Diarmuid,

Do you feel all right again—I hope you are well from the cold.

I thought I'd told you, I believe I will come up for a little while in November—it is really cheap for such a long ride and now with the fast train only one night to sit up. I'm glad you liked the sugarcane and this might be the first time in the world any was hung on a wall—I wish it had all its green top spreading out all over everything, like a crown, a beautiful green, it would have looked better, and made the royalties seem even flashier.

Our fall roses are in bloom and we have michaelmas daisies and dahlias but no chrysanthemums yet, and it is a race between them and some chewers at their stalks, of an invisible nationality. Some sawyers just ate a pine tree down in the front yard and all night they chewed in unison, you could hear this bad rhythm going out the window, the jaws of doom, like this—oeurnk oeurnk oeurnk. It was a twin pine tree too and they did them just alike simultaneously. It is time to plant bulbs and I have a bewildering miscellany by ordering from those old ladies out in the deep country that put ads in the farm bulletin in hopes of "pin money" or of swapping a pieced quilt top choice Double Muscadine or Road to Dublin pattern for a white rooster. But the poor old ladies are mixed up about bulbs.

Yours,

Eudora

After Russell received some Mississippi sugarcane from Welty in early October, they exchanged several fanciful letters discussing its effect on the agency's office space.

October 16, 1941

Dear Eudora:

My cold, like most colds, has passed away, leaving a faint mugginess of spirit but no other effects so that I can tap away with some energy. Your sugar cane, hanging on the walls, is drooping as it dries and it has a barbaric appearance as if this agency is accustomed to explore jungles and probably our visitors will soon be expecting to see a couple of heads on the wall—maybe a dried human head or that of a rhinoceros. It mightn't be a bad idea, too, to have a couple of [g]uns leaning in a corner so that people would say "This is no agency to be trifled with."

Your spider lilies are behaving strangely and I don't know what will become of them. They have a misplaced ardour for this climate inasmuch as I went to take them up along with other tender bulbs and found them putting out little sprouts as if it was spring. I think its a kind of nitwitted performance for frost will come soon and then they will have to think twice about what to do and so will I.

We are anxiously awaiting the copies of your book which ought to be along any day now. There is a finality of fact about the appearance of a book that is always pleasing. The masterpiece may be a masterpiece in mss. but no one would say so. But the printed word has a kind of magic about it and when I open the book I shall expect to see rabbits and genii hopping out of it

yours
Diarmuid

October 20, 1941
Dear Diarmuid—

I was glad to have your letter this morning saying you were nearly well again. I did not guarantee the spider lilies against unreason—to the contrary. I am sure they will continue to sprout deliriously, and they are acting just as if they were home, where most of my bulbs are up 3 or 4 inches. For the first year they will probably do exactly as they would here, they bloomed at the same time, and it will take them all the seasons to learn to do your way. In the meantime they are nitwits.

It would be grand to have the shrunk human heads hanging up, and have little tiny spectacles on their noses and little gold fountain pens stuck behind their ears—editors. You would have to add it on to your letterhead, what you do. You would have to wear cork hats, and dress for dinner. You could have traps set in your office and a big net would fall down on the editors when they opened your door. This would be good to get new writers so they could not change their minds too, so whimsically. When your writers do badly you could shrink their heads too, 10%. All the way out to the elevator would be a dense jungle with a path people would have to hack their way through. Cornelia Otis Skinner[35] might not like it much at first, she would have to wear boots and cotton in her ears for gunshots. Now I am scared to come near too.

I think I will leave here around the first for NY, but that is all I know for sure. If there is by chance any money for me by that time, I have a little plan ready, but I won't set my heart on something that depends on editors. With a little more time of my own than I can have here, I want to try something, I feel ready to try, but I can't honestly put the word 'novel' to this mythical product yet so it would be nothing for you to speak about.

[. . .] I'll be glad to see you and if the book comes and something jumps out that will be the test. Good luck to all, including me.

Yours—

Eudora

Welty and Russell celebrated the appearance of her first book with parties in New York and at Katonah. After her return to Jackson, Welty received Russell's account of favorable reviews appearing in the New York Times, along with his own assurance that readers' admiration for this book would only increase with time (11.18.41).

In his next letter, Russell reported that he had spent the day spreading manure around his garden to enrich the soil for the following spring. "If the garden can but reach one per cent of my imagination I shall be crowing around the neighbourhood for in that sunlight region of the mind cabbages were three feet in diameter, beans were two or three feet long, the tomatoes were as large as footballs and all the plants had smiles on their faces" (11.21.41).

November 24, 1941

Dear Diarmuid,

I know what you mean about size in vegetables, as you can tell from this picture of me admiring a large Mississippi tomato one day—notice they are having to build their house around it, before they can sit down and eat it.[36] This may be due to maneovres and not to manure. But a place in Racine, Wis. sells packages of Gigantic New Guinea Butter Bean seeds, advertising "Grows to an astonishing size, the Beans measuring from 3 to 6 feet long and weighing anything from 10 to 16 lbs., and even more. One bean is sufficient for a family for several meals. The Delicate Buttery Flavor is much appreciated." There is a picture on the package of a man standing beside one of the beans, showing how small man really is. My mother would not let me plant the seeds but I wrote a little

rhyme for the seed company to use for their advertising if they wanted it
(I guess they didn't) that said:

> You may have seen the Atlantic,
> But have you seen the Gigantic—
> You may have seen beans too many,
> But have you seen the New Guinea—
> You may have been charmed by other means,
> But have you ever been charmed by the
> > Gigantic
> > New Guinea
> > Butterbeans?
>
> NO!

I would send them to you but I am afraid their power has gone, this was
so long ago.

[. . .] Katherine Anne wrote and said she was in despair over her novel
with 20,000 words more to go. That must have been what kept her and
I am sorry for her, though to myself I imagine one thing that's stopping
her is that her purpose in writing this story has to narrow down as she
goes instead of broadening out. [. . .] I think she feels things often, over
and over, and writes in a sort of synthesis, which is why she cannot ever
believe it is the way she wants it, and cannot quite let it go. It is not a very
direct way to write but it is a way to write very perfectly. It is a little like
the way they make the sound- track of a song in the movies, take the best
notes from a hundred different recordings and put them together, and it
is the purity that you miss, the clarity and integrity of the single original
impulse. Aesthetically I agree with you but the finished object she makes
has an extraordinary kind of beauty that no doubt comes from this very
much-divided source. This is a kind of rambling letter. It makes me glad
to think you believe my book might have some kind of little future. I care
very much what you think of it because I wrote most of the stories when
I could not imagine whether or not they communicated anything and in
some kind of hope that was wild enough that by some kindness of the
gods they would reach someone who would know rightly and would give
a sign. [. . .]

Yours
Eudora

In December 1941, Welty visited New Orleans with John Robinson, then returned with him to Jackson to attend the wedding of his sister, Anna Belle, on December 7. After the wedding, they learned of the Japanese attack on Pearl Harbor.[37] The following day, the United States declared war on Japan.

December 8, 1941
Dear Diarmuid,

"Excuse my not writing" (as an old lady with flowers to sell wrote me) "but must plead company." I was company myself in New Orleans and they came back with me and were my company, but today all is quiet again and now the teeth-grit of war is to begin. One thing I would like to read more of in Orage is his opinion of Swift, to whom I have the same kind of devotion.[38] Do you remember what the Houyhnhnm said when Gulliver described our art of war—"That although he hated the Yahoos of this country, yet he no more blamed them for their odious qualities than he did a bird of prey for its cruelty, or a sharp stone for cutting my hoof. But when a creature pretending to Reason could be capable of such enormities, he dreaded lest the corruption of that faculty might be worse than the brutality itself." I was glad you liked the story about Ida but I can tell it is going to be a trouble, for which I am sorry, but she rather catches you up—just as every subject does really of course—and you have to write more than you thought you would.[39] I do not mind if you cut it, but all the time I was cutting it myself down to about 5,000 words, having the idea somehow that that was the limit. [. . .] Tell John another Jackson store besides the bookstore has decided to offer a few [copies of *A Curtain of Green*] for sale, the department store, and they have placed four copies in the window, along with 50 articles such as long pink suede gloves, with a sign: "VOGUE'S 50 GIFTS UNDER $10.00," mine (the combined 4) being the 51st. It is hard to tell how well they are going to compete with 50 other objects, non-books, but I think they are just as pretty as the gloves. [. . .] Your Elysian fields sound fine, and I hope the manure will make them thrice-blessed (or is it thrice-happy?) Maybe the gods will truly be looking for some such place to sit by the time your grass is up.[40] You are right, there is nothing to do about the spider lilies, they are bound to grow on until next summer. I thought maybe I had found some purple ones for us in an old lady's advertisement of "blue phantom lilies" but when the bulbs came they looked like nothing on earth. Maybe nothing comes up but a little blue outline. Every camellia in this part of the country looks ready to bloom at any moment, and I become more and more anxious for you to see them all. If you could come as hoped could you come sooner? In New Orleans they declare February would be the best time. January, February and March are their blooming times, each plant having its favorite days but since you like azaleas too February would give a sight of both. Azaleas were blooming in New Orleans last week—that town rather bothers me, it is both timeless and seasonless, all the trees are evergreen, and there is always something blooming that makes you jump. I do like seasons. It was nice there though, sitting in a little back courtyard under banana trees and palm trees and smelling the sweet-olive flowers in the air. I brought back a boxfull of plants from someone's garden, some small odd kinds of native iris that bloom in little blue clusters, some croceum (?) bulbs, cuttings from an old-time yellow small rose, some exotic kind of hybrid amaryllis, and some seeds of a thing thought rare by the grower, hibiscus manihot, which has palmate leaves and yellow flowers with dark centers, and I will send you some to plant early if you have seedboxes and it will be an annual. Down there they have tree-dahlias, which grow up and branch as tall as most flowering trees, but are very dainty, with single lilac-colored flowers, large but delicate. The boy I know also has a golden spider lily which is a different kind of amaryllis and of which he is proud and he says smugly that he doubts if I ever find one. The old gardens in South Louisiana are the places to find all things. I just noticed how terrible a letter this looks, quite solid, no paragraphs or breaths.

At last I will have time to read "The Root and the Flower" which I have been saving.[41] [. . .]

What will happen to us? Since we have no relation to the war will it allow us to continue? Of course I can, but what about you? For myself, I guess I will try Johnny Appleseed next. The other day I wrote the New York Public library to ask if it was not too extraordinary a request that they would send down to me, to read, their little stock on Mr. Appleseed, for I wanted to note down a few facts, times, places, etc. and they wrote back that it was too extraordinary. That is, they gave me an itemised list of books and pamphlets and said I could not have any of them. It would be silly to burden a child's book with such like but I thought it would be well for me to know these things myself. When we are young we think that books are written out of complete knowledge, so I might as well learn the little available. In New Orleans I found a beautiful old little map of Mississippi showing the river running the way it really does, not like in your atlas, but north, south, east and west, and over the cuckoo's nest, and bought it, it was a dollar, and there was Benton on it. Judging from where it is on this map, I have been there, but simply didn't know it.

Yours

Eudora

As a Christmas present, Russell sent Welty three sketches done by his father, A.E.

December 12, 1941

Dear Diarmuid,

The beautiful presents came yesterday—safely—I wish I could tell you how much I like them—I do really believe I love them enough for you to have parted with them—It is wonderful to have these very ones and to see that they are instant and fragmentary and still partake wholly of the same beauty—and to have three—wonderful to see each one, each alone and different from the others—hills and sea—beings of light—two walking—and then to see all filled with a radiance and mystery from the same source—I will take care of them and see them every day—I guess frame them but I meant more—They must have given me some primitive kind of happiness besides the other kind—no one would have taken them away from me but the first thing I did was to hide them—Then I realized what I had done—I am glad they came early so they could come on a day of their own—It was a day that anyone *might* have got a present, it was like a spell, silver to look at, rain in every breath of the atmosphere, on every leaf and blade of grass, but not falling—when you took a walk it was quiet and still, the tree trunks seemed luminous, and violets were cool and filled with weight in their heads when you picked them—Today the drops are falling softly, the birds are singing clearly, and even in my room upstairs I can hear the thrashers walking around under their roof of the magnolia-fuscata branches, thinking the world is green and filling with small brown funny birds all over—Thank you again for sending me the beautiful and magic sketches—I never thought such things would come to me—

Yours

Eudora

December 23, 1941
Dear Diarmuid,

I gather the war may be having a depressing or stagnating effect on the business, but maybe that is just the first shock and things will begin to go on again. People get used to terrible things quickly—the more terrible the thing the more quickly they get used to it, it seems—it is part of the kind of ignobility that can put one in despair. Though what hurts now is to see people come alive at cruelty—to give their attention at last and give it to that, to be aware at last, and aware of that, and to be eager to inflict their own. All of a sudden in a calamity they turn receptive and eager and wait lovingly to be acted upon, even fooled, while if something gentle and wise and holding truth should be offered to them in their lone lives they would turn rigidly aside. Plunged safely into a mass feeling they show off and preen their anger and horror, when they have never in their lives given any hint or sign or indication of a feeling of their own, an elation that might have been greater. I suppose it is a small thing to be concerned about at such times—but sometimes I am in despair about people and it feels good to hate them as a kind and to give all your love to a few and to flowers and animals. I cannot feel a wish for destruction of anyone but O Lord how I want to protect the rest. To keep a few separate and apart. I don't know what I will write next, but I wish it would be something that could make an individual and tender life when seen alone seem sacred and inviolate from all beastliness and violence that besets it. People must be taken one by one in the world, that is the way they are loved, believed, or understood, and when we are told to think in masses, we are lost for the one thing that is the essence and holy is gone. This may sound confused—it is what I have always felt but I may never learn how to say it. I would just as soon write about Johnny Appleseed because he was a singularly unencumbered soul that postulated freedom for himself and then acted exactly as he saw fit and it was a good way. Without adherents, bodyguards, disciples, gangsters, or anyone, without force or coercion, only with gentleness and a firm steady head and hand, he did what he did and never harmed a living thing. I would not want to point morals or a lesson but for its own sake it would make an account worth writing down, if not by me, by somebody. I somehow do not feel it as a children's book; so maybe I'm not the one. I really sort of hold on to Johnny Appleseed in these days, what little I know of him takes on all its meaning, more all the time, in my head, which proves he does have something of the genuine legendary personage about him.

The sketches are in little frames now, narrow ones of natural wood, which was the best I could do, and they look nice and please me every time I see them.[42]

I keep wondering if the little camellia will get to you, for it seems to be taking a long time finding its way through mazes of troubles and terrors, I guess.[43] I forgot to tell you there is some mystery about its origin and the lady as she was digging it up was heard to say to one side, "Damn it, I hope this isn't an Eleanor Fairoaks!" I said, how do you tell an Eleanor Fairoaks, and she said, muttering, "Lightning markings." Then she put her fingers in both her ears and said, "Don't tell me if it is one, for I sold my soul for its mother." So you may have something that will make you rich when it is big, and if it ever comes and it flowers, watch out.[44] I had a wonderful dream about going back to the original camellia that took all night that I will tell you about some time. In an office you can't sit listening to dreams. First there were all the billions of camellias in the world, that was how it started. Then these just narrowed themselves down to millions, each showing how it was a variation of what, then these narrowed themselves down, and so on, back and back, further and further, and all the time I had to hold on fast (it was like being in a strong wind) or I could never keep it straight or learn it exactly. It was like a wonderful problem in deduction but it had all kinds of importance attached, I forget what. So the plants narrowed down and narrowed down, all night, and finally there were only three left and still I held on, and then all of a sudden there was only one, the original bush, and I looked and the leaves stirred and I got to see it.

But immediately there was a little sound like the closing of a jewel box, fast and final, and that was the end. It was such an undertaking of the mind, I would never in my waking moments consider starting back so far.

Yours
Eudora

Below them the river was glimmering, narrow, soft, and skin-col-
ored, and slowed nearly to stillness. The shining willow trees hung
round them. The net that was being drawn out, so old and so long-
used, it too looked golden, strung and tied with golden threads.

Standing still on the bank, all of a sudden William Wallace,
on whose word they were waiting, spoke up in a voice of surprise.
"What is the name of this river?"

They looked at him as if he were crazy not to know the name
of the river he had fished in all his life. But a deep frown was on his
forehead, as if he were compelled to wonder what people had come
to call this river, or to think there was a mystery in the name of a
river they all knew so well, the same as if it were some great far tor-
rent of waves that dashed through the mountains somewhere, and
almost as if it were a river in some dream, for they could not give
him the name of that.

—"The Wide Net," May 1942

At first, in the hushed disappointment which filled the Chautau-
qua tent in beginning moments, the music had been sparse and
spare, like a worn hedge through which the hiders can be seen. But
then, when hope had waned, there had come a little transition to
another key, and the woman with the cornet had stepped forward,
raising her instrument.

If morning-glories had come out of the horn instead of those
sounds, Josie would not have felt a more astonished delight. She
was pierced with pleasure. The sounds that so tremulously came
from the striving of the lips were welcome and sweet to her. Between
herself and the lifted cornet there was no barrier, there was only the
stale, expectant air of the old shelter of the tent. The cornetist was
beautiful. There in the flame-like glare that was somehow shad-
owy, she had come from far away, and the long times of the world
seemed to be about her.

—"The Winds," August 1942

CHAPTER TWO

January 1942–August 1943

By January 1942 Welty and Russell were planning for her next book, a group of stories that were all connected to the Natchez Trace, an ancient trail running from Natchez, Mississippi, to Nashville, Tennessee. The setting of the Trace was inspiring Welty to write more ambitious, longer stories that took her much longer to complete. A few months earlier, she had told Russell, "I see whenever I think about the Trace now a kind of wanderer and all the gloom he walks in and the flicker of poor little uncertain lights about him that give him hope and the stubborn radiance he lets rise inside him and all that he passes by or imagines is there in a sort of panorama" (5.41). In "The Winds" and other stories from this period, Welty was exploring her characters' impulses and desires from the inside out, often presenting events through irrational or dreamlike perspectives. Editors and even Russell were puzzled by these stories initially, but Russell encouraged Welty to continue revising them. Some of her letters discuss her hopes for these new works alongside descriptions of gardens and natural settings. "For me ideas must go far off into excursions of their own, once they start," she told Russell in July 1942, "like somebody that walks along a little road in some country and samples the various berries and breaks off a stick to climb over the wild places with and drinks out of the brooks that come, and on and on, and you have to wait till they come back before you know what they found, but you had better be there when they get home." A few sentences later, seemingly changing the subject, Welty added, "The strange bulbs came and God knows what they really are or what will happen to them down here but they are in the ground" (7.13.42). The artist was following the lead of the gardener, who believed that "you have to see and watch what each [plant] wants" (2.17.44). Patiently revising these new, more complex narratives, Welty allowed her fiction to unfold at its own pace and to lead her in unexpected directions.

Russell's efforts, too, were bearing fruit. Welty's stories were earning higher royalties from magazines, and she won a Guggenheim Fellowship in February 1942. In the fall, her Natchez Trace novella, *The Robber Bridegroom*, was published as a separate book, and by late 1943 she had become the author of a third book, *The Wide Net and Other Stories*. Her professional successes were overshadowed by worry over the safety of many friends and family who were now in the military: brothers, cousins, and close friends, especially John Robinson, who joined the U.S. Army Air Corps in 1942. An additional urgency now underscored Welty's discussions of gardens and Nature. As she had told Russell just after war was declared, she longed to create fiction that could "make an individual and tender life [. . .] seem sacred and inviolate from all beastliness and violence that besets it." With the world at war, Welty was more conscious than ever of "individual and tender life," the kind that gardeners protect and friends cherish.

January 7, 1942
Dear Diarmuid,

Snow today—and nobody sorrier than the fig trees. If you could see the camellia bushes in the yards your heart would go out to them for the indignities they are suffering—just as they were prepared to shine forth all in bloom people have run out and covered them from top to bottom—just in anything—stakes are driven round them and then carpeting, dish pans, curtains, flowered cretonne, blankets and old sheets are put on them. They will be all right I guess and some day will be uncovered but now some of them look like Egyptian mummies and some like ballet dancers on skinny legs and some like ducks with little tails sticking out and some like whole assemblies of matched ghosts, white with blue borders. There is a maniac here (really a surgeon) with a yard full of huge bushes which he erects canvas tents over and heats all night by gas heaters inside, one each—an ideal place for drawing tramps, I should think, and I am a little envious of tramps that could come in out of the cold to a nice warm tent and a stove to heat coffee over and a Pink Perfection to curl up under for the evening, imagine waking up and finding that you're in bloom. [. . .]

Yours—
Eudora

January 19, 1942
Dear Diarmuid,

O God, what a day, too grand, I had a digger poised but will lay it down and work on The Winds, thanks to the good news, and hope I can fix it.[1] The brain has not been working lately and all I can do is make rugs, but have made two—that's enough—it must be my brain hibernates in winter. In bloom—crocuses. Hyacinths on the verge. I am making a list like a tickertape of things to order. Also breath-of-spring is blooming outside my domain and must be stolen. [. . .]

Yours
Eudora

February 4, 1942
Dear Diarmuid,

I haven't any story today, but I will write and tell you that I have a daphne coming, is that a nice thing? It is the garland flower so it will be convenient to make garlands. I will make one for your genius the day you find him, to put around his neck. The rain lilies were starting to grow last week, so I sent them to you quick. They are just little low pink flowers but I like them and some day after a rain look out and they will all come in bloom before your eyes. Zephyranthes—a kind of amaryllis—is what they are.

I was glad to have the figures—people are always asking me point-blank on the street how many copies I have sold of my book and how much money they gave me. But I'm still being introduced as "our poetess."

[. . .] I'm afraid my brother will have to leave this month for the army, and three more of my friends. There's not much to be found out about it—all I know is that it will be soon and far from here and that all their hearts are gentle. I was asked to be in charge of the volunteer publicity to "popularize" and "sell" all local war doings in the paper and radio and said I would not, but the way this has to be done is just another little sign that the emotion behind what we will do has been falsely made—and what could be a surer proof of the real lack of validity in what we have done—

A cardinal has just started singing in the holly tree and I must say he looks handsome—and in charge—and it is beyond any doubt spring, and all kinds of old gay itinerant souls that I always look for are show-ing up. The first one is the sassafras man who comes in boots and cap, looking like a general this time of year with the gold roots strung on him, in bunches all up and down and across him, and on his shoulders like epaulettes—he sits on the church steps in the sun, enjoying life, and people come to him. He ties the roots in bundles with little strips of old inner-tubes, but when my brother bought some this year he got it untied and handed to him loose, because the sassafras man said he had to save tires.

The little camellia seems to be basking in some springtime of kind treatment. I am sure these are its first flowers and I hope it will know how to make them beautiful. Don't let anyone point at the buds, for that is supposed to be bad luck and they will not open—or maybe it is really only bad manners and they know it. I have a white one in the house that is almost open—I go in and read by it. (Yes, it is so bright.)

Yours

Eudora

On February 6, 1942, Russell wrote, "Harper's Magazine have also just phoned up to say they want THE WIDE NET and that they consider it a work of genius and one of the funniest stories they have ever had. Price $250, on account its on the long side. Probably will be published Juneish, plus or minus, which refers to time and not to money. The camellia is still opening, bit by bit and gloriously, with the stamens peeping out, the whole thing looking too extravagant for our cottage— it should be housed in a palace. As soon as its full out I will give you a literal description of what it looks like, in case I have some wonder that has never been seen before."

February 9, 1942

Dear Diarmuid,

Three letters and all kinds of enclosures and things, and even how the camellia opens—I would like it like this every day. [. . .]

After some more stories accumulate we can see how they do and what combination would be the best for a book. So far no one-act plays or anything have entered to throw things off but something may at any time, for I feel the way you feel always in spring, as if it might be pos-sible to go in some place that is different, by a different way, and as if it would be easy to be far away and doing something spacious and free.

People from the country are in the markets selling their jonquils and hyancinths, that are blooming before ours, and I long to speak out and ask them things.

Good luck

Yours,

Eudora

In late February, Russell reported, "The camellia suffered the most terrible tragedy. The buds almost came out and then one day Pammy came in and said she touched one and it fell off and I was furious and went to look and touched one of the two remaining buds and it fell off—and later the last bud fell off. I think it may have had something to do with the clayey soil in which it came." He added that he had spent several hours outdoors the previous weekend; since the ground was still frozen at Katonah, he spent the time waxing his car (2.26.42).

March 6, 1942

Dear Diarmuid—

Your letter was here when I came home and by the way you went at shining up the car I can see spring hovering in the air and you just biding your time. I am sorry about the camellia. That is an old grief—but it is a shame for you to have it the first time, and with your good care. No one seems to know just why the plants sometime lose their buds indoors, there are lots of theories which I think are guesses and superstitions, and I think you may be right about the soil in the case of your little bush. Re-potting would be good for it anyway, just so you don't disturb it about the roots. Your good soil in a slightly bigger pot with the ball set into it and not any deeper than it is now, with a little peatmoss sprinkled on top and the pot buried in a half-shaded place, will keep it fine till the cold comes next year. I hope it never does this again. Sometimes in poor soil like ours the roots ball in the center and we find watering from the bottom in the house and burying the pot in the ground all summer keeps the earth softer and of the same consistency and lets the roots grow. I read in a book that potting soil for camellias should be above all things porous and might be the following mixture—2 parts cow manure, 2 parts sandy loamy soil, and 1 part peat, to which is added sufficient commercial fertilizer to create a chemical balance (you will know what that means). But I believe any good soil you have up there would be such a kind and welcome change that the camellia would put out a whole array of grateful buds, and then certainly have the grace to flower. I have a bush that is the same as yours and when the flowers are open I will send you some just to look at, I can't bear for you not to know what you have got. Our bushes have been a little hurt by freezes coming at the wrong time, in spite of being covered night after night during the cold spell, and have been at a standstill with their flowers, but today is beautiful and I hope they will open to the warm sun soon. Usually by this time all is in flower. On the Coast they were blooming. I wish you had the little green-house you might build and there was a cool-greenhouse partitioned off for camellias, because when I see them all coming out each kind is so different from all the rest that you can't know how beautiful camellias are from one or two. I don't care about number, but each kind is beautiful. When you go around the countryside you see that each little community of any age has its own variety, grown from seed by some lady once and cuttings given away, and there you will see a great parent bush in some yard and little and middle-sized ones scattered in the yards around it, all a camellia known only to the one place. I am trying to collect cuttings of the ones that are the nicest and after years go by I'll have them all in one place—whatever kind of instinct that may be.[2] [. . .]

I *know* I wrote you about the rain lilies, but the letter probably got lost. They are not like the zephyranthes in the picture in Vaughan's, being larger flowers and pink, but they are kin to those. They are native to the Americas and I understand have some loud Cuban cousins but these that I have are delicate and graceful and grow low, and some day after a rain you look out and they will all come in bloom before your eyes, that's why they're called rain lilies. They multiply like rabbits and are tender (like lettuce) so you will have to lift them over the winter if you want to keep them. Have you a seed-box planted? Lots of little pinks are ready to be transplanted here and all kinds of little odd things. Hasten the day.

Yours,
Eudora

March 19, 1942
Thursday
Dear Diarmuid,

Thanks for the letter and check which came just now. We are all all right, the storm went by overhead but didn't swoop down here. It went down on my poor little pets, the people in Lafayette County,[3] the ones who personify the elements and seasons when they talk and say Jack Frost and "Old Mr. Winter", and who somehow get all the calamities. I was working in the garden and knew what was coming by the sudden heat and electricity that filled the air and the black clouds with a sulphur-yellow sky under them and I could only begin hoping that the schools out in the country had let out and the children had got home, and they just had.

[. . .] I'm glad the camellias got there and I'm glad to know about the potato—I knew you could send gardenias that way, but somehow doubted if camellias would endure the indignity.[4] I was a little worried because at the express office I had to sign a paper saying there was no bomb in the box, and of course that is a fine excuse for them to just take all packages to a vacant lot and drop them in a bucket of oil and never send them. We are still all in bloom here, for each bush has its own time. I'm sorry there were no white ones to send that day. There are some kinds that begin blooming red and then as days go by they bloom pink and finally white. I guess they use up all their red in the first energy and delight. [. . .]

Your spreading house sounds fine and you will be having company all the time, I can see that. It will soon be like this up there and you will be seeing buds on the Dutch iris and the leaves will all be coming out everywhere in a beautiful golden green and the redbud will be against it looking like what I see now out the window. I have some little species tulips, not many, but they are what I would like to have more of some day, and they have small long narrow buds like arrow-tips. They all have green-purple stems and the most wonderful colors, to read about, lemon yellow and pink and green even in the leaves. I like originals of flowers, the single and bright-colored kinds, and they all have fragrance too, all the things that have been bred out, for size. Of course camellias have been bred that way, so long that no one knows what the wild one looks like, but I think they have sometimes arrived at perfection. The Chinese especially knew what to breed toward, but their kinds, the most simple and fragile, are alas the most expensive.

[. . .]

Have to go out and admire everything.

Yours

Eudora

Western Union
March 23, 1942
      HAPPY DAY THE CHARMS WORKED THE GUGGENHEIM
CAME AND I AM DIZZY—EUDORA

March 23, 1942
Dear Eudora:
      Isn't this a happy day? [. . .] I would have got quite angry if Guggenheim hadn't given you something.[5] Now you will be able to take another trip up here this year, if you want to, with a bottle of rum in your pocket and a pineapple packed away in your trunk. [. . .] As soon as you calm down tell me what you are going to do on the Gugg. Go to Guatemala? Fish in the Restigouche? Build a greenhouse? Horseback in the Sierra Nevadas? Get a new hat for Easter or buy a boat with a hammock and float on the Mississippi
      yours happily
      Diarmuid

March 27, 1942
Friday
Dear Diarmuid,
      I wanted to be told back by you and Henry and John[6] that I had got the Guggenheim, then I believed it. It was something that befell something else in a whole array of things that were somehow started up, and I am still surprised, and working the whole day long in the garden I would forget it and then if I thought of it I couldn't help but wonder if it was so. [. . .]
      As to the hat, I saw the aunt of one of my friends downtown and ran up to her and said "Oh Aunt Mary, I just got a Guggenheim," and she said "A Guggenheim *what*?" I think she thought it was a hat.
      I haven't felt yet any assurance to come with it that I will be entering any new phase—I go from change to change knowing about it and very aware, and I know it is coming, and for sure there is something, a state of mind, that is like a place, which I would like to reach and long to reach, but I still don't know the way, and where I felt in the dark before, I still do, and still have only a blind hope and only moments of a waiting intensity to go by.

[. . .] I have lots of energy and full days working, but on flowers, not stories—there is so much to do outside that I may never get through and never get to stories. I only think about the kind of day and the feel of the earth that day, and the planting and transplanting and spading and digging and weeding and watering, and then I am asleep and doing the same thing in my sleep. About a month ago I made the mistake of sending off for a whole lot of catalogues from fine places, just to look at the pictures and find out about West Coast plants and bulbs, and now here they all come, the pictures all but speaking from the page and saying "You can afford it now, don't turn over." There are some strange bulbs there, I will tell you, in case you don't know it, they get them from the Cape of Good Hope and around. Some sound curious, I would hesitate to say infernal, but I think it, and some sound the most beautiful you can imagine, and the prices are to match them, $5 a bulb, or for bulbs that have flowered, $10. I think they must weigh quite a lot too, for they say the express charges are often as much as the price of the bulb. Do you think they are of enormous size, or just of densest gravity, with all that much of a thing contained inside them. They could be changeling bulbs, because if I remember, one way to tell a changeling from a real child is to weigh it, the changeling weighs entirely too much. Or maybe the bulb is just resisting being dug up, and is getting strong. This is enough. What I love are the little bulbs, originals, and some day I hope to have and see some fritillarias and species tulips if I can find any—maybe I will go to those countries—goodbye—

This letter is being written at different times as I come into the house and must not make sense. There is one from Asia Minor (tulip) with beautiful narrow pointed petals pink-and-green tipped, that does not open on any day until one P.M. and then it is more fragrant than any of the rest. I might bring you one back. I must say it has taken a long time to wake up to the sun. In my garden is a little Clusiana species tulip open and nodding and looking beautiful. In the ground—I wish I had time to draw a map! maps—I have Canterbury Bells, delphiniums, phlox, forget-me-nots, sweet-alyssum, oxalis and those things, wild lilies from Florida, butterfly lilies, rubrum lilies and Easter lilies and phillipenense, "blue lilies of the Nile," Jacob's Ladders, Mariposa tulips and other tulips, crinum, stocks and many things, in various stages of seeds and shoots. The time to leave it—when will that be, because we have to water as soon as the heat comes, which will be soon. I guess we are not much ahead of you in our late Spring—Jackson is pretty with all the trees coming out in leaves shinier than the blue sky and more shades of green than there are shades of yellow in the fall, and the flowering trees in arches and cascades, peaches, almonds, plums and every color of quince, and in our garden are irises blooming, violets of all the violet colors, bleeding hearts, trout lilies (1), hyacinths and the late narcissi, and spireas, and a Lady Banksia rose is all gold in the garden across the street—How is yours?

Yours

Eudora

April 5, 1942

Easter

Dear Diarmuid,

[. . .] I know no transformation came along with the Guggy, but that was just what would have been nice—why get a tap on the head at all if you are not going to turn beautiful or glamorous or become full of strange powers—however it would have been only for a year and you couldn't do much in that time. Only revolutionize everything and change the world up.

I wanted to ask you about growing tulips from seed—species tulips—I know it's a dangerous enterprise for me to undertake, but not long ago I sent off for the seeds and now they will be coming and what happens to them will be on my head. Would you freeze them first? They will probably be here tomorrow. All I can think of is to fix some good kind of drainage system in a seed box, and just plant them—and I don't mind how long it takes, but would like to know. I thought maybe you had done this in Ireland.

It is a beautiful Easter day down here. A little boy came running by flying to an Easter egg hunt waving his basket, and said he hadn't been to one in a month. We drove through the colored section where all the clothes are the most imaginative and really the most effective on shining dark skin, when you get right down to Easter egg colors. The negro men this year have a style all their own—not copied from white people, but theirs, and it is a delight. Pants come up as high as the points of the collar, almost, and bell out and come to peg tops, showing 6 inches of sock (bright). Shirts are satin. Coats are long and come as low as the bend in the knee behind and are a light perishable color. Hats are up to 10 or 12 inches wide in the brim, gently turned up like a saucer, some colored and some black with wide satin bands, and all have one, two, or three full length turkey feathers stuck in the back. This is a back view but does not tell you how they walk. When they ride bicycles their coat tails float far, far out behind them, like gauzy dragon fly wings. As in bird life, the females are far surpassed, no matter how they try.

[pencil sketch of man in long coattails and broad-brimmed hat with feathers]

I will close with a dream—it was about an iris—The flower floated for the whole dream in front of me, in slight motion and a little larger than life so that all the pattern of it was shown closely—then going off from it stamped or printed on the air were fainter images of the iris, and it showed how by giving off its form or its qualities of color or fragrance, all these being distinct images each one, it set people to paint or to dance or to plan structures and systems or to follow after some romantic thing, all depending on the image thrown off by the iris, and then it suddenly appeared in cross section and was identical with the floor plan of a great church. This is a crude account for it was very intricate, and very delicately shown, and I had the feeling that it could go on giving off images like a fountain, for as long as I could dream it. Some time when you are not very busy advise on the tulip seed.

Yours

Eudora

April 20, 1942
Monday
Dear Diarmuid,

[. . .] I am glad you thought the new story ["Livvie Is Back"] all of a piece. It was a supreme effort, really, that I made to have it so, but I thought the odds were against me, and was worn out and depressed afterwards. If there was any way to get the envelope back out of the slot in the post-office after mailing, like with a long hook and a string—you would never get a story, though I will race down in the middle of the night, I'm so anxious to put it in.

How are your little gladioli? There is no telling, is there, what you might not get? The tulip seeds came, and I heard the cook screaming when she found them in the ice-compartment of the refrigerator, a little file of envelopes. Also, all kinds of bulbs came, moreas, asphodels ("the genuine ancient's") a blue-shell flower (eustylis) that grows up like the tigridias but is contained in the tiniest bulb, no bigger than a pea—all of which I hope will bloom in the late summer. Couldn't you come to see them? Don't answer to me, just write the cook. Remember, moreas are fugacious, and some of the flowers only last 4 hours, so you will have to be prompt. I have a little fleet of lilies coming up. Here now it is iris and rose and tulip and sweet-shrub time. Just to take a walk at night, all the streets have their own sweet blends of scent, and a street after a little rain, just the right street, in the moonlight! I hope this letter did not come on your busiest day. Chinaberry flowers are simply unbelievable, they must be smelled—not obstreperously, but gently, as if by accident, as you come into their drifts—to be believed. We go out just for that. If you ever do, in the next 30 yrs., get a crate of chinaberry flowers without a card, that will be from me, and you and Henry can line the office with them and all your visitors will go into swoons—or is that what you want?

Later.

I hadn't thought of the connection between the iris I dreamed about and the fleur-de-lis, but it was time I had for something is going on somewhere, in my subconscious or unconscious, that I discover like new every day or so. The day your letter came I had just exchanged my book at the library and got "Mont-Saint-Michel and Chartres," [by Henry Adams] without thought of connection, then you recalled medieval France. Another time I was sketching idly and drew Reynard the Fox without a doubt—which I remembered when I came to a sentence in Adams telling that Reynard's head was carved on the handrest in a seat in the choir in Chartres cathedral. The crowning thing (you see—it even makes me pun before I know it) is that I was fascinated by a fine hat that I could not afford, no other hat would do, and bought it, it was on my birthday—and after that, standing idly before a little reproduction of one of the "Tres Riches Heures" which I have framed on my wall, I saw the hat, feather and all, on one of the ladies, same style, everything—it is a different color, but it is exactly the color of its little trees meant to be in their spring leaf, that clear marvelous vert de vert that could not be found today except in a hat prohibitively expensive—and this painting was the one done to celebrate the month of April, which is my birth month. All this is very trifling but it depresses me rather, because I don't understand it and it makes me feel that my mind is inferior if it is in little, sort of tricky, prodding things, that magic-like connections have to be made. I suppose the subconscious mind as well as the conscious can take a great

liking to some time and place in history and see it in everything—but why? Isn't it mysterious? I have never known much about the thirteenth century in France, though I like it very well—enough to have cut out and framed some of the "Tres Riches Heures" a few years back to hang over my bookcase, and on penetrating through the superciliousness of Henry Adams in this book I find the things I do most greatly admire, in the directness, simplicity of belief, gaiety, strength, aspiration, purity, exuberancy, etc., of that time reflected in all that he relates, but I have not got this *passion* for it that lies underneath. I feel depressed, though not scared to go to sleep at night or anything. Maybe you noticed that in my new story the Natchez Trace turned into a moat for a minute. I was writing fast, in the center of my concentration, and put that down, and just left it in. How can I speak of this to anyone—they would think I am cracy [*sic*], and maybe you do, and maybe I am. It all may be just spring fever. Then longen folk to goon on pilgrimages.[7] There may be somebody in the world now thinking so hard on the 13th century that in my openness of dream and vacancy of mind I caught it. I guess it will pass—although now I am determined to read and ponder all I am able on the time, and force the connection through and see what is so marvelous to me. I have to, when I can't doubt it.—I had to say this to someone.
    Yours
    Eudora

Late April 1942
Dear Diarmuid,
    [. . .] I would be glad if I could come up in May and that is my hope but there is no end in sight of the work to do. The garden has an emergency every day, transplanting, pruning, spraying against all the plagues we have, mulching against the heat of summer or they faint like ladies in the swoon of the afternoon, painting the swing and the chairs, preserving the strawberries that are coming in, and you know all the rites of spring. I have a little malaria at night, but hope to get over that too. At last the tulip seeds are planted, and what a thing—they stick to the fingers like beggarlice,[8] and I had to shoot them off the end of my thumb like marbles. It's a good thing I didn't have to conk them like croquet balls to get them in their rows or I would still be planting them four years from now when they are supposed to be blooming, with everybody standing around in derision. The weather is wonderful and soft and fragrant and

the nights are lovely, the garden under the moon is like an island floating in light, and today at long last it is about to rain and the birds sound low and consultant. The mocking birds walk around as you plant and dig and open their mouths if you come to a worm, and if you don't put it in their mouths they scold. The blue shell flower is coming up—all these below-equator things are so immediate and instant in what they do, you have to watch and you hate to go away. One of your little gladioli is likely to flower as a tier of small princes sitting cross-legged in order of honor up the stalk, each with a little instrument that he alone can play.

Yours

Eudora

May 4, 1942

Dear Diarmuid,

Quick work on the story.[9] [. . .] About the hibiscus, I don't know, never having seen a yellow one, and the boy who gave me the seeds is drafted—but he just hung them on the Christmas tree and said wait and see. I doubt if they take on the size of altheas but I wouldn't trust them in front. I heard mother telling a visitor that she doubted if mine got "big enough to do much damage this year." You might transplant the seeds to your landlord's garden for observation. They are slow to germinate, mine are just a few inches high now but look as if they are about to spring, sort of big crouching leaves. Did I tell you how instantaneous the south-of-the-equator bulbs are? I just barely got them into the ground in time. If you would care for any spider-lilies this year I can bring you any number from one to a hundred. It has never rained here either, after promising, and every thing has to be watered every evening. I made paper hats for some things. Also a plague of plagues is upon everything, even my camellias whose every leaf I watch—coming overnight, and I spent all day yesterday spraying bad concoctions mixed by my mother. Do you know what eats mariposa tulip buds? I should think anything with refined taste might, but it does break my heart for they were just showing color. Now is the time when all the swamps will be filled with strange rare things. Do you think I could buy a ticket on the bus and get on carrying a bucket and spade and wearing hip boots and patting a snake-bite remedy bottle in my pocket, and get off in the middle of the swamps; and get back on the night bus hung with lilies and irises and orchids and snakes and with water hyacinths in my hair, and not attract unfavorable attention? My mother will not even answer this question, much less say "Use the tires and go, rather than that."[10] When I take the trip up I will see all kinds of invaluable things from the train window—why is it you always see such grand things from trains? There have been times when I could barely stay on and I would almost get off at the nearest stop and see a house I could live in and how I could fix it up and where things would grow and imagine the view as being daily for the rest of my life.

Yours,
Eudora

In late May, Welty visited New York, spending a weekend with the Russells at Katonah.

June 8, 1942
Jackson
Dear Diarmuid,

It was lovely to be there and I feel homesick to come back, but I guess the time is far away. Did you air-spot and did Henry come out and did you see the roses—that would be the last I know and now I have to start thinking of you all in the old absent way again. Even if that might be the truer way sometimes there is something so comforting otherwise. I enjoyed coming out so much, and was glad to see the house so big and the garden so beautiful. I never thought I would get to see so many irises. There was a light over the sky after rain one evening on the way home (by that time I was on a bus, and the countryside was closer) that I wish could have been on your pluie d'or iris—it was sort of like it, everything was, the sides of the sky going up gold, and down below where the hills are gentle, reflected gold light. [. . .] Maybe some day I will write a story of the imagination that will really do what I hope, really be an incantation to make what I feel or have delight in come alive. When I fail in a story I blame myself, some flaw would not let the story come through, but if I make the story as well as I can it is because the story itself has been allowed to get a start and grow in its own life. I feel such a line, like a boundary, between those that have life and those that don't. But I can't tell where the Robber falls, if it is wrong and dead, or if it has life, because it really was written in a kind of dreamy way, a dreamy concentration rather. This is what Katherine Anne said once that no 'artist' would allow himself to do, she sees the highest virtue in calculation, [. . .] she said nothing written out of a dream could be even respectable. I would just as soon write out of a dream, out of music, out of love, out of a beautiful day, out of anything except out of craft—because I think no stories perfect but all of them seem more like a little road, leading from one thing bigger than the writer into some other thing which should be also bigger than the writer. Perhaps it is all because I love magic things instead of clever things. I am sure K. A. does too, only she thinks by being clever enough you will be magic, and I don't think you ever will. Do you? She is magic in spite of her cleverness. I am not magic but my heart lives in that country, and some day something might just happen. I would work like a slave for it if it did. [. . .]

In our garden are hemerocallis, larkspur, single dahlias, and loaded gardenia bushes smelling sweet night and day. One day lily I like very much is named J. A. Crawford, like a plumber—the clearest yellow, and the clearer they are the better, for me—very slender and airy, turning different ways. I have worked hard and now there is a nice rain. I hope the cutworms will stay away up there and that all is growing. I have looked up all the plants you wrote down and some sound possible here if I can find them. Lots of them you can make dyes out of and eat for vegetables, so when you come down here some time I will be wearing a gown of allamanda and serve you a datura-moringa salad with jacarandas.

Take care of yourselves and love,

Eudora

June 12, 1942

Dear Diarmuid,

Thanks for the jackpot. [. . .] It is awful about the cutworms—are you going to try the third time—you must have pinks. Here is an old Greek charm against mice—not much help—"Take a sheet of paper and write on it as follows: 'I adjure you, ye mice here present, that ye neither injure me nor suffer another mouse to do so. I give you yonder field (here you specify the field), but if I ever catch you here again, by the mother of the gods I will rend you in seven pieces.' Write this, and stick the paper on an unhewn stone in the field before sunrise, taking care to keep the written side up." They might eat the letter all the way down word by word and just leave the last word, 'pieces', that would be their way (lip-readers). I wonder why they shrank from the cosmos. Some spanking-new rabbits ate all the leaves off my birdsfoot violets, ate on till I got within an inch of their little tails. What made them think they would like violets for their very first meal? And you read that if there is anything mice love it is tigridia bulbs—how did they get on to the delicacy—there are so many more mice than tigridia bulbs—I guess such are their life search and dream and in their craniums is stamped a little mouse-vision of a tigridia.

[. . .] There has been much hard work in the garden, and it is a hot steamy rainy time with beautiful longlasting sunsets and soft black nights with wind from the gulf coming in the south and the cardinals and mockingbirds singing all night again. Every evening between 8 and 9 you can watch the Calypso daylily opening—it is a night daylily—palest pure yellow, long slender curved petals, the color of the new moon. To see it actually open, the petals letting go, is wonderful, and its night fragrance comes to you all at once like a breath. What makes it open at night—what does it open to? in the same progression as others close, moment by moment. Tell about night flowers.

Yours,

Eudora

June 20, 1942

Dear Diarmuid,

We are having a fine rain—I felt so glad, I began to write a letter. By now I hope you are well again—are you?

[. . .] Do you want to examine my letter from the Virgin Islands?[11] When he asked me pointblank if I had ever seen bluejays sitting on the hot rail of the railroad track, I started out all right, but then I wavered. I ended by saying if they did not sit on the rails, I wrote that they did because, unlike him, I had not spent my life watching where bluejays sit, but only in assuming where they sat, although, until I saw a bluejay *refuse* to sit on a rail I would continue to assume that it did, and besides I told him he did not know this town that was in my story and that there the bluejays not only sit on rails in the summertime, they skate on them in winter. Maybe you had better answer the letter too, as my agent. Remember the censors are opening the letters both ways, and for all I know, so are the bluejays. [. . .] Today I have something beautiful in flower, and drew it on a scratchpad—It is Eustylis Purpurea—that only blooms from eight to three-a. But I think it will have fresh flowers from day to day, and all from the tiniest bulb I have ever seen—no bigger than this * . Maybe a little bigger, but for some reason there is not a thing on this typewriter the size of a eustylis bulb—they ought to have a bulb keyboard, with bulb drawings on the top row and italics below. I can no longer write to you on this typewriter. Something I did turned out to be smart. I wrote to Oakhurst Gardens in California, one of the strange bulb clip joints, and offered to exchange with them—I would send them spider lilies and they could send me something wonderful out of their catalogue.[12] I made it casual and unsuspicious. They wrote back that they would do it but doubted if I wanted to bother since they would only allow me $5 a hundred in exchange, up to 1500 bulbs. I can send him two or three hundred bulbs this year so imagine my delight. He asks 25¢ apiece for them in the catalogue, so he has thought of a way to make money. By now you might have 100, look and see. Do you know Mrs. Hegarty, a recent introduction from Ireland? (A lily. Schizostylis.) I am in a dazzle what to pick out. Tigridias, clivias, Peruvian scillas—they sound nice, tigridias do well here. I certainly do not want any Kangaroo Paws whose flowers and stems are covered with yellowish wool, they make me want to take my spider lilies indignantly back. He hasn't any of the things from the Bahamas. Watch out for the hibiscus manihot plants, mine are high already, and look like conquerors of 50. Did the cutworms retreat?[13] I hope they did. Our wonderful longed-for rain is still falling, the air out the open windows at seven o'clock looks like moonlight with it and the white mist rising up from the earth to meet it.

Yours
Eudora

(Welty enclosed a drawing of a flower, labeled "Bloomed 8 AM–3 PM June 20.")

June 26, 1942
Dear Diarmuid,

[...] Are you well from the cold? It was a sadness I felt, not a dullness, in your letter. It is all right to sustain hope, but it is time going by that is felt in the night, almost speaking the word Waste, and I feel without any solution a longing to cherish in some real way what is itself real. Now and then an image comes in my head, or maybe it is a dream, of some one bringing cupped hands together and holding something safely. She is just an intent figure in a blowing wind. Perhaps she holds the key to the joy and tenderness that people dream of giving or finding but cannot give, or simply some little flower. You might imagine her too.

[. . .] Our rain lilies are blooming too, for the second time—there is something serene in their beauty and miraculous in their almost instant flowering. I dug, sorted, cleaned and packed 400 spider lily bulbs and sent them to the man in Arcadia, and now if he will send me his, there will be a nightblooming, fragrant kind of rain lily, white, coming to me. You know the St. James lily or sprekelia that you like was named that for Saint James during the Crusades for it was the color of the bright cloak of that Saint that is still in the stained glass windows of Chartres in a story of his life there.

[. . .] As for my coming to N.Y., I need to, it can be worked out, with luck, and I only hope it will be possible for civilians to travel by Fall. Just so it's possible to start, I can get there somehow. I would like to stay for a little without hurry. I was born with the feeling that if time and hurry were forgotten, something quiet and wonderful would happen in their place. Maybe because on summer nights in deep content and quiet, lying on the grass, unhurried and so in deepest waiting, that is when you see the shooting stars, and the touch is almost made between the sky and the earth.

Yours,
Eudora

July 13, 1942
Dear Diarmuid,

[. . .] Edna F. is here and I hope will like it and get work done. There's a lot of talking about writing around here though since she came—mostly future writing.[14] I like Edna and think she is good but I think the breath should be saved and if writing must be talked about the requirement should be that it's writing completed that has had life, before it's vivisected. I feel like trying to find some old silent niche this morning, that I must have had somewhere around, just to be still, for that's all I can be about my own evolving ideas, if I ever have any. There was something starting off in my head that I wanted to try in N.Y. if I can come away. Everybody is different, but for me ideas must go far off into excursions of their own, once they start, like somebody that walks along a little road in some country and samples the various berries and breaks off a stick to climb over the wild places with and drinks out of the brooks that come, and on and on, and you have to wait till they come back before you know what they found, but you had better be there when they get home. I think you might whistle to them, but not talk about them.

[. . .] The strange bulbs came and God knows what they really are or what will happen to them down here but they are in the ground. Have a good time up in the green woods and water.

Yours
Eudora

During the summer of 1942, John Robinson was being trained for the Army Air Corps. Welty sent this letter to him in South Dakota. The plant she reports on is one Robinson had given her, a Leila camellia.

July 1942
Thursday
Dear J—

[. . .] It is a still morning, rains every day, I think with pleasure and comfort of my little plants and the roses are growing and blooming. When it is just a little cooler and they all come out the way they do in the fall I will miss you then. Leila has numbers of real buds, I will not count for it's bad luck, but around a dozen and more coming every day.[15] I attend to the vitamins.

The little boys in the neighborhood came to mother and said they were the Junior Commandoes and would like to take over the little house—you know the one, down in the back[16]—and collect scrap metal in it.[17] So mother was helpless. Pretty soon she asked the leader if they would not walk on the plants she has coming up down there and he said, "No ma'am, the Junior Commandoes don't walk on the plants—however I believe the Black Legion was in here this morning."

[. . .] Had a nice note from Charlie,[18] though he was a little depressed from the bout of fever. I wrote him one day, with some silver bells to plant, and told him how the Philippinense looked—you should have seen them when they all came out. Six and eight bells to the stalk and all lined up. The hibiscus manihot is almost opening its first flower, I am eager to see. Miss Cook[19] has some old botany magazines from England, 1837ish, bound copies, that I have been reading—astounding! There are lots of rare plants always being sent in to the editors and they put them right away in the stove—which I finally gathered was the conservatory. A

North American Mr. Drummond from Texas was always sending them odd strange seeds with laconic notes of culture which they quoted with a caution approaching rigor. They have a heated discussion going on every month on whether plants give off excretions daily like animals, and if not why not? The magazine is on the affirmative. The engravings in color would take your breath, they are lovely, I wish I could see them every day. [. . .]

I go over bulb catalogs every night and order and some have come. There is a chance you might see the flowers up in spring—there is the feel of dirt for you, and what it does, it makes your hopes seem matters of truest fact. Well, flowers are older than war.[20] Species tulips are hard to get now but I love them best. You know, the little wild tulips that still have lightness and grace and perfume and the clear delicate colors that I guess all original flowers had. One is Clusiana, that you know, the white and red striped tulip with violet blotch. One is Sylvestris, yellow to green and very fragrant, the buds with reddish tip which disappears as they open. Eichleri comes from Turkey and is crimson, and on the outside of the flower is a patch of gray, pink, and yellow—the basil blotch is shining black. Marjoletti comes from Savoy and is bright yellow with a green star at its base. Some of their leaves are bronze green with pink edges. They are all small and sort of bow in the wind and flare up.

[. . .] I sent you some stories one day to look at but they may have gone to the wrong place. It's raining gently, thundering gently, the pine needles come down like arrows and it does feel like fall in the air, a little touch of clear cool. It is the kind of air you wish to see in painting when you have felt it in the world, with color implicit around every object, a kind of coming to life of the atmosphere after the fainting away in summer. Over at Belhaven[21] I hear a piecing together of some Beethoven with my mind helping and helping at every note. Write when you can and soon.

My love to you.

E—

August 8, 1942
Dear Diarmuid,

[. . .] It's a shame about the wild life taking your vegetables. Didn't they even leave you 10%.[22] Could you have fixed up some kind of all-purpose scarecrow that would scare all those different kinds of animals with all their different tastes and also the Japanese beetles—some sort of composite affair holding a little lethal (or lethal little) kerosene bucket in outstretched glove. Well—next year. The Auratum lilies look beautiful to me in their pictures but once I planted some and they didn't grow. Our cement-like clay doesn't drain them much, I'd guess. I had a Rubrum this summer, did I tell you, that was a wonderful exotic thing. From pictures I think I would like to try a Martagon Album some day and the Ochraceum lily from Burma, have you had those—greenish yellow and smell of spice. I sent you a handful of silver bell narcissus the other day that a lady "spared me" from out in the country—at least I hope they are silver bells—the petals come forward over the trumpet and make a globe or bell, an old fashioned flower in the S. I held the bulbs to my ear and didn't hear anything, but we can plant them. Edna has given no hint as to when she might be leaving so my trip hovers vague. My brother will be coming home to his room next week, on 2-week furlough before the army, and she says it will suit her to move in with me. [. . .]

> Yours
> Eudora

Welty was a regular reader of the Mississippi Market Bulletin, a state publication that ran free advertisements for farm tools, seeds, livestock, and other miscellaneous items. She had put Russell on the Bulletin's mailing list; in July, he asked Welty about two items he saw advertised there, the "Blue Wonder Lilly" and "California beer seed" (7.15.42).

August 13, 1942
Dear Diarmuid,

[. . .] I also enclose another communication about beer seed and think I may uncover something yet. Now that we can't buy beer around here because there are no caps for bottles, they *say*, you could put a few seeds in a fountain and embarrass the beer manufacturers completely.

I would love to see the watercolors. Be sure to save all you do. [. . .] The fragrant white night rain lilies I planted last month are blooming fragrantly and nightly and whitely. They are lovely—Cooperea, or something? They will multiply, and I will divide.

> Yours
> Eudora

Russell replied, "The more I hear about the beer seeds the more intrigued I become . . . I can think of nothing better as a parlor trick than to bring in a jug of water and then nonchalantly drop a few seeds in and say PRESTO! LET IT BE BEER and all the guests would sit up thinking 'This really is magic!' [. . .] I see a kind of wild divinity about the end of your letter—Man proposes and God disposes and you 'They will multiply and I will divide' [. . .] My respects to all and the garden" (8.17.42).

August 31, 1942
Dear Diarmuid,

I should have written—everything has come, your nice letter, the books, Edna's book, the H. Bazaar—and Edna has gone.[23] [. . .] It rains here every day of the world and hundreds of toadstools come up all over the yard, I don't like that, and mold gets on victrola records and on shoes and envelopes stick to the typewriter before you can get them addressed and the type seems to run on the damp paper. But there's a breath of cool in the air, just a breath of fall. My friend John Robinson, of New Orleans, is in the Air Force now and what can I do but think about his life, which is dear to me and close to mine. I know it is the same story everywhere. Six yellow rain lilies opened this morning—they never did bloom in their lives before and while I was weeding they opened right under my eyes—lovely, clear, and fragrant with a cool fragrance—I took them as a sign. I feel as if I could just *turn into* something that would keep people safe, if I knew how. It is nice to have Edna gone, so I can fall into my own dejections—the comforts of home. It would be nice to be there painting and saying "oh-oh!" to each other, for something is always happening with water color. [. . .] Down here the colors shift by the moment, probably from our nearness to a big river and the ocean, and cloud shadows and a kind of haze come drifting over what you are painting, and the sky has a little green in it instead of the violet of the north, and none of our foliage is set in any deep summer green but is always grayed, or blued, or silvered by our weather and all these things make you want to paint with water color, to catch changes quickly and to show them with light and transparency, the way you can when you leave plenty of white. [. . .] Forgive such a dull bad letter, I will write some day when something good has happened. Give Henry my best.

Yours
Eudora

September 12, 1942
Dear John—

Mother just came in with a double-handful of roses. It's nine o'clock in the morning and I'm getting dressed. Have to get out early in the mornings to go on with some work Aimee has browbeaten me into.[24] [. . .] I bet we both ordered the same thing out of the La. Market Bulletin today, a white-flowering pomegranate. The prettiest things are blooming now, little low dark, dark red amaryllis affairs that are dark as wine and sparkle like wine, with bright green in their throats—I planted them in front of some camellias. We have had a dreadful time with no yard man. The other day we finally got one, aged 14 in a heavenly-blue turned up hat, who wanted to sharpen everything. He could open his mouth wide and drink out of the hose turned on full force without knocking himself down. He was so fast at the lawnmower I ran out and stood in front of each little camellia to keep it from being mowed down before he could stop. He was black as sin and twice as fast, and might have been the Devil—just popped up. Smarty is barking frantically—the Junior Commandos must be running through with their bugle. [. . .]

The yellow hibiscus is so wonderful, how does it manage to have a flower a day ready? Mother thinks it turns into okra after blooming without doubt. I think it is beautiful at all hours of the day, and when it begins to fold itself together in the evening, with a little flush of rose on the backs of the petals that has come from the sun all day. Write when you can and send a picture of you at work. I will keep it positively secret, in a drawer, like goldfish that have never seen the light of day.[25]

All love to you
Eudora

September 14, 1942
Dear Diarmuid,

Many thanks for the contract and the check. [. . .] here I still am in Mississippi and the time goes by. One brother has his induction orders for the 23rd and the other will leave soon too, and I wouldn't want to be gone during their furloughs, so around the middle of October I'll see how things look for a trip. I will need it and will be glad if it can happen. It must be lovely up there, and it is here too—I love the Mississippi fall.

Muscadines got ripe and I made some preserves and stuff. Roses are blooming and three gardenias (wrong time). Your hibiscus plants scare me, in pots, because mine are stalks 12 feet high. Better put them in the hall so they can go up the stair well and bloom in somebody's room. [. . .]

Yours

Eudora

September 28, 1942

Dear Diarmuid,

I was glad to hear about the article to be in the *Atlantic*.[26] What next will you bring out? You can't stop now. [. . .] I planted some species tulips and "peruvian scillas" and white spider lilies—the lady said they were white, so will wait and see. I have "got a hold of" the beer seed, from the Louisiana Market Bulletin, and when it came it was so repulsive I couldn't bear to drop it in my fruit jar of sweeten water and leave till it tasted good.[27] This could never taste good. It looks like something off an old pond, and came wrapped in a piece of bread paper as it still is. I may have drunk worse home made beverages than this would make, but just can't think I would swallow this. I am going to send some of it to the lady that wrote me in Miss. and see if she will drink it. If I never hear from her, I will assume that she did and is out of the world. Mississippi is looking beautiful now, leaves are turning and all the fall wild flowers are out. [. . .] I hope to come up after my brother leaves for camp and before the other one is called, which would be for about 10 days, or I could wait till November, but something tells me we might not be allowed to travel by that time. It will probably take three days to get there with trains and buses the way they are, and no connections attempted anywhere. I'll probably be walking on my hands by the time I arrive, so you'll see what you're waiting for, a performing client.

Yours,

Eudora

The Robber Bridegroom *was published in October 1942. During that month Welty visited New York, then went to Florida to see Robinson, who was training in St. Petersburg.*

October 31, 1942
Jackson, Hallowe'en
Dear Diarmuid,

Are you painting a landscape today, or witches? [. . .] It was lovely to come on this little trip as always and thanks for such nice times. The weekend was wonderful to the senses and it was nice to be with your family and wear all your clothes and paint in your woods [. . .] .

I had a nice two days in Florida, going swimming and seeing fine sunsets over the Gulf, one bright day and one stormy. Little sandpipers, mother and young, were always running along the shore like tiny waves, all moving as a unit and instantaneously. We could just stay until dark, on account of the Coast Guard, but late enough to stir up phosphorous when we swam. I didn't care so much for all the things they grow there— things grow too quick and lurid for anything, and there is too much orange color, and too many things stay exactly the same the year round. At a house where I went, there was a papaya grove that was bearing fruit from trees planted from seeds two years ago in sand (with some old iron scrap for nourishment). There is a nightblooming jasmine that everybody plants around their houses that has little trumpet like flowers that open at night so potent that it would lay you low. Staggering scent—I got tired of it. [. . .]

Yours
Eudora

November 6, 1942
Dear Diarmuid,

[. . .] Have you been doing water[color] again? I want to try some crape myrtle trees when they get bare—they are beautiful in form and texture and their color is soft, brown, and mottled—like that on little deer. A kind of amber, with pure violet shadows. If I can get sort of down under, and paint them against the sky. But that means at my house that I will have to sit in the middle of the sidewalk. I could just draw it on the sidewalk, in chalk, and everybody would have to go around it. But if I manage a good enough one of one tree I will send it up for your inspection. It has golden seed pods.

[. . .] Well, this is too long a letter. The little moreas are still blooming with utter freedom, 5 or 6 new flowers every day, all as lovely as anything. Roses are good now. [. . .] The Peruvian squills are making little rosettes for winter all over the ground where I planted them. The hibiscus manihot made its seeds, do you want any? Maybe some time it would be fun to plant some mimosa seeds in some wild place about there—they wouldn't make trees or bloom, but they would come up fern like and make a kind of ferny glen, the leaves are very delicate—sensitive—they close up if even a cloud goes over the sky.

Yours

Eudora

Sweet-olive in this letter—did it last?

Mid-November 1942

Dear Diarmuid,

Here are the seeds and I hope they grow—when the plants come up, set them far apart, and behind bushes, for the flowers come high up and the stalks are prickly. You can tell I put them in front of the gardenias, close together, and got pricked every time I pulled a gardenia. It was really my next door neighbor that sent you the sasanquas, because as I was going around her garden she heard me say I had a friend who had never seen a sasanqua. She gave me 3 times that many that I could not send, and insisted that they would open when you got them, but I sort of doubt it—the whole beauty of the flowers is their extreme delicacy of texture and color, and their wide-openness, the things I fear that get lost in the mail. They are the Japanese race of camellia, while the Japonica is Chinese, in the usual pattern of camellia confusion, and grow wild in the high mountains there—sasanquas are as they always were, while Japonicas are of course cross-bred to infinity. See if your camellia has made any buds yet—I can't understand it if it hasn't. Mine are as fat as anything, some are showing color—this is properly the time of year when they threaten you with having flowers during the first freeze. They are sort of alarming plants.

[. . .] If you are going to be a citizen can't you specify that you want to be a Southerner, because I feel that you are more near and kin to us.[28]

Yours,

Eudora

November 13, 1942

Dear John—

Your letter was nice to get, on Monday. I wanted to answer, but we were cleaning house and instead of typing at the typewriter I was painting windowsills and washing the curtains. How are you? These are heavenly days—frost in the night, bright days—To ride down Pinehurst St. toward the west when the sun is going down, riding under the tallow trees, you know the ones, that turn ruby red and have pearly white flowers—so beautiful—that is the place I saw the new moon, this time.

[. . .] I've been watering the camellias and making stakes to put their covers on over—one of these bright nights soon we will be a-dashing out to tuck them in. Their buds are of the best—you would admire them, and I think Leila has grown about 7 or 8 inches, 7½ anyway, and put out the best of buds. They look like little candle flames shining in there to me as I go along from bush to bush. A little old Pink Perfection making its first buds—it's 3 years old—made 5 and is going straight ahead to open them, I found them pink today. I hope they won't be struck by cold.

[. . .] *Somebody* has brought a bad chrysanthemum plague here. Six different bugs, by count (mother's) are on our flowers—though I think some of them are after the other bugs by this time and have lost sight of the chrysanthemums. One kind has long black silky wings which it *folds* about it—another kind sort of armored and stinks when disturbed, though does not leave. They don't care about Flit or anything—arsenate of lead, anything—when I spray them they only shrug one wing and chew on. They have eated [*sic*] all the chrysanthemums away. I showed them to Seta[29] and she dreamed about them. Mother said one day that she just thought I had brought those bugs back from Florida—all 6, one of each on my hat no doubt—ask Mrs. C. but none of this mattered to Mrs. Lester Franklin. The other day as I was going out via the garden I saw her back in our chrysanthemums—she called out "Did you know you had a little humming-bird in your garden?" "Yes I did," I said in my good faith. "Well it's ME!"

It pleases me for you to like Livvie still and it is good that you think the newer work gets better instead of worse, for that is always the hope. [. . .] I hope you are fine and all is well and things will be the way you want them—that the work will be good—but combat intelligence—my dear, please not, please not.

Love,

Eudora

Welty, Russell, and the garden writer Elizabeth Lawrence all enjoyed
the Mississippi Market Bulletin. *Welty had met Lawrence when visit-*
ing her friend Frank Lyell in North Carolina, and she had given Rus-
sell a copy of Lawrence's 1942 book, A Southern Garden. *Like Welty*
and Russell, Lawrence took an interest in the "California beer seed" as
well as the "Blue Wonder Lilly" that Welty seems to have purchased;
Lawrence thought that this plant could be a scilla hyacinthoides, *a*
hyacinth that bloomed once every seven years.[30]

November 22, 1942
Dear Diarmuid,
[. . .] It has been like springtime here, we go around in our shade
hats and stare at the bulbs coming up and the spirea starting to put out
flowers, and don't know what to do. Maybe it is going to be a mild winter. Leaves haven't fallen yet here and are at their prettiest, all shades of
pink and gold. Enclosed are some Miss. Bulletins for reading if you have
a cold. I wrote the lady about the 7 year lily, but she probably will not
answer for 7 years.[31] [. . .] Is that sale of the book good? It seems more
than I imagined, but my imagining was vague. I just cleaned out montbretia bulbs from a bed, and used to think spider lilies multiplied fast.
Ha—from a space 4 ft. long I took up by count (it's a long Sunday) 986
montbretia bulbs, not counting those I didn't get. If things can be said to
petrify, what this dirt did was to bulbify. Each one sends out long rays of
root like a star, and each star end becomes a bulb, and then sends out its
own rays, a whole universe down there.
Yours
Eudora

In this letter to Russell, Welty apparently enclosed another letter in-
dicating that her mystery bulb was not scheduled to bloom for some
time.

November 25, 1942
Dear Diarmuid,
[. . .] Here's some mail you can read. Come down to Tuscaloosa. I'm
furious about the 7 year lily, no wonder she advertised it for sale! 25c shot
to hell for the next 4 years.

[. . .] I had to write a poem to the squirrels and put it on a stick in the garden—

Squirrel squirrel burning bright,
Do not eat my bulbs tonight!
I think it bad and quite insidious
That you should eat my blue tigridias.
Squirrel, Sciurus Vulgaris,
Leave to me my small muscaris.
Must you make your midnight snack, mouse,
Of Narcissus Mrs. Backhouse?
When you bite the pure leucojeum,
Do you feel no taint of odium?
Must you chew till Kingdom Come
Hippeastrum Advenum?
If in your tummy bloomed a lily,
Wouldn't you feel sort of silly?
Do you wish to tease and joke us
When you carry off a crocus?
Must you hang up in your pantries
All my Pink Queen zephyranthes?
Tell me, has it ever been thus,
Squirrels must eat hyacinthus?
O little rodent,
I wish you wo'dn't!

[. . .]

 Yours
 Eudora

Happy Thanksgiving, 1 and all—

December 4, 1942
Dear Diarmuid,

I hope the colds have all gone away and that the weather is not frigid at the door. We have had springlike weather for the last 2 months, making all kinds of things up and happen, like spirea and quince flowers. But yesterday a cold wind came out of the north and blew all evening, and when they said it was snowing in Memphis, that's when I dashed out to the camellias. My camellias looked like fools this morning, with dizzy looking stakes and the most outlandish things hanging on them, and twice as humiliating for them as it needed to be, for no freeze came. Their buds are as fat as little apples and showing color—I talked to them this time—just begged them to watch out. We have of course had no yard man since summer, and it hasn't rained either, so all we do is against the concrete earth—it makes spading and digging real labor, no matter how we water and try to soften the clayey ground. Your camellia baffles me. You never by any chance cut any of the wood off, did you, to shape it or anything, because they bloom off the old growth—no, I know what it is, just temperament—what their reasons ever are, God alone knows. One in the next street just changed its flower this year—color and formation both, an eight year old plant, it has always been scarlet and double and bloomed for Christmas, and now is pink with a circlet of single petals and a chrysanthemum-like cluster in the center, blooming Thanksgiving. The *new* Professor Sargent, as they would say if it were a movie star. Next summer, when you have yours buried in the ground, I will send you a little of the fertilizer we make up for our bushes, providing we can still get the stuff, and you can put a spoonful or so on, once in April and once in June. It will taste like home cooking to your plant and it will then cover itself with buds—I hope. I trust Mr. Aswell will have the grace to cut his flower off instantly and give it to you.[32] I looked in the Reader's D. and saw nothing of your story. Have they ever "said anything"? Maybe owing to the nature of the article they are going to let you know supernaturally. William Maxwell, that we met from the New Yorker, wrote me in care of you and you forwarded the letter, to ask me to send them something— wasn't that roundabout, he could have phoned you.[33] Of course there ain't anything—the cupboard is bare. It looks like records coming—with the added money from the Wide Net—isn't that wonderful? How could I have left out such a grand rhyme as hippeastrum epigastrum—it's a wonder I didn't feel a short jab of reminder from my own epig., a kind of "ahem"-pain, at the time. I ordered some bulbs from S. S. Berry, in Redlands, Calif., some of those wonderful kinds of daffodils.[34] He wrote me a long letter back, as long as this and just like this. He said a nice order like mine was such a surprise in the middle of winter—the poor man had to go to out and dig up 1 each of about nine different kinds of bulbs. Squirrels stood over me while I planted them, so I went on and marked each spot with a little stick and a tag on it with name of bulb.

Yours
Eudora

December 16, 1942
Dear Diarmuid,

[...] My dread of Christmas is going a little, for my two brothers are going to be together for the day, I think, if not here, and my little sister-in-law is going off tonight to Virginia to try to get near—she says they may just have to start walking toward each other at some point, but we are all crossing our fingers, that they will make it. It is all luck, for my friend John had his furlough all set to come and the day it was to start he was sent off in the other direction, to an officer's school, and just won't get a furlough. [...]

Yours
Eudora

December 26, 1942
Dear Diarmuid,

[...] Christmas got by, a lovely soft day with hyacinths blooming and an Iris, Stylosa Marginata. To think of your snow and our spring, but today it is raining and thundering and gloomy. I worked in the garden Christmas morning so it was not so bad. [...] I have been sick but though it looked like a cold and acted like one I guess it was just low spirits. [...]

Forgive the rambling letter, I will try to do better next time. I hope the new year is good to you and is full of good stories, polite writers, and handsome flowers. [...]

Yours
Eudora

February 15, 1943
Dear Diarmuid,

[...] I hope the white impatience cuttings are thriving—is that like balsam?[35] Did you ever see a white flowering quince—I am trying a cutting of that. [...] Do you know anything about OWI jobs? I wrote Clifton Fadiman and asked him if I might get one.[36] If they draft girls, girl writers will head the list of the ones they'll get to catch rivets, etc., I know (I can't catch things.) I told him of my experience in publicity, etc., which is what I'm doing at the moment with War Savings Committee here (a little boring).[37]

Well, a camellia grower in Mobile sends his latest listings, and is even more raging against the Japanese than ever—he has always had a rival grower there who is Japanese—this time he calls them "insincere rats." A wonderful rat term, but this is all mixed up with homage to flowers. My wild tulips are coming up all around. The little Clusiana sowed itself—

yours

Eudora

March 19, 1943

Dear Diarmuid,

Everything's fine—if I'd held my hand to my ear to hear the time to come, and held the other hand out to get the money to come on, it couldn't have been finer.[38] It sounds lovely and I look forward to the day. We are having a thunderstorm now, and that has a spring sound. Is there anything you'd like me to bring up, in the plant line?

Don't be surprised to see me at some odd, previous moment in the city, because it looks as if I might drive John Robinson's car up to him in Harrisburg, Pa., on my way, and it is complicated—the car is in Fla. [. . .] It would be grand to drive up through the spring. I think I will put a digger in the car. We have some (½) little pink and green spots here and there, peach trees and willows, and redbud in the woods but not dogwood yet, or the yellow Jessamine. Elizabeth Lawrence, who wrote "A Southern Garden," wrote that this was the worst spring they had ever had, and I feel the same, with even next fall's chrysanthemums killed. But things look a little gay in one border now that the species tulips have opened—the Wild English tulip with reflexed petals like little Florentine slippers, clear yellow, I love those. And Algerian iris.

[. . .] I hope spring is coming in and soon little shoots will be pushing out of the earth to your satisfaction. I hope to see you soon, and write if you can think of any plants.

Love,

Eudora

Welty visited New York in April. She was able to spend some time with Robinson; he was now stationed in Pennsylvania, and spent one weekend at the Russells' Katonah home.

May 5, 1943

Dear Diarmuid,

I'm writing in a green shade, on my upstairs back porch—home again. I can't tell you how fine it was to be up to see you, and I wish I were back. Thanks for all. It's so truly an event in my life to be there and it stays in my head before and after, each time, something good to have—"I will hold it closely," as they used to say in fairy tales, of tokens and treasures. I left the little willow trees and came here to fine plain summer. The train got to Jackson just as the sun was coming up this morning, and the whole town was full of green, and our house asleep, and I came in by the garden.[39] There were the roses in full bloom, Shirley poppies, larkspur, columbines, day lilies, and some strange new lily, and irises. Eros is a beautiful one, but smaller than the one we saw—needs lime? I put it to Mother about the lime at breakfast. I'm about to go out now and weed in the shady places, and plant the St. James, and I think when they all bloom at one time it will be magnificent. I got your letter of March 29, when you sent the Robber contract and had just spaded for two days—I think flower crowns should come with such energy, not tiredness for being virtuous. So that you shouldn't ache, but sit regally, sending for food and drink. When all of this vegetable garden grows up and bears, paint me a picture to look at, I think of something thick as Rousseau's jungles,[40] with one of the tigers showing his face between ripe ears of corn. I haven't been to bed yet. [. . .] There were lots of wild flowers in the upland valleys around the Chattanooga mountains, and I had your little book. There was trailing pink phlox, I know. Also many other things, and how I wish the train had gone slower. (Or stopped.) As we were going through this beautiful valley it was being plowed and planted in many places and we came to a little water-stop, and it was just at sunset with the light on everything, and children were playing and birds were flying very close, and a man was sitting on the porch with his feet up reading a paper, and women were standing over rakes talking at a gate, and I saw a soldier jump silently off the train, without his hat, blouse, or anything in his hands, and go across the tracks and over the fence and down a little path. He was running, but then slowed to a walk, and simply strolled away into the little place, and we went off without him. You could smell the fields and horses while the train was standing there, and hear the birds, and it did smell wonderful, and was nice.[41]

I'll send you the spider lilies before long—they won't take much of your planting time, all they like is to be put just under the surface. Mother says the day lilies had better wait till fall, for they wouldn't bloom for you now if taken up. No, she says there is one that you could try planting now, a late bloomer. I'm sorry I don't know its name, we call it after the lady who gave it to us, but it's a nice flower, and not Fulva or Flavum. Give my best to Rose and the children and to Henry and I'll write soon. You are right about the way it is bad for me here, or could get bad, but it is much to imagine about friends, and how they are, and to write and have notes and letters, and I keep my hope about a visit down here. I think I had better put in a little camellia food too, and you can give the gardenia a bite of the same.

Love,
Eudora

May 11, 1943
Monday
Dear John—

I got your letter and was glad to know where you were Friday. I hope when you leave it's for here—it will be nice, the day you come to Mississippi and have a furlough. Look for it to be summer—you can expect to smell chinaberry trees. [. . .]

Diarmuid wrote to tell you that if you settled in the neighborhood to let them know so you could come out again. Did you go up to the city again this weekend? Last weekend was fine—I hadn't any plans, I was just staying on for a chance to see you again. D. says the trees are getting green now and the seeds sprouting, and all the daffodils are out.

Would you like to come to Rodney?[42] He has got me a commission to do an article on it for Harper's Bazaar—I don't know how. I'll wait for you, we can take a lunch. I don't know what I will write—my only idea is to note exactly what's there—loess bluffs and bottoms and the river, what grows and did grow once, which is really its history. [. . .]

Today there are little five-minute showers at intervals and I rush out to dig after each one—just like the robins, to take advantage of a sixteenth inch of soft ground. They pull up worms and I put down petunias. I think it might well rain tonight, I hope so, and fall on my little plants. You will be pleased to see Leila, so many new leaves you can't see the old—beautiful sight, and I am very proud.

[. . .] Let me know what happens—but I had a letter today from a boy stationed in N.O. that was censored—with the scissors—He is a writer and Jewish and rather eloquent, and the letter was nothing but ribbons—Write so they won't cut your letter—

Love to you and luck—Come soon—everything when you come—
Eudora

May 15, 1943
Dear Diarmuid,

Thanks for the letters. Everything must look beautiful—especially today after the day's work. I wish I could see all the little shoots and leaves—and hope there has not been a nibble through the wire. The weather sounds lovely and soft. Your St. James lilies I planted on Friday and on Monday half of them were up an inch, and now all are up 3 or 4 inches—lucky I got them in the ground. I put them near my acidantheras. Elizabeth Lawrence, who wrote the garden book, wrote that she had got hold of the beer seed, "and here are yours and Mr. Russell's, which I started to send him, and then realized I hadn't his address (forgot for the moment I didn't really know him)" so I sent them on.[43] I have to stop Elizabeth in time, for she is going to plant the seeds. But do you think we ought to try to make beer, either? I'll copy the directions from my beer seed lady to refresh your memory, before sending her letter to Elizabeth—"You put the seeds in a Jar of Some Kind with Sweeten Water one day, the next day it ready to Drink. if Enyone let it Set over a bout 4 day it might make Eny one drunk. We all way use it Just as soon as it Tasted Good. it mighty healthy to. a ½ tea cup of Seed in a ½ Gallon fruit Jar of Sweeten Water Will Serve 4 Or 5." Elizabeth sent me six Butterfly Tree seeds too. She got them through a seed exchange and has sent in your name and mine to it, she said, for the lady wants to get in touch with seed persons. She wrote Elizabeth: "I am one of a seed exchange have been president of it for several years. our seed list almost as good as a catalogue. If you are a seed person I'd like to tell you more about it. We need a member in your part of U.S. There is no writing only at Seed Exchange time and our list should be out by Oct. 15. We have a membership fee (.25) to help with expenses and your seeds cost you nothing. Well I better be careful for I don't know your business ever once in a while I offer this to a commercial grower not knowing their work." What is the Butterfly Tree? The seeds are from California. I started to divide with you but if one sprouts and has butterflies I will send some to you then, by wing. I do think if there's no writing only at Seed Exchange time, there ought to be just a password for seed persons—did you ever join in Greenie, by locking little fingers? If anybody you've joined in Greenie with ever says "Greenie!" to you, you have to have something green on you, usually keep a leaf in your shoe, or they can extract some penalty. I stayed joined in Greenie till I was 16 or 17 years old—it looks as if that ought to make me Irish—[44]

[. . .] The sun has been hot. The little petunias I transplanted have to have covers all day. The best time to work is between six and eight-thirty, A.M. and P.M. They are wonderful hours anyway. There was only one daylily I could send now, the rest being in flower, and that was "Miss Newman" (local name). But later I can send more beautiful ones, and have marked Hyperion, Harvest Moon, Calypso (the evening one), J. A. Crawford, Modesty, and others that I like—the clear or pale yellow—Harvest Moon having the faintest touch of orange, but delicate, and of a beautiful long slender form. I found my little wildflower in your book,—the tufted primrose. It's Oenothera Speciosa, a Mexican primrose that's become naturalized from Miss. to Fla. and in the Southwest. It is in flower everywhere now. I sent you some camellia food that you could make a little sprinkling of around the edge of the pot, and I trust that little plant will have the flowers it ought, this time, or go up in blue flame. My yellow ladyslipper that I thought was dead has come to life. Do you know the yellow and white and purple fringed orchis? There are supposed to be ever so many of them down beyond Rodney, toward the river.

Yours
Eudora
I still have hopes to come back again—Have the slight fevers again but hope to drive them out soon and take hold of some plan then—

June 1, 1943
Dear Diarmuid,

I keep thinking of that African plant.[45] The fruit I imagine is a tempting fiery color, the foliage blue-green and pinnate, the flowers cinnamon, in little puffs—the flowers are as sweet as the fruit is sour and smell like nutmeg, the seeds are dragons-tooth shaped and jet black. What's the name of it? Your garden sounds beautiful. And now that the first radish has been solemnly eaten, all should follow cornucopia-like, ending with a glorious prize melon. I think the St. James lilies will probably bloom this month—I am watching for their sudden flowers. Are your iris in flower? We have one or two Japanese iris, one rich purple, one white. And the gardenia bush that was not killed is full of flowers. But the beetles came to eat the roses. We had strange weather too, when yours was cold—mostly winds, but Saturday it rained for the first time in many weeks and I expect it will rain all of June.

[. . .] My "Russian lily" is going to bloom—what it is I know not. The Rodney article got interrupted by galley proofs to the book. Do you really think that the Purple Hat is all right—somehow I wanted to jerk it out for good this time.[46] I just wrote to Katherine Anne yesterday and gave her a lesson story from the plants about not wanting to let your stories go—how I saw the Peruvian squill eject its seeds from the pods with such force that they bounced, and that's what we ought to do with our finished deeds.

I hope somebody wonderful will appear today in the office with huge, fruity manuscripts, never before read by the human eye. I have to stop now as we have no maid and no little yard-boy on Wednesdays any more.

The birds are singing beautifully.

Yours
Eudora

June 9, 1943
Dear Diarmuid,

[. . .] How is the garden? What are your melons doing? It is a good thing they are planted by the spotting post, so no dirty work on the melons can go unspotted.[47] We've had prostrating heat and have to revive things after supper every night—even the dogwood tree hangs every leaf down each day. A little rabbit ate the tops off my acidantheras—I know this rabbit, he was born here, and thinks acidantheras are just the tender things for his little teeth. He is always passing through with a little sheaf of leaves of some precious thing in his mouth, and I have to move the hose to let him by—he has got me. He is close enough to spank at all times. (Dear Dorothy Dix: Should I spank my rabbit?)[48] [. . .]

The Rodney article gets nowhere—I will try harder, though, and maybe before breakfast it will be cool enough to let the brain work—I'll put a cool leaf over my head.[49]

Love to all—
Yours,
Eudora

June 23, 1943
Tuesday
Dear J—

I think I saw you in the movies—To my surprise I did walk right in on the OCS film—last night at the State. It was fine—I think I saw you twice, once from the side and once from the back, with a lot of other men—just for a second. [. . .]

It's five-thirty and I've been watering the poor flowers since 7 o'clock this morning—going out at intervals to move the hose—even the dogwood was hanging its leaves straight down. Just a minute ago a big black cloud came up out of the south and there was a clap of thunder—but enough water *couldn't* fall on those hot things. In between times I worked on an article (Rodney) and it ain't very good. I sliced a lot of peaches and put them in the ice tray for my supper—too hot to try any pie-making, or doings. Every morning when I get up I think I will cook something splendid before night, but when the temperature goes up to 98, I eat fresh. *I've* been 99⅗ and taking quinine.

[. . .] Little boys with pants rolled up are wading in the Belhaven lily pool, with dog friends. The gardenias are still blooming, mimosa still blooming. Petunias now, and just before phlox. Something called the "Russian lily" is going to produce a flower, what, I know not. The camellias are all doing beautifully, putting on summer growth.

[. . .] Lightning and thunder. Please, rain—This is about the end of the second month without any, except for one lovely afternoon. Could I send you anything? I miss you when I taste something grand like frozen peaches and wish I could divide that instant. A P-47 came over twice—it had probably been to Norfolk in the 20 minutes. I hope you are fine and that it is comfortable—whatever and wherever it is—[. . .]—Bath just ran over. I guess I should put my typewriter in it.

The P-47's come over about 7 AM, turn about all over the sky and play like dolphins and are gone in 5 minutes.

Love to you—
E
You would love our little tender onions—

June 23, 1943
Dear Diarmuid,

I was glad to get the letter, and thanks for the iris clipping too. It does look to me as if yours ought to bloom—did it ever? Mother is sometimes against the La. iris for having too much foliage for the flower, but if you got the ones I meant you to have (and not something awful which showed up this year here) you might like the colors. Your rains sound wonderful, even the torrents. This is about our second month of drouth—only one rainy afternoon, though the weather makes a phony threat every day, with stage thunder. I begin soaking the flowerbeds in the morning at about 7 o'clock and am still moving the hose around when it's dark, just stopping it in the worst heat, and yet this has to be done every day or two or plants die. I hope the woodchuck changes (its) mind, though the kerosene rag may just make it eat the beans, it is such a perverse number. [. . .] What were your paintings? Did you do the morning meadow with the shadows?

Yours,
Eudora

July 8, 1943
Dear Diarmuid,

[. . .] Hope the spirit animals go back the way they came.[50] You need a bottle tree, in the African manner, to lure such things inside. We have been eating corn, snapbeans and onions and butterbeans out of the backyard but our tomatoes (Mother got a special kind like they grow at her home in the mts.) were a failure. Figs are almost ripe and I wish I could send you some. The days have been hot so that you go to bed at night on a hot pillow, but gradually a little breeze comes. We had a small cyclone the other night that cleared the air. While it was going on a little poet from a nearby camp passed through town and phoned me—he said "I would like to show you my poems" but the lightning kept striking the wires and I would reply "oh, ouch! Thank you—gracious!" [. . .]

Yours,
Eudora

During this summer, the Allies were known to be preparing an invasion somewhere on the Mediterranean coast as part of the Italian Campaign. In early July, Allied aircraft bombed Sicily for several days before ground forces arrived. Welty was sure that Robinson, who was being shipped overseas, must be involved in this effort. She wrote most of the following letter before learning that an amphibious invasion of Sicily had occurred in the early hours of July 10.

July 9, 1943
Friday night
Dearest John—

I hope you are well—I hope you have comforts—food enough, and a place where you can sleep well when you sleep—I hope all that is dangerous to you never hurts you—

I've been working fairly hard—This is evening—The moon is up—It was new 3 nights ago—

[. . .] The camellias are putting out their second growth of summer— I planted spring bulbs—hyacinths, white and pink. Then I sprayed the camellias and the small white flowering quince—

My hope is when you come to the moment and the spot where you can send a message from, you will pick the quickest way—To hear how you were just the moment before, that would be the best of messages—

[. . .] I miss you and could never tell you how I look forward to the day you come and dream about putting all kinds of things out in front of you for a welcome so I will probably know just how—All my love now as I can tomatoes—

Yours,

E

At midnight—where are you? This was the night of the Sicily invasion—

July 12, 1943
Dear Diarmuid,

Thanks for the check for the Spanish omelet of "Petrified Man" which came this morning. How is the garden, did the creatures withdraw themselves, and leave any vegetables? A great big owl has been sitting in the top of one of our trees for the past hour and the birds are nearly insane. He hoots not at all, but is about the size of a Collie dog and looks like one.

I finally heard from John—a letter written on the boat, and I think the signs point to Algiers. [. . .]

Have you done any more articles? It has been so hot here that I could not think, was "mindless," as Ida M'Toy says, and maybe up there too the most alluring thing is a little shade to lie in. We are planting our second crop of beans and tomatoes. Peaches are ripe—figs almost.

Yours

Eudora

The next letter was one of the earliest V-mails that Welty sent to Robinson during the war. Short for "Victory Mail," this type of letter was designed to reduce the weight and space needed to ship mail overseas. V-mail letters were written on special stationery, received by the military, then photographed on microfilm. After the film was shipped overseas, facsimiles of the letters were printed at about one-fourth their original size.

July 19, 1943

Dear John—

I just now got your little letter written c/o the Fleet Postmaster on the boat—it went clear around the world, and came in at San Francisco. [. . .]

Here it is hot. I got up early and watered a little, so I could weed a little. Mrs. Fox[51] sent Jake up with some figs—he came hollering "Figs, Mrs. Welty!" from down the street. They were wonderful. I wrote a letter to Rose Russell—she had asked what you were doing now, so I told her riding along the mountains above the sea in your Jeep in high delight, in Africa. The yard man came and we put him in the house because it was too hot, then we worked outdoors. I ate lunch downtown with Bessie—she'd sent for a Western Union boy and got a poor old one nearly 90 years old—he said he'd been sick a long time, and had trouble with his mind, and couldn't carry anything heavier than a telegram.

We had some pretty Editor MacFarland Roses this morning. And a garden club lady sent over the most beautiful strange lily—very pale, silvery pink—rather frosty long slender petals—yellow stamens—seven flowers coming out of the top of a long pale green stalk. Mother took a look at it and said, "Lycoris Squamigera." It is very wonderful, you should see it—it smells good too. I've been thinking about bulbs. Here's the way the camellia border will be

(Drawing with map of plantings in Welty's side yard: Herme, Duc

D'Orleans, Tri-Color, Elizabeth, another Herme, P.P—probably
Pink Perfection, and Leila. Daffodils are among the Herme and Duc
D'Orleans, with species tulips and spring star flowers around the Lei-
la. Pink, white, and blue Roman hyacinths are in the front row.)

What do you think? Think of the color of the camellias too.

I think it will be on the abundant side, as things have all multiplied
and grown. A cardinal is singing just now. It's the middle of the afternoon. Not a breath stirs. I practiced knitting so I can begin your sweater.
I was so afraid Mother would groan when I wanted to try to learn, but
she very calmly said she thought I could. I hope to know enough by the
time you send your measurements—I go along all right for a while, and
suddenly I forget how I do it—it used to be the same with swimming,
I'd forget how. I hope for a letter soon. At the same time with this I'm
sending you some clippings, etc. by air mail, so you can see which comes
better, and let me know. I am eating a Praline and wonder what you are
eating. How is Bill? It's nice to think he is with you—tell him to stay
close. I left out the little Algerian irises in the diagram, all of them I
transplanted back behind the bulbs, they make a shimmer of blue when
all is bare, earliest of all—

    Love—

    E—

July 28, 1943

Dear J—

I got the letter you wrote in the Mediterranean, July 9—it will be
good to have the next one after that and I hope the landing was all right
and when you pulled out your maps there was everything just as you had
thought. And all in its right place and like in your special map, the castle
and all. Maybe you are eating off the trees you wondered about, right
now. I hope delicious—

The first letter came too—the one on the boat. [. . .] I'm so pleased
that the Jeep's name is Eudora. I hope it will behave well. I never knew I'd
have a Jeep named after me. [. . .]

This is a cool day—cloudy. Birds singing. Mermaid roses out, 7. I
hope all is fine with you. I hope it goes all right, days and nights.

    Love to you,

    E—

August 6, 1943
Dear Diarmuid,

I hope you've chased the cold away and all goes well in home and office. Did your watermelon win? Or is it time? I had a dream Pammy was in—she told me that as soon as she had finished reading a set of Dumas she would pass it on to me. I *hope* this is a dream. How's your garden? Ours is worse than a jungle—we can't stir out to weed on account of a plague of swamp mosquitoes blown in from the river—the kind that cluster 30 at a time on your leg. We run out and change the water sprinkler and run back again as though through fire. Did you find the What-Is-It that eats your vegetables? Regardless, I pass on to you what our cook said when rabbits got our beans—she told Mother she should have had a jug. Empty. You put the jug out without a stopper and a rabbit comes up to eat your beans and the wind moves over that jug and it says "Mmmmmmmmmmmm! Mmmmmmmmmmmmmmmmmmm!!"

I haven't been able to do a thing with the story I was telling you about. For a while I had good ideas but this seems to be just a bad time. The weather has been hot, around 102—so that just the act of typing seems erratic. You will want to fire me for a client. [. . .] I tried to get lycoris squamigera but the place that advertises it has sold out—I wanted to send some up to you too. They are wonderful—prettier than anything in the amaryllis line I ever did see.

Yours,
Eudora

Saturday. Your letter came today—only 5 days to come. Whatever Mary Lou wants to do about the article will be all right with me, I'm sure, so when she sends it I'll probably send it back to her.[52] The Auratum sounds beautiful. John Robinson is on the Sicilian front, moving with the infantry, which has me upset so—I got a letter yesterday afternoon he'd written July 18. He said everything is ripe together and out of season—and that he couldn't bring himself to touch anything in a small garden but when he got to a rich absentee landlord estate he et hearty. He said it was so beautiful there. Do you think this will all end soon, and the war be over early—you did once.

I'm trying to work on the story and maybe I can get it going a little more smoothly by tomorrow. We have some Philippinense lilies in bloom—they are great tall things about 8 feet high with long white trumpets that smell sweetly, and underneath are some others of the family blooming sitting down on the ground. I know not why of any of it.—E

I can't think about the fall—I wish I could go somewhere to think about it—like the next town—I'd be so glad if I could see you and Rosie now and then—but that's all—nobody else there.

August 18, 1943
Dear Diarmuid,

The copies of the English "Curtain" came this morning and thanks for sending. They look like brave little efforts, nice too. [. . .]

The article arrived from Mary Lou and I did a little piecing with it on top of hers and hope she will be satisfied. I put the Indians back in, and took out some plants—did a little weeding—and in other ways tried to preserve the contrast in the place and keep the length she'd brought it to. Did your yellow hibiscus come up. Mine is suffering these days and no amount of water seems to be enough to take it through the heat. The paper said it was 105 lately but today a most wonderful, cool breeze is blowing—but you can smell on it the black grass and scorched fields. This morning is almost fall-like and I am going to plant a row of bulbs before the spell lifts. Last time I wrote you, I wanted to be a hermit, I think, but the cool wind's a little alleviating today, no matter how horrified people might be inside. If your hibiscus blooms will you save the seeds so I can get another start from you. I hope something exciting has happened there and glamorous clients glide in. [. . .]

Yours,
Eudora

In the next letter, Welty describes a neighbor's night-blooming cereus. (In Jackson, this flower's imminent blooming was sometimes announced publicly, so that neighbors could come to watch it. In the 1930s, Welty and a group of friends who enjoyed such events called themselves the Night-Blooming Cereus Club. Their motto: "Don't take it cereus. Life's too mysterious."[53]) She also tells Robinson about receiving copies of her second short story collection, The Wide Net and Other Stories.

August 21, 1943
Dear John—

I hope for your little rest. [. . .]—The locusts are singing—Do you have locusts in the evening—It is cool a little, like fall, but has not rained. The evenings are long, the sunsets very beautiful. Later—I have been sitting on the curb with Helen waiting for her bus. A little creature sat on the other side of her, a cricket—locust—going with sounds, very eager sounding, kkk, kkk, kkk. A night-blooming-cereus opened down the street and had three flowers—We went to see it and looked at it with matches. Do you remember all the intricate little things inside? The colors too, to be a night flower. It smelled good. The little stamen like a minute replica of the flower, and opens too, just like it. The lady gave me a cutting started in a pot. The Milky Way was looking dense and beautiful. Sunday—Dorothy[54] came and brought us a quart jar of boiled peanuts and 12 Easter lily bulbs and the last little tomatoes from Utica. We read in the swing where it was cool. All the dogs in the neighborhood were barking about something. A train was going over Pearl River Bridge. You will be glad, 'Livvie' won the O. Henry Prize. The camellias look nice and I am watering them. I do it all day. Russell Fox advertised some clover seed as 99.9% pure for sale in the farm bulletin—right next to a lady wanting a bird dog that could do it all. The squirrels are eating the green pine cones, or their seeds, and throw the husks down as fast as they can out of the treetops, like sports in the bleachers gnawing peanuts. Monday.—I hold to this letter thinking one might come from you to answer. Tomorrow might really be the first day one could come. Much love to you. The book [*The Wide Net*] is printed and came today, I wish you could see it. I still water the garden.

My love to you—
E

The following letter, Robinson's account of the Sicily invasion, is the only extant wartime letter from him to Welty.

Sicily
Sunday, Aug. 8
Dear E—

I am trying to write this on the Jeep—we have no windshield and it is not too bad. It is seven PM and we are based for the night in a valley under some old olive trees. That is, I suppose they are old, the branches are growing out of huge old trunks which have been drastically pruned. The sun is going down clear. [. . .] I still can't quite get over the scene of war. I think Tolstoy is modern in this respect, the disorderly scene which has order, the stragglers, the simplicity of battle. One of the things which has amazed me at the front is that one rarely sees the enemy. He is dug in or hidden and is described by his gunfire. When I think of war I think of an odor, a burnt smell of flesh, powder, vegetation, intermingled. Of corpses lying around under trees in the moonlight, killed by artillery fire, everything burned, of bodies by the roadside, and I wonder what they were doing when they were killed. Wrecked vehicles along the mountain roads, tanks, trucks, piles of unused ammunition, and in places canteens, clothes, blankets left behind in hurried retreat. Deaths of people I know. I ask about people I like with fearful misgivings. [. . .] The boy who won all the money at poker coming over, he was very obstreperous and over-talkative in a way, and childish and I think I thought of him as silly—he was among the first killed, jumped up to throw a hand grenade and was killed by machinegun fire. The paratroopers have been very brave. [. . .] One I knew talked an awful lot about the battle and knew all, but I think he never saw it. Others are very silent, they visit a day or two, say little, and are off again. Even a Lt. Col. was the same, just dropped in one day, stayed two days and dropped out again. They are wanderers in a way. They look like wanderers when you meet them in the road and talk to them. They are usually alone, and have everything about them, no destination, no plans. I can tell a wanderer I think. [. . .] Are you writing much now? I got your letter written on July 7 yesterday, sent to Camp Bradford, must have been one of the last sent there. [. . .] I like very much the idea of the sweater. I wear a no. 40 coat if that helps. [. . .] Your letters are most interesting, and I enjoy getting them. My love to your family and Joe and MF.

Yours,
John

August 26, 1943
Dear John—

Your long letter came safely this morning and I have read in it all day. Nothing has meant quite this to me. I should have written before now to thank you for sending it. There was no doubt in my heart that you had been on some great crest, or the crest of the truth of the whole event rose up in you—because it could in you, and you stopped and wrote this when you could still see all. I will keep this—I have kept everything. I haven't even told Mother any of these things—you did make me see them, as well as I could when you told me so carefully and clearly, but they went to that part of my life where things stay secret—somehow like the tenderest things. [. . .] Your letters did come in such a strange little order—first the postcards—the absurd wonderful postcards of Sicily— saying all about you was gilt and champagne, the first I heard after the worst time—then the V-mail that afternoon, which I think I answered in a light-handed way—I couldn't seem to be sure you were really all right—then this morning this magnitude of a letter. It had acquired 3 more airmail stamps coming here and a sizeable paper-clip on the out- side holding all, was it yours? but the seal was unbroken and it was safe all as you sent it. So then I could be sure of all. I felt very full of riches for the two days. And in a kind of profound rejoicing that you were all right.

I bought a little desk—you know I never had one. This one is beauti- ful—I had seen it at Casey & Casey [in New Orleans] and now a prize fell in my lap and you are so well—something overflowed. Maybe with the foreign money you put in your letter I will buy a fine quill to write with except I think the money there is too pretty to spend, if I were an Algiers lady I would never spend any. It is so late—a little tiny green grasshopper is on my arm, riding. I think I will write you tomorrow. The size 40 helps and the sweater is like a long tail instead of the little birds nest of before. I hope you will find the new orders good.

Yours with love—

E

August 28, 1943
Dear Diarmuid,

I came home from a few days in New Orleans sort of hoping I might have a letter from you and there was a little stack, with one from Henry, a grand surprise. It was nice to have them all. Much seems to be hap- pening, vacations, money falling around, melons getting ripe, articles, and I can't think of anything that hasn't happened. Have you tasted the strange melon? How is it? You were going to name it the Russelliana, and

I hope you won't take it back after taking a taste—I hope it is something very special.[55] You may be printing MELONS on your letterhead next, in bigger type than Literary Agents. MELON SPECIALISTS, maybe. [. . .] I am sorry the vegetable garden back of the house has to be given up, but those little creatures coming in must be annoying beyond endurance. I suppose you will not leave a sign, "Have Moved to Top of Hill." Could they all be starving there the way they are here—it is on account of no rain here, since May, except for a solitary afternoon, that little squirrels and rabbits come up the front steps and literally press their noses against the screen door. They (squirrels only) sit in treetops now eating the seeds from green pine cones and toss down the shells with one paw just like sports in the bleachers at baseball games, and they would eat all the buds off winter flowering shrubs if we let them, and they have eaten summer bulbs down to the ground. It is sad. Ponds and streams are drying up too and there is little water for anything to live on. Our town was asked today please not to water gardens any more as the drinking supply is low, but with the temperature at 107 as it was yesterday and must be now, things cannot live without water. This typewriter, in a room, is a little stove to touch. It would be worth doing without a little drinking water to save camellias—I have had one to die, but the rest are alive. We will have to have a rain before I can dig your daylilies, so put off the frosts up there. John won't be home soon, I think, but he came through the Sicily fighting all right. He wrote me a remarkable letter of great length about the whole scene, from every little thing that grows to the livid things at the front where he was most of the time—just after he had had his first bath of the war, in a little river, and before going on in to Palermo,—where he had a day or two living among gilt furniture and drinking champagne between orders. [. . .] This is a long and dull letter to send after the good ones from there but when the heat abates I will try to make it up by wonderful scintillating notes such as were never really cooked on this little stove at all.

Love,

Eudora

P. S. I forgot to tell you that a night-blooming cereus opened down the street the other night and was beautiful—3 flowers opened, between 9:30 and 10—They grow out of one edge of the *leaf*—how do you account for this?

Deep in the swamps the water hyacinths make solid floors you could walk on over still black water, the Southern blue flag stands thick and sweet in the marsh. Lady's-tresses, greenish-white little orchids with spiral flowers and stems twisted like curls and braids, grow there, and so do nodding lady's-tresses. Water lilies float, and spider lilies rise up like little coral monsters.

The woods on the bluffs are the hardwood trees—dark and berried and flowered. The magnolia is the spectacular one with its heavy cups—they look as heavy as silver—weighing upon its aromatic, elliptical, black-green leaves, or when it bears its dense pink cones. I remember an old botany book, written long ago in England, reporting the magnolia by hearsay, as having blossoms "so large as to be distinctly visible a mile or more—seen in the mass, we presume." But I tested the visibility power of the magnolia, and the single flower can be seen for several miles on a clear day.

—"Some Notes on River Country," 1944

CHAPTER THREE

September 1943–October 1944

During the summer of 1943, Welty had closed a letter to Robinson with the phrase "I still water the garden" (8.21.43); unsure how he had fared during the invasion of Sicily, she tried to maintain a hopeful outlook. Throughout the following year, Welty continued to hope for a swift end to the war, and to worry about Robinson and other friends and family who were in harm's way. After her second collection of short stories, *The Wide Net*, was published in September 1943, Welty began working on a story set in the Mississippi Delta, where Robinson's relatives lived. She encouraged Robinson to write about his wartime experiences; he sent her Christmas presents that included a leather portfolio, where she planned to keep her writing—"it will hold all I ever do or keep," she told him (12.7.43).

In 1944 Welty spent almost six months in New York City working for the *New York Times Book Review*; she hoped to get an overseas writing assignment, since that might enable her to see Robinson. Welty enjoyed New York City and the time she spent with the Russells and other friends, although she missed the Mississippi countryside and her garden. Robinson's military assignments were keeping him away from the front lines, so she worried less about his safety. But Welty was dissatisfied with the Delta fiction she was writing. "My thoughts seem to be more and more in ways I cannot write in," she told Robinson in July. She felt he understood the ineffable experiences she wanted to convey, something "so here and there—anywhere—like lightning bugs all around you, in a field, in the Delta" (7.18.44). Such evanescence characterized many of the natural scenes Welty described, whether she glimpsed them in her garden at home, traveling in the Mississippi countryside, or between skyscrapers in New York. Sketching these scenes, Welty was also tracing her own yearnings—her hopes for her art and her desire to be reunited with Robinson.

September 1, 1943
Dear John—

A soft grey day—one little cardinal giving a few notes—not raining, but oh it might—first cloudy day since it was July—The potted plants set out, like so many little urchins' palms in a row—There is a delicious smell of mist—The fall flower catalogues came in the mail—strange new irises, and amazing looking things coming out of big bulbs like roc's eggs—Erasmus? The fox-tail lily—so expensive—I think I still like hyacinths and the white daffodils best—

Today a big beautiful amaryllis opened many flowers—the white kind with pale pink lines, and rose stamens with gold hoods on them, and the most delicious fragrance, like a cool magical something you could drink—

A little wind blows—the porch floor is misted over and is reflecting the sky—the swing makes a creak like the note of a bass viol—A little white tail is going down the street like this [*drawing of the tail wagging above a line*] over the terrace—I know this tail, have seen it often and some day I am going to raise up and look at the owner—I think it may be one of those short-legged dogs with long white hair and intent little faces—

Judge Lyell[1] just phoned and told me a joke he was sending the Lions Club paper. Mother is playing bridge at Mrs. Fox's. I stayed home to read—stories by Sylvia T. Warner[2]—Dry. And to watch for my little desk—Henry Volkening sent fond wishes to you—He was writing on his vacation, out on a hill, watching a little dancing leaf, way up in Pa. [Pennsylvania]. 8 Canadians bought "The Robber B"[3] according to royalty statement today. Who do you suppose they were? I see them as all together—like a party in a bar all deciding they'll try something—This is a wonderful afternoon to play music—So quiet—nothing to hurt the eyes—the long glare gone—(for you too?)—Now rain—maybe—

Love to you-

E

September 12, 1943
Sunday
Dear John—

After following after Amaryllis Belladonna[4] I find it is a native of S.

Africa as we should guess, and my bulb book lists 4 kinds—elata, deep rose—major, pink—rosea, maxima, dark rose—and speciosa purpurea, purple-rose with white center. A place in California lists them and I ordered 1 doz. major, they sounded so beautiful there. My bulb author says you have to grow them in pots, in the cellar—but he is from Boston—I consistently flaunt him. I'll put them right outdoors. One flower I have wondered if you might see along the coast is the sea-daffodil—pancratium maritimum. It seems to bloom in summer there, a little bulb, that grows about 5 or 6 inches high, long buds striped with pale green that open one evening and last till the next evening—6 to 9 flowers in an umbel, and they resemble pure white daffodils, so delicate as to be almost transparent. The fragrance is supposed to be a little like vanilla. The staminal cup is toothed and the recurved segments are very long and narrow.[5] I thought you might have seen them on the shore once where you swam. Maybe you smelled them after dark and didn't know what that could be.

[. . .] It's a beautiful day—birds singing, little rain lilies, white, yellow, and pink, blowing in the wind. The only other thing blooming much is hippeastrum advenum, two little bunches. Yesterday at sunset, while I was ironing on the back porch, I counted 38 robins on the grass in the one place seen from the window—feeding a little but mostly just poised quite still—just that moment of the day.

I hope to hear soon. Much love to you—

Yours—

Eudora

September 13, 1943

Dear Diarmuid,

I got two letters from you and one from Rosie—a nice thing for Monday. It sounds nice up there—have spider lilies shown up? Buds are sticking up here. [. . .]

It was grand to have Rosie's long letter about the children and if you did take the pictures I hope you will remember to let me have a print so I can see them. The Wide Net jacket is up on my bookcase looking nice by lamplight also. [. . .]

Yours,

Eudora

John says he has been in a garden in Palermo where an Englishman (gone) had a whole greenhouse of orchids, one (a tri-color) named after him, and an Italian gardener remaining through all lovingly tending them—and thousands of amaryllis belladonna—

September 17, 1943
Dearest John,

It's a fall day truly—cool, winds blowing in the trees, little winter berries forming, and the camellia buds growing full. It's time for spider lilies here—which I never think I will like, but something about their color makes me glad to see them when they come. They are buds now, like candles along the edges of walks, but might be flowering when this letter is done, you know their speed. Do you see these? I put information from your letters into my garden notebook. Soon maybe sweet olives. I have been over a large part of S. W. Jackson this afternoon on foot (bond survey etc.—I regret to say what I do is ultimately for Aimee) and saw many small sights on W. Silas Brown, Earl, Hiawatha, and S. Gallatin sts. A little girl (this was the first day of school, pets wagging outside the schoolhouse) racing along the top of a wall and jumping into a deep bed of late verbena, and looking up as I passed with the most *sisterly* look—It was fall-like in backyards—leaves were falling—some big old chinaberry trees were the most stately I saw, near an old firestation—with a ring like a fairy ring of roller skates left around it. [. . .] I looked for quinces on everybody's bush, but all were dried in the long drouth, if there had been any I could have made little gatherings one by one and made jelly tonight. I have to believe you went where you thought—not elsewhere. I'm writing to an address that I feel to be old, though—since that day you climbed the mountain to look. I hope you are well and safe. Do you need your sweater? I am waiting just a little now on the address but this week being the first we can send things to you I long to have it on its way, for it might be cool and the wind might be blowing. I wish I could send you something very fine, splendid, that you would exactly need, at just the right time. [. . .]

Sept. 21—Tuesday. [. . .] Sent you a V*mail this morning—I forgot to tell you that the Leila is superbly decked in buds, the finest any camellia has, long and full and pointed, and a delicate light-green. It is unlucky to count them, but I can tell at a steady glance that there are twice as many as before—I hope when they are flowers you can look at them to your fill—this spring very early. I have felt that Leila had an intelligence about things—some camellias are so dumb—always putting on growth at the right times and considerably when she did—making and protecting her buds judiciously and generously, shading them just so (many let their buds burn in the sun this summer) and in flower she has a graciousness that seems truly special, opening them where they look loveliest together, spaced just so, just the most beautiful number at one time. A sense of timing. Not a one of her flowers was harmed by cold and not a bud has been harmed by the burning heat. I do nothing but just attend in spirit, and think of that time when the flowers will shine in that wonderful color I told you about. [. . .]

Mother came in with some fine single dahlias, the ones named for her in the neighborhood, the Chestina. She sent her best to you and wished you could see the flowers. The roses have put on good growth, and Mother says she is undecided about whether to remove the mulch and plant a little fall crop of greens under there.

There is a blue sky, small silver clouds. A thrush is singing by himself. I must go now. When I got your letter I played the Mozart and some of the other things to think how they would sound in Sicily with maybe ocean sounds behind them. Don't forget how the Mozart symphony is, ever. I must go. It is so good to hear from you and it changes everything sometimes when things have happened in the world that make a fresh mystery of how you are. Please take care of yourself. [. . .]

Love—

E—

Enclosed a four o'clock from corner of N. State and College Sts—

September 21, 1943

Dear Diarmuid,

Thanks for the English reviews, which I got several days back, and enjoyed looking at. I sent you and Henry some books today, they having come from H.B.[6] Are your spider lilies up? Ours were buds looking like candles yesterday and today are like flames. Houghton Mifflin wrote that they took pleasure in sending me a check for $20 in payment for use of my story in 1943 Best Short Stories, at request of Martha Foley[7]—am I supposed to get this? Anyway, I owe you two bucks enclosed; but do not remember anything about this. Also Whit Burnett wrote me this letter,[8] have you seen his outlay? I thought it looked a little tiring—aren't all stories stories of the human spirit? I thought it looked a little fearful. John sent his love to all of you from Sicily and says he would like to visit you again, and Pammie and Will. Tell Rosie I will answer her letter soon. We are having cool days, fall winds.

Love,
Eudora

September 24, 1943
Dearest John—

Happy day—your letters came from Africa—with many delights—[. . .] It was so nice to hear. At this moment I don't see how I lived through Sicily. Your letters came so fast today—I felt the ink wasn't really dry, I held them delicately—8 days, the airmail. [. . .] This is a wonderful day—cool, bright, little wind blowing—cardinals flying about, squirrels shaking out their tails in the tree just out the window—in a minute I shall dash to the garden. What will I plant today—I don't know. [. . .]

Much love,
E

September 27, 1943
Dear Diarmuid,

Thanks for the H. B. money. I'm looking forward to the pictures. It's so nice down here now—sun, little winds, such nice smells (cotton seed mills—smell like ham cooking) in the air all day. For some reason some species tulips are up—could some be fall blooming or are they out of their minds? I see in the paper your temperature going down—are you painting leaves? You didn't name any colors. I saw the Time review[9] but they say those things just because I happen to live in the South—but nobody else had better say I am un-human. My little desk came from N.O., the piece of the hinted prize money, and is nice. [. . .] I wish all of you were traveling down here—for October days—they are our nicest, just about. Love to all, signed on my desk.

Yours,
Eudora

September 28, 1943
Dear John—

[. . .] Did I tell you how quickly the letters are coming? [. . .] It is lovely to hear so well—You know I live in a glow because you are in a house—and have 2 balconies instead of one—

Lots of love—

E—

This is such a picnic day as would lead you out—We still have windy sunny days but so many mosquitoes the yard man builds a fire on the grass to mow it—the kind they have on the Coast—Roses are pretty now—I am looking at a vase with a Hoover, a Dainty Bess, a Lady Hillington and an Editor MacFarland—it's getting to be the time you like them—

Much love to you—[. . .]

October 18, 1943
Dear Diarmuid,

It was nice to get the letter on the new ribbon, and with a picture on the back. Now I can see how it [the Russells' yard] looks from the porch and it must look like a stately park. How much work and how long did it take you? Now you can see the deer coming a long way off. I guess you have plenty of wood for the winter fires now. Did a cold snap come on you up there too? It might have snowed—for we had a frost Saturday night—astonishing—it killed the bean crop. The spider lilies, if they sent up leaves, aren't going to bloom—that's a notification. I think it was the drouth, or else they were down too deep for their liking, but most probably it's the drouth. They are probably multiplying like demons. Mother has started dividing her daylilies and yours will be there in time to be planted, I hope. We had a fine rain Wednesday. I was listening to a Schubert Trio—No. 1—and it began to rain—andante, then scherzo and presto, and rained all day. I have a new ribbon in here too, as you see, and had been trying to write a little story—so far it isn't very good, though. I don't know what has been holding my brain in such a clamp for so long—I've *wanted* to write things. I am glad you don't give me up, as maybe you should. Yes, I read the Nation review and she says all the things about me I always say about Carson McCullers![10] So I get slapped right back. [. . .]

You were right in your prediction, Pamela wrote me she thought she couldn't make it over this way.[11] But I wrote to her how she could and do hope she can come, for just a little, anyway. Remember October as a good month for coming down—wouldn't that be nice, I wish for it. We took a walk Sunday and the trees were a little golden and bronze, with sumac, thistles, asters, coreopsis, and such things everywhere, and the Chinese tallow trees that grow on this street have burst their little pods and now translucent silver berries are all over them, with bright red leaves. It is a shame you lose your good paintings to admirers[12] and I wish since you had to let it go I could have borrowed it first (maybe you could lend only) since it was so good of that fine country from the lookout. Was there a lot of blue.

Yours,

Eudora

October 25, 1943

Dear J—

Saw your mother in the P.O. yesterday, about noon—she was looking well—She had on a blue dress—some beads with little elephants. She said she hadn't heard lately and I said, "He's all right"—a gesture to go with it, I think. That was a beautiful day. Dorothy[13] came on the bus and we took a walk to the top of that hill looking over the waterworks. The cold had come with the sap in the leaves and everything was colored—it was a windy day, with clouds flying—some dark, almost navy blue, some silver, some sunny, some pinkish—and the sky between the most radiant dazzling soft blue—from the hilltop you could see all over into Rankin county—[illegible: Brandon?] but for the trees, I know—areas of light and shade, clearest colors of gold and rose and red and violet and yellow and a wonderful lime yellow (pecans) and you could see the Capitol and the old asylum building looking like a castle and those fields between very bright, and in the north you could see as far as the water tank at Madison Station. On the hill was a very old tattered cedar tree, two of them, bleached white, and a chinaberry—you know it's an old home site. Every few minutes things changed as the light changed under the clouds—we would watch it travel. We sat down in the grass which was warm. Our hair blew straight out. We smoked cigarettes. The wind blew and smelled of goldenrod and woodsmoke. Some birds were flying against the wind and being perfectly still in the air with their wings beating, they enjoyed flying in that direction best, it seemed. Then they would perch on the very tip of the cedar tree—mocking birds. Little balls are making on the chinaberries. Pecans a little green yet. No muscadines. I picked some sweetgum leaves and some pecans and tallow tree leaves coming home, and I sent them to you in a long envelope with some book reviews—

[. . .] It's cold tonight—I'm writing by the fire. Maybe I will hear tomorrow since it is the even month since you wrote. I hope this will be over soon. If you are where you can't write I wish you could have this fire—and roof—or for myself that I could be there. Have worked hard in the garden. Love to you.

Yours—
Eudora

October 29, 1943
Dear John,

[. . .] Charlie was sending word about the belladonnas that they were "beautiful but tricky"—must be very carefully planted—This is too late to tell me—but I was careful as I could be—Do you see African iris? Mine's blooming—! Sky blue—a flower a day—

I am writing a little story[14] and will soon send—not quite done—I'd be glad to know what you think—You know what I try—I wanted the next book for you—but will I ever be able to do things well enough to agree for *this* (any) to be a book I want for you—No—but you will understand both wish and reticence—I couldn't do without sending the stories to you as I write them and if I feel I have learned nothing at all, often, there is that moment of pleasure that comes too—and I rush something to you. [. . .] It's late—Goodnight—

Love—
E—

November 1, 1943
Dear Diarmuid,

I was so pleased to get the letter saying you sold the "Curtain" to Sweden, for which I was unprepared, and even the money with it, gotten so swiftly. Many thanks. I enclose the signed contracts. I was sorry to note clause 7, that my name is only going to appear in its customary form, as it would be fun to be called something else (Swedish). [. . .] It is raining a little bit this morning, for the first time in a long time, so things may be looking better around here. The leaves have been wonderful—unusual for us—and I wish you could see Chinese tallow trees, which have Oriental looking leaves*, very fat and simple with delicate points, and in the fall the leaves turn wine colored on one side and either black-plum or chartreuse on the other, and the little pods pop and very translucent little white balls come out in clusters of 4 all over the tree, shining like glass. They are small, leaning, decorative trees—silver gray twisted bark—mostly though they grow tall eventually. I have about finished the story I was telling you about, but be prepared for a bad length—about 30 pages, it looks like—and I am not sure it's good either.

Love,

Eudora

* Enc[losed].

November 5, 1943
Guy Fawkes Day
Dear John—

A grand bright day. Yesterday we got hold of a sack of sand, a load of fertilizer, and some old cast-off sticks to put up around the camellias—very rare—all within 30 minutes. It was all coincidence—I won't go into it V-mail. Those earliest little sweet jonquils are coming up—also white hyacinths. [. . .] The leaves are still beautiful. Miss Flo Lehman was on the bus[15]—I said "Beautiful weather" and she said, heavy-lidded, "Gawjus. We'll pay for it." Some people's winter grass is up. [. . .] The yellow hibiscus is blooming—some sturdy specimens survived the drouth—I have one flower on the desk, stuck in a jigger—beautiful—you remember that wonderful clear yellow—and maroon eye—and perfectly round petals. Toscanini[16] was playing on the air Sunday. Can you ever hear such things? He played London Symph, O. to Magic Flute, and Beethoven's 9th.—All rather breathlessly fast—

Love,

E

November 10, 1943
Dear John—

[. . .] This is a little siesta for me. Have worked hard outdoors. Part of the time we were moving a fairly big camellia from our next door neighbor's over here—not behind her back—3 random colored men were spading, while all the ladies stood around like surgeons, guest-surgeons, at an operation wringing their gloves. All went well. It's by our side porch steps now. It is a little dark red flower with white lines in it that you have seen out in the country a lot. The money from Sweden I told you about went for a General Washington—semi-double white with occasional rosy dots and markings—do you know it? I remember Charlie thought it was nice from having seen it. A place in Augusta sent me a fascinating catalogue. [. . .]

Must tie up head and go now. I wish your watch band would come. It is still pretty here—the prettiest leaves have blown away—we had nigh onto a cyclone the other night with lightning and thunder—paying for Miss Flo Lehman's beautiful weather. The camellias are all right and the rain was good for them.

Mother sends love. She has a rake over her shoulder and two smocks on. I have several vests, like the vaudeville character that's going to shed them, only I'm probably going to add on. Much love to you. Tomorrow's Armistice Day.

Yours,
Eudora

November 13, 1943
Dear Diarmuid,

I hope you are all feeling better—one by one all having flu—I hope all the germs are gone, or probably worn out. Is Williebelle[17] still there, to fetch and carry? I hope all is better now.

I think you are probably right about the story [. . .]—but it's still too new for me to think how to work further on it.[18] [. . .]

No trips look very possible right now—I fix hopes on the spring. It got to be very funny weather lately—we had two or three tornadoes in the neighborhood though nothing in the gardens were hurt much. I put some of the Swedish money into a fine new camellia bush, named General Washington—semi-double white with occasional pink dots and markings—about as double as a gardenia flower. It's sent off for, to Ga., and I look for it daily. I wish the trip would work from there to here and would be at camellia time, because all the plants look very promising and fine.

Love,
Eudora

Hope your landlady hasn't snatched any more of your good work—landladies could as easily like the *worst*—

November 25, 1943
Thanksgiving—morning
Dear John—

Are you having French, British, or American table today—I wish you cranberries—Maybe you're having a picnic. Maybe you're having a little seafood dressing—oysters? I hope you will send me a little report. We are making a pecan pie. Mother and I haven't eaten yet. I got up before day to take Dorothy to her bus—it was cool, clear, the sky just pale—before I got home it turned amethyst and clouds like petals everywhere—and a little *fine* moon, rising—the streets and buildings and the Old Capitol looked like light and dark pearls—I went by the fair grounds hill and river mist was everywhere, I watched the sun come up. Some church bells began to ring. I went to see how my little new camellia Gen. Washington, had spent the night—it looked well—I told you about it—it came yesterday, all crated, and looked like a small traveling peep show, with platform over the ball and little sack curtain all around—the express man was so interested—I pulled the curtain and showed him it was a camellia—he said "red or white?" I said white—he said "My mother's got four red ones!" It won't be blooming for a year or so but it is a nice little branched plant about 18" high with longish lighter-colored leaves, and fills in a space in my border that kept saying "Camellia" plaintively. Everything looks well now. I worked a while—Thanksgiving seems a good day to get ready for the Christmas bulbs—I can't tell you how pleased they have me, very excited—do you think they will do all right planted in Hattiesburg Sharp Sand? I have Hattiesburg and also Pearl River sand. I have a little can of bone-meal saved for them, marked "Africa" in the garage. You are sweet to send things, I don't quite see how you did it. The way your letters came (finally), I saw it all in reverse action—sent off the packages—then, have packages wrapped, don't know why I don't send them—then, hunting for string—when *I* know all the time they were sent. I was never so glad as to get the letters—at the end of a month I was scared and I wrote you so, in spite of effort not to say a thing. The letters are tremendous, they make me see all, I feel carried away, I am amazed all the time, and yet not surprised. I love them a lot. This will be a nice day another day with family MF and Joe[19]—and a little

music. I hope soon. Lots of love—Happy Thanksgiving to you—
Yours—
E—
Mais[20] I wish you were here—Mother sends love

December 7, 1943
Dear John—
Your letter came, of the 18th, both parts—Don't be leaving your little fire—when you just got it. I wait very anxiously to hear. I just won't think of anything else, unless you tell me I have to. It's so strong a positive to feel—and now you have a fire and two human beings in the house.[21] I know a map is in your head—more of places than a map—but oh for you to come home at night to the other thing. I hope very much for it. I think I use hope out of the future too, as well as out of the present and past, I take it from both directions—Our times are so mixed up—and the present moment seems to absorb them all. [. . .] I study my map too but with all my energy on the one spot. The heart of things, where you are needed by all that makes sense. I went to Utica and a light like the grass, a sort of golden sedge-light was over everything. Chinaberries, trees on the hills. Smells of cotton seed mills here. The portfolio has letters from you in it now. I keep it on top of the desk. On one wall by it is a drawing of hyacinths and on the other wall the boat you sent me—all colors fine with it. I am hoping to put work in it soon—it will hold all I ever do or keep. Every day I think like now that I have never seen things so beautiful as you have sent me.[22] It is warm and cloudy—why is it so much like spring—even the air. We worked hard moving shrubbery. I am pleased beyond everything you like the book and sweater, and proud. Leila is fine. Belladonnas, much foliage, parted in middle, like one of those beards. I hope it is not so cold and rainy. I hope everything goes well and you are fine. Much love. I sent you one day a very small picture for a wall in a house. Violets are thick and 1 narcissus.
Love—
E—

December 10, 1943
Dear Diarmuid,
I hope Pammy and William are up by now and there won't be any

more of that. I can just hear Pammy's clear little directions from the bed as to what can be done next as that is a regal situation.[23] Many thanks for the O. Henry [prize] money—why did they bother you with it? It was nice to get—they hadn't notified me or anything so I wasn't quite sure. How are the camellia buds? If they only open this time. My plants look pretty well, though I had to wash each and every leaf of some of them with whale oil soap, because some caterpillars or something had laid eggs there—I remembered Blake's saying—that the caterpillars always choose the fairest leaves to lay their eggs on, just as the priests always choose the fairest joys to lay their curses on, or something.[24] I must read INDIGO[25]—and it looks very fine and prosperous maybe, hope so. Did I tell you FAREWELL MY LOVELY appeared down this way in Pocketbooks and I was crazy about it—he has a new one out this winter, I saw somewhere, THE LADY IN THE LAKE,[26] but it's not here yet. We have had mild, warm days—exactly like spring—the onion grass is blooming everywhere—and a spray of forsythia, madly. This is very dangerous weather—everything comes up and puts out leaves and buds and then we always have a grueling January. A few iris and pansies and daffodils are already blooming—all the hyacinths are up—even a daylily bloomed. John wrote me he was sending me some bulbs from Africa—I hope they come—a surprise kind of iris, he said. He is still there, I hope, but he gave me a little hint that he might be somewhere else soon, a wilder country. He does not like the brass hats and I think is anxious to get back with the men—although he is in the thick of all kinds of things in Algiers, which he likes. He went far up into some Arab village and saw them making leather things and sent me some beautiful, wonderfully worked pieces—one is a big portfolio, that looks as if meant to hold a mighty lot of writing. This is the most colorful fall we ever had, and I didn't paint a thing. I take long walks to the country but someone is always along that wouldn't want to stop and pause respectfully while I paint. The leaves are still on the trees, dark bronzes and purples now, and the sky has been lovely. I sent you and Rosie some nuts one day, so look in the express office. The cottonseed mills are running and they make the air smell like ham cooking. Joy! only you can't eat it. A camellia is blooming today, the kind called Pink Perfection—clear shell color, petals exactly so, that I don't believe you like as well. I wish I could see all of you. [. . .] I hope everything up there is fine by now—family, business, watercolors, everything. [. . .]

    Love,
    Eudora

December 15, 1943
Dear John—

We got our boxes at the same time, we wrote the same day—so it was Christmas, as near as it could have been. I hope you got my letter too. [. . .] It's the middle of the morning—very cold. I was looking around the garden. I wish you could see all the little bulbs coming up—of course small now, but I like to see them when they first show in the ground—and today, in the cold, below freezing, with snow clouds, there they are, little firm rosettes of hyacinths—so green. The only thing about waiting another year for you to see them that is good, is that there will be more, they will multiply. Nice little clumps now—you remember when I found my first white and pink Roman hyacinth bulbs, from the lady from Terry when you bought her flowers on the church steps. I had never known where they came from. I've covered the belladonnas with pine straw, not knowing if they like it so cold. I watch out expectantly for the surprise iris—suppose they should come blooming. You know how in the country now little straight rows of narcissus spears are up between road and house, between the cedar trees. There are more berries on the holly trees this year than I ever saw before—they look between every two leaves. I saw so many near Raymond,[27] late the other evening. [. . .] When you get this, it might be the New Year. All I feel about it can turn into only one thing, hope, but if it starts out of my love now, maybe so much energy of the heart can make it shine as bright as if it could stay its first way and you will know it is a daily kind of hope, not ever idle. [. . .]

Much love to you
Yours—
E—

Christmas 1943
Dear John—

What is your Christmas? All day I was thinking of you—I wish I could see you and see how everything is—good or bad—and if I could find some little Christmas thing—Here it was dark and cold—but small white hyacinths in bloom—About 2:00 I went over to your house and saw your father and mother, and D and baby and wife, and A. B.—Sat at the table while they ate 2 turkeys—Saw the tree—I carried my gold-stitched purse[28] all day and dazzled people throughout the day—Brought everything down for the Christmas tree this morning—I hope you are warm and all right—that you have a roof and fire—a good place to sleep in—a good day, a good night—and then one little thing for Christmas— My love all to you and I think of you as if all days were Christmas and counted very much like this, it is every *day* that matters so much—It is 8 PM—raining a little—We had egg-nog—the tree—music in afternoon— sandwiches for supper—With love—please take care—I hope you are fine—Tell me if your Christmas was all right—and now—Goodnight, my love to you—

yours—

E

January 13, 1944
Dear Diarmuid,

The pictures came along with your letter this morning and I'm so pleased to have them—I've been wondering what your things were looking like by now and in this season. I like them both but especially the one of the hills and the three fields. In the other one I like the contrast between the smoky and yellow sky and the turquoise ice, and also that wet hill on the right hand side—all the hills I like, the progression of colors in the 3 on the other side too. [. . .] I could frame these in beautiful icicle frames today—we had a rare, icy storm, and the scene outside is like a glassblower's—the pine trees like big glass fans. I woke up to hear my poor camellias chattering their leaves in the wind, and ran out to cover them all but a coat of ice was on every leaf and bud. I snapped off some hyacinths that were blooming and they were not frozen through, so I took heart. But all is laden and bending, and many trees will probably break. At least our cold weather is coming when it should, January—lots of times, like last year, we have summerlike weather then and everything, all the fruit trees and flowering shrubs, put out, and are killed in February. We have some quince in flower, and a little forsythia and spirea, but no fine show of things to get killed now. If our spring is nice, I wish you and the family could come down and see it. It would be easier than you think. If you took the streamliner, you could get overnight to either Meridian, Miss., or New Orleans, and I would meet you, and the round trips don't cost very much and being in Jackson and looking at flowers doesn't cost anything. [. . .] I am glad all the flu has gone out of your house, it sounded like a curse or something. I hope it never comes back. Have you tried any more bottled Old Fashioneds?[29] It didn't do any good to warn me they were bad, I wished I had a lot of them—in a row, when I read your letter. Maybe this summer we can all make wine. My mother wishes you could come, too, all of you.

Love,

Eudora

[*drawing of camellia bud:*] Yours should be about this size now

January 14, 1944

Dear Eudora:

The camellia has flowered! It's so beautiful that Rose carried it down from our bedroom to the kitchen so that we could look at it during breakfast. Ever since it has showed color there has been tension in the house. [. . .] There is another bud to come later. This is all for the moment but I had to let you know that affection has paid out in the end

love

Diarmuid

January 21, 1944

Friday

Dear Diarmuid,

I was gratified to hear the news about the camellia. If it hadn't bloomed this time, I was going to have it excommunicated, because no camellia could have fared better at any hands than yours, and then to have no flowers! It would be different if you had a garden full and were wise to all their tricks. So I am glad it did open a flower as hoped and that you thought it was a nice kind. Did Pammy like it, or did she frown that a camellia was just a flower—after she had bothered to get its name in her head. There is one variety that has fragrance, and bees stay around it all the time—maybe you can grow that one day. My plants look all right, though they have been frozen, sleeted on, snowed on, and came through a terrible drouth just before. The outdoor plants look more pleasing and symmetrical than those grown in pots, because just as you say all the plant goes to the flower, indoors. When they get to be trees they are something like the holly tree in form. In about ten years or so there will be a tall hedge of camellias all the way around the yard on one side, if they keep thriving, and I will put a bench out then, and you must expect to sit on it and enjoy such grandeur. There are fall and spring flowering, early and late, single and double, red, white, pink, solid, striped, and variegated, though of course just a small representation of the family.

Most of them stand for some story sold, though some are raised tenderly from stolen cuttings. There was an old German here when I was a child who was poor and loved flowers, and he went around the town with a pillow slip taking camellia cuttings at every garden, and he planted them and now in the house where he lived—he is dead now—there are alleys and forests of camellias. Alas, the people who rent the house don't care a thing for them and chop them down and leave big trunks, and let all the flowers die on the branches. I usually go by there every spring and shake my finger at the house. Little hyacinths are blooming here, and the quince bushes. I hope all of you are still well, all Russells and Volkenings, and no more flu has sneaked in the door again. I hope the other bud will open now, I'm tense about it too. It might be a little different.

Love,
Eudora
Sometimes they throw a white flower.

January 21, 1944
Dear John—

[This letter contained handmade valentines: EW's drawings of daffodils and other flowers, glued inside lace hearts, with the following verses written on reverse side.]

When these do crowd upon your sight
Wish you were here with all your might.

When you will early jonquils see,
Dear Valentine be.

See how the hyacinth grows—
And next the rose—
What e'er is mine
Now zealous flowers to be
Your valentine
Happy Valentine's Day

[. . .] Much love to you.
Eudora

January 23, 1944
Dear John—

See, I just put a new ribbon in the typewriter—pour le printemps[30]—so this will christen it. Such a soft, half-cloudy, half-sunny day—breezes—one of those Jan. days that just leads you out of the house. All morning I worked in the garden—mainly to look—pulling up the first weeds—combing the pine needles out—I took care to disturb not no snakes—especially remembering where I found one asleep in the fall, planting bulbs—and how I covered him up again. There was a cardinal singing the whole time, sitting in the bare redbud tree, tail straight down, head thrown back, he looked like an arrow about to shoot, and singing marvelously. He and I—we presume about its being spring. The paper said it is clear and cold there today—I think where you might be until the garden and all look faded to nothing. I hope you are in the city. The quince bushes are flowering a little, not the white, and the yellow jasmine—I have some jasmine here, in a glass before me on the desk. I am at Aimee's beck and call. She owns a roll of film in my camera, so whenever she wants a picture taken, she phones me. She has seized film from people. But when the camellias bloom and look glorious I am going to take you a little snapshot in my garden so you can see how it is. [. . .] I was playing Offenbach—Gaite Parisienne—while cleaning up, and I was doing I don't know what pony trots and steps and arabesques, and then saw a man in a leather jacket, smoking, looking in the window—he said "I'm the termite man. I've finished looking and you haven't got any termites since last year." [. . .] How are you today? I wish I could see you. The day is so tender here—so springlike. The pear tree starting to bud in a hundred places.

Love to you—
Eudora

February 8, 1944
Dear John,

I hope everything is all right with you—They say the weather is bad—about all they will say—I hope and pray you are in the town—Letters don't come very well, to tell me how you are—3 from Italy altogether—but your next letter,—or now, the letters written now,—will tell me rightly how I can feel—But always it is if I could only see you—Is it an illusion that then I could help you in some little practical thing—but it is always in front of me—I wish I could run out of the house and find myself there, and could know in the next minute from this how you are—

I have worked hard—I took a walk to Helen's[31] about 6:00 and thought how the sky itself has taken on such dimensions this year—over Pinehurst and St[ate] and all—it seems so obviously a wider and busier world than what is below the horizon, all the varied ways it can look, distances—in one hour a storm was coming up—It's because I think that your mind bears on the sky—flights and the evening sky—and the times I know of that you flew and dived—I see what a vast unsettled place it is, it is a whole geography I am ignorant of—and the moon that rises is so important to you—Tonight here there is a storm, a little one—a swelling wind, flying drops—a spring storm, not a winter—it makes the house creak, but it could not hurt you if you were in it, I wish I could send you our gentle storm. I know even if you are not in the terrible place you think so much of the boys for you have done what they will do, and of your fliers you like—will you yourself be careful too—I tell you this so much because of no way to have you safe by sending love—though it is new each day as if it would next time know how to make you safe. The letters you send are good to have—I am glad you have seen some beautiful things there—I hope they were not too much harmed, that you would know how they should be—I see so well all are a part of it, that you describe—of the war but of the world too, most greatly—maybe I understand about the island house partly for I know some things, like some people, or one person, can show us the whole intent of our lives by their rarity that could light up everything that the rest had kept dark— we come under their magnitude and we *know*—and the most passionate hope was not too much—Please take care of yourself—Send me a letter telling me to send the candy and any things you need I could get.

Love,
Eudora—

February 12, 1944
Dear John—

Tonight they say things are a little better in one place—how glad you must be for that, how hard you must have worked—doing so many things at once about it—in more than one place. This is Saturday night— cold, we had a freeze last night and tonight. The pink magnolias were hurt but other things are not. I don't know about the cabbages in Utica.

I covered the tender advanced things. Dr. Shands's yard is tented tonight and his heaters burning—it looks like *anybody* would snuggle in, curl up by the stove, and lie there and read if they wanted to, under the flowering tree. They would think, what a wonderful man Dr. Shands[32] is. I wish I could tell you how beautiful the pear tree is out of my south window, and I had forgotten it. The homeliest little stranger of a dog has been got with puppies by the Dalmatian next door, and is barking at the moon from there. She is all white except her head, which is all black. Of course he is all spots. I keep thinking of her puppies—they will be divided in the middle, black and white, some each way, and the black half will have white spots and the white half black spots. The father sportingly ate a paper sack with 6 narcissus bulbs one day when my back was turned, named Firetails, and maybe the puppies will have other little features. Maybe they will have handmade placards on their backs too—complete little Mardi Gras floats. Mother is up and mostly stronger—wanting to go to the Jitney.[33] I take her and call her The Brain—I just ride her over and carry the basket, and she points. The OCS Joe files papers for is the Judge Advocate. I will tell him about your trials. They sent love to you and hoped you were not there. Edward [Welty] wrote—was asking about you. He is in Air Borne Engineers now, but until borne off he is a camouflage teacher. Much love. I hope you are not so very tired, and that things will be better there, in each of your places, soon—long before this comes. Oh John—to get a letter that you were well and safe—Such a grand Valentine from Seta. Just the kind I would have got for you, my favorite kind—a bear that dances—fat and gray—with a tassel to pull—and across his stomach [*drawing of a heart*]

It is cold—spring is still waiting. It is a quiet night here, but for Mrs Black and White, clear and moonlit and the midnight stars.

[*Drawing of a moonlit tree, with caption:*] The pear tree in the back garden and the moon from here, 1119 Pinehurst By hand.

Yours,

E—

February 17, 1944
Dear John—

Green leaves. The nights down to 20 and the hail storms we had didn't keep them back, and Jefferson St. is like a bower, and down toward the river, golden green—now hanging with drops. Mist—rain—and last night a rolling and luminous fog like a S. Holmes story—or Christabel—

Belhaven looked like a moor—of Cathedral Engloutie—and in the afternoon a strange thunder—Paul said he thought it was an air raid—I thought, thunder 16th Feb., frost 16th April—god forbid. I am not consulted by ladies about covering camellias. The Crystal Springs kind in the yard is covered with flowers around the bottom, like a hem, and those big elegant Chandleriis are opening. The Leila has one coloring bud and the rest of hers very full. You should see the wild tulips (Sylvestris) (and Clusiana) putting up their buds near her. The Silver Star daffodil, silver white parianth, wide fluted primrose one, is out, a little flock this year. [. . .] Diarmuid is fine and sent some really good watercolors he did out in the bitter cold—one of the picnic places under snow and the frozen lakes. The camellia he got has a flower and Rosie called it a gardenia and Pammy squalled "Not a gardenia, Mother, it's a camellia!" I was glad to hear from you the N.O. camellias are all right. And the Beins well.

A thousand birds are flying and shaking off the raindrops—sitting in the trees, little robins, their breasts the only bright things under the sky. Saw Mrs. Aunt Alma Shands in the market—wearing a camellia—of course Dr. S. and I are of different schools. He is very lordly and indiscriminating the way he treats his camellias, while I think you have to see and watch what each wants. [. . .] There is a fascinating thing beginning in the Atlantic this time, Osbert Sitwell's autobiography—a fantastic, gothic, ironic thing, surely the last Britisher who will have written like this.[34] The family stories—his father, "surveying with an appraising eye the comparatively" (to his) "small garden at Weston, a house then already in the possession of my brother, nonchalantly remarked, somewhat to the surprise of the owner, 'I don't propose to do much here; just a sheet of water, and a line of statues . . .' and then suddenly reverting to his other principal interest—medieval times—by, as it were, catching the eye of a periwinkle, effected a formal introduction of us to it in the following terms: 'The Periwinkle! A charming flower and a common term of endearment in the Middle Ages.'" I must go now—Sir Periwinkle— hoping you are well. With much love

> Yours—
> Eudora

February 28, 1944
Dear John—
I was so glad to get your letter—I'd been real worried this time. [. . .]

It sounds nice now where you live—better now, with the stove. Joe and MF came and will be here for the whole week—they were over yesterday from about 2:00 on, it was so good. I wish you could see them. We all just sat and beamed at each other. [. . .] I knew we wouldn't go on a picnic, our kind, without you—such things must wait, wholly. [. . .] Sometimes we just sit still and wish for you. I had a strange feeling you might get here—Or did I see a little gleam of it by mistake. Your camellia has 3 flowers—so beautiful. Many more to come. You would be pleased at its growth. Last year there were 3 buds and they opened one by one and this year there are so many they can open by threes. They are more beautiful than I remembered, which will show you. Mother says she would not be surprised to hear of a climbing Louis Philippe. So maybe that is it. It's fine, not too surprising, that you find Charlie's camellias and the one you know of Washington in flower there. If you see the Leila let me know. The things I have flowering around it are small–growing irises, 3, and "Epicure" daffodils and many little blue and white star flowers, and the small tulips with the points of their buds just parting as of now. I am so pleased about the French translation—Will you get to see it? Will I? Maybe you will have all ways and versions of the Wide Net that are *possible*. John Lane[35] is going to bring out the book in England. The birds are singing so—oh such rain as we have had—days and nights, heavy and light—and in between showers, birds singing—It's like nothing so much as Mexico.[36] Redbud is fully out now, the plums and the peach trees, I saw a peach tree in a bare yard under the new moon. Onion flowers, bluets, buttercups under foot. Confederate violets. I was going to send you a translated bit I made in the Baudelaire but it did not get good enough—though made at the Baudelairean hour of two or three in the morning—It was so good to hear from you. The letters mean everything.

Yours with love,
Eudora

February 29, 1944
Dear Diarmuid,
Many thanks for the English money—and so painlessly, without the figures. I'm late answering because I took a day's jaunt to New Orleans to see what was out in bloom. Camellias and azaleas, and all the way down along the river was yellow jasmine and many redbud trees and little peaches and plums. The drinks are very scarce in the bottom of your

glass. This is all I found out. I took a picture of one of our camellia bushes in full flower, the same kind as your little one, to show you what it will be like one day. How is William? I hope he is up and merry. An anxious time that must have been, but I hope all that is over for the winter. You would like the species tulips blooming now—yellow with long slender petals, half of them reflexed, on long arabesques of stems—Sylvestris. If I get to come up in a couple of months, what fleurs do you want me to bring? [. . .] I am still aghast at the sum you whispered to Mr. Weeks.[37] Have done a little work on the story and cut out about 1500 words so far, and believe it is better.

Love,

Eudora

PS I owe you 30¢, as I won cash from the New Yorker for a Most Fascinating News Story of the Week out of the local paper.

Perelman is on Information Please next Monday night, let's all send in amazing questions.

March 3, 1944

Dear J—

This seems like a good day—don't know why—but do. It is 5 min. after 11, AM. I have on your angel with the red eyes, over which a spray of sweetolive is hanging. Offenbach is in my head, I cleaned up the house to it and at the end a grand dusting round to the Marriage of Figaro. (I dreamed a student came to me and said the Leila camellia was the Mozart of camellias.) [. . .] Am dashing out to meet Dorothy on the bus—I phoned her to come look at the Leila. It is glorious this morning—A spring day brought a good 6 more flowers out on it—soft sunlight, some clouds, bird sitting on the camellias and singing—the birdsfoot violets and the Confederates are thick under the trees—This is the best redbud year we ever had—so full—in early morning and late evening it is rosy but paler than the blue air and seems to just hang in the light. The robins sing very drowsily and springlike now when the sun goes down. Redbirds—mating. I bought 3 tubes of watercolor, new blue, rose madder, and gamboge yellow, and I am liable to paint. Much love to you and I wish I could see you.

E

Welty in a camellia
[shed?] in Jackson. This
photograph, taken by
Charlotte Capers, ap-
peared on the cover of
a promotional booklet
publicizing Welty's first
collection, *A Curtain of
Green.*

Trellis and bench in
the backyard of 1119
Pinehurst Street.

The backyard photographed by Welty from the roof.

Drawing sent to Russell from Yaddo (in Saratoga Springs, New York) in a July 14, 1941, letter. Welty's comment at the bottom of the drawing reads, "What wild lily is this? Drawn from life. (Sunday) Life size. Saffron, lemon, or coral. Ought to be called 'Turkish Slippers'—grows in bogs—" Russell identified the flower as a Canada lily.

Chestina Welty with delphiniums. Welty's caption reads, "No one else grew delphiniums in Mississippi."

Chestina Welty sowing grass seed.

No. 108025

John F. Robinson, 2nd Lt., A.C.

Hq. Co., 3rd Bn., 180 Inf.

APO 45, c/o Postmaster

New York City, N.Y.

(CENSOR'S STAMP)

Eudora Welty

(Sender's name)

1119 Pinehurst St.

(Sender's address)

Jackson, Mississippi
USA

July 19

(Date)

Dear John--

I just now got your little letter written c/o the Fleet Postmaster on the boat--it went clear around the world, and came in at San Francisco. But it's a joy to hear, it doesn't matter if it reaches back. I hope when you get ready to come you won't take the long way and take that long.

Here it is hot. I got up early and watered a little, so I could weed a little. Mrs. Fox sent Jake up with some figs--he came hollering "Figs, Mrs. Welty!" from down the street. They were wonderful. I wrote a letter to Rose Russell--she had asked what you were doing now, so I told her riding along the mountains above the sea in your Jeep in high delight, in Africa. The yard man came and we put him in the house because it was too hot, then we worked outdoors. I ate lunch downtown with Bessie--she'd sent for a Western Union boy and got a poor old one nearly 90 years old--he said he'd been sick a long time, and had trouble with his mind, and couldn't carry anything heavier than a telegram.

We had some pretty Editor MacFarland Roses this morning. And a garden club lady sent over the most beautiful strange lily--very pale, silvery pink--rather frosty long slender petals--yellow stamens--seven flowers coming out of the top of a long pale green stalk. Mother took a look at it and said, "Lycoris Squamigera." It is very wonderful, you should see it--it smells good too. I've been thinking about bulbs. Here's the way the camellia border will be

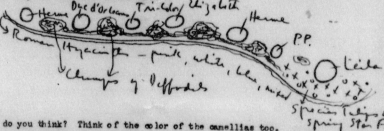

What do you think? Think of the color of the camellias too.

I think it will be on the abundant side, as things have all multiplied and grown. A cardinal is singing just now. It's the middle of the afternoon. Not a breath stirs. I practiced knitting so I can begin your sweater. I was so afraid Mother would groan when I wanted to try to learn, but she very calmly said she thought I could. I hope to know enough by the time you send your measurements--I go along all right for a while, and suddenly I forget how I do it--it used to be the same with swimming, I'd forget how. I hope for a letter soon. At the same time with this I'm sending you some clippings, etc. by air mail, so you can see which comes better, and let me know. I am eating a Praline and wonder what you are eating. How is Bill? It's nice to think he is with you--tell him to stay close. I left out the little Algerian   irises in the diagram, all of them I transplanted   back behind the bulbs, they make a shimmer of   V--MAIL   blue when all is bare, earliest

Letter from Welty to Robinson, July 19, 1943, with a drawing of the camellia border in the Weltys' side yard near their screened porch.

Nov. 12

Dear Diarmuid,

Here I am in Mississippi, and thanks for the letters here and I got the two big checks. You are probably having a holiday today and maybe the lilies had come and you got them in the ground. How are the azaleas looking? Yes, if the camellia doesn't act right this year, burn it. It has gone far enough. I came back and looked over some of the antics of mine while I was away, and think the whole tribe should be taught a lesson. Maybe they can hear this low rumble of discontent if we practice it around them, and will heed, fearing the guillotine.

The Italian Wide Net--how much better is the Mediterranean title of Primo Amore--is here and I didn't know I could write so beautifully, I opened the book and loved the way it seemed to sound. So admire myself in other languages. Are the leaves all fallen there? They are still on the trees here, some of them bright and lovely--we had a nice little rain yesterday to break the drouth and today is fine and cold. Nothing is like that Arizona air though and that fine, fine cold, and the yellow aspen trees. The whole state is amazing and beautiful, and I'm trying to track down some books about it--such old country. The Indians there though are starving, truly, it is said. People seem to be investigating, but not doing anything about it yet--

Glad the little brush didn't break and no telling what it will paint. The paper flower I thought was one of those

First page of letter from Welty to Russell, November 12, 1947.

Mittie Creekmore Welty, Chestina Welty, Walter Welty, and Eudora Welty in the family living room.

Welty holding a gardening hat.

Diarmuid Russell at his home in Katonah, New York.

Diarmuid and Rose Russell.

The pear tree in flower in the backyard of 1119 Pinehurst.

Welty's drawing of the pear tree by moonlight, part of a V-mail she sent Robinson on February 12, 1944.

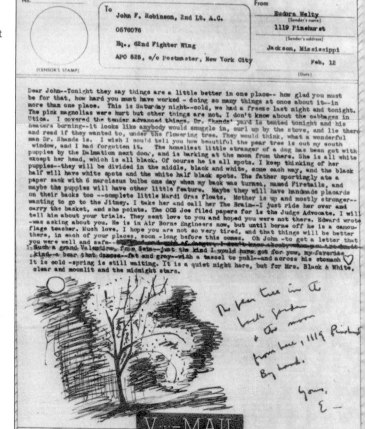

Snapshot Welty sent Robinson of a camellia he had given her, captioned "Leila camellia in Oct. Note buds." Enclosed in a June 23, 1943, letter.

View of the perennial bed.

1119 Pinehurst Street, the Welty family home, is now a National Historic Landmark. Since 2006, the house and the restored garden have been open for tours.

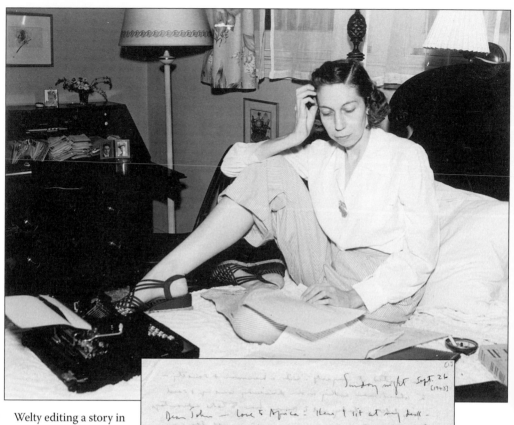

Welty editing a story in her bedroom. The desk she drew is behind her, with Robinson's letters in the pigeonholes and a picture of Robinson in a frame. The angel pin she wears was a gift from Robinson.

Drawing from a letter Welty sent Robinson on September 26, 1943.

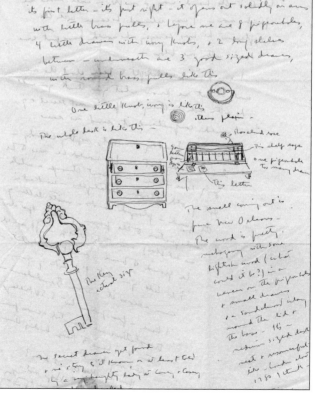

Handwritten letter from
Welty to Robinson,
October 18, 1944.

Welty working in the
backyard of 1119 Pine-
hurst.

Left: Art and Antoinette Foff and John Robinson in San Francisco. Right: Welty and the Foffs in San Francisco. These snapshots were in a November 13, 1947, letter to Robinson.

Welty's drawing of a shell flower. Sent to Russell in a June 20, 1942, letter.

Welty in her backyard.

Welty and Robinson during her first trip to Europe.

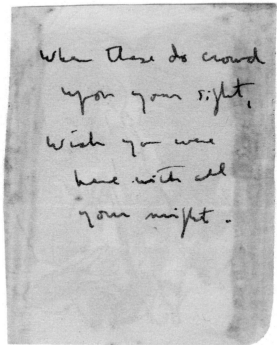

When these do crowd
upon your sight,
Wish you were
here with all
your might.

Welty enclosed numerous drawings of flowers in a January 21, 1944, letter to Robinson. Several drawings have verses on the reverse side. This purple flower, which appears to be a violet, is framed by a red heart shape.

These yellow flowers are perhaps the "early jonquils" named in the verse.

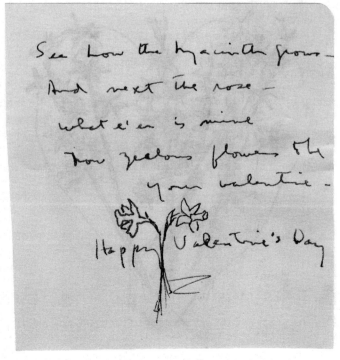

See how the hyacinth grows—
And next the rose—
what e'er is mine
You yellow flowers the
your valentine—

Happy Valentine's Day

These pink, red, and lavender-blue flowers may be Roman hyacinths, which flower in February.

March 6, 1944
Dear Diarmuid,

I don't seem to have a bit of paper—I would answer your red letter in kind except I have to bear with a ribbon that won't write red. Many thanks for the royalties. Didn't expect any. And for the contract again—it is my instinct to send anything like this to you by return mail, so pardon, and I won't enclose it this time. Maybe Mr. Weeks is not going to get in touch with you at all but will send an armed man to meet you by the old stump and catch in the act of blackmail or extortion—so be careful. The story hasn't been shortened any further, but any day I may get it down on the floor, which is the best way, and cut it with scissors and pin it this way and that and squint at it. I thought May was when you said to come. It would be nice to dash up then and sniff your springtime. I would like to see your tulips on their best day. How do they look now? We are having a thunderstorm at the moment but it has been the most wonderful spring sun—at last—after 6 weeks of black rain—and everything popped out like magic. The camellias had a good season and my best kind is in full flower right now under the driving rain, alas. It is called Leila. I dreamed a scholar told me that the Leila Camellia is the Mozart of camellias. My species tulips and some early other kinds are blooming, and the fine, pale daffodils, and the Dutch iris is about to open. There is so much work out there to do. [. . .]

Love,
Eudora

March 13, 1944
Dear John,

A good long letter this morning which was nice. Yes I was upset about the beachhead, the paratroupers [. . .] If you could just get a leave [. . .] and come to this exotic place. It looks very nice now, all green and sunny spring light. Mrs. O.H. Backhouse (daffodil) is blooming. [. . .] No I don't think it's necessary for anybody to write. It's a thing I think of as a secondary thing in my life which gives me intense pleasure (I mean secondary in that it is work—definition)—it is not quite like gardening. If I feel something and try to say it truly then the easiest way to do it is writing a story, for me. Since there is so much wrong being said about the war, by all agreements, I know you would say what is true and what it is *like* (I try to express it all by that, do you see) because of everything. I thought you might because of it's being possible. The sun is very warm. Dutch iris, blue. Wisteria is hanging in the tree next door. I have weeded. Mittie had a daughter, March 10, we have been up there most of the time lately.[38] They are fine. It is a sweet little baby, fat. Mittie very smiling. Walter, a faint voice calling from Boston, "Is she all right?" I knitted a sock for you in the maternity ward—the others waiting looked puzzled. Diarmuid says some daring southern birds have arrived in Katonah and he hears their misplaced songs in the morning. He is holding up the Atlantic for $700 for my Delta story, I want to feel his head bones. Of course they had said in some editorial that I had produced nothing for a year and had offered no explanation. I have been cutting it—down on the floor with scissors and pins and a finger to my brow. I hope you are well and I still like your stove and your being in the town fine. For you to be well is everything, enough.

Yours with love,

E-

March 18, 1944

Dear John—

[. . .] I wish you could see Peruvian squills—maybe you are looking at one right now outside your window—has something sent up scapes with cones of seed-like things and these turned blue or purple like berries and then they've begun opening into starlike azure flowers from the bottom up, just like slowmotion fireworks until finally they're all rayed out like an umbrella of blue flowers? [. . .]

Love to you—

E

March 18, 1944

Dear Diarmuid,

I was glad to get the note about Mr. Weeks and as you guessed glad of the reprieve for working for a little while on this story.[39] It might be good for the story. Also maybe I will write another one by that time that you might give him the choice of, with so much money at stake.

This is just a note this time for I am involved with a baby being born in our family and a brother home on furlough (not the father, though everyone takes him to be and he just goes on and takes the congratulations) so I will have more chance to write next week. I hope all of you are well. Is it any warmer? Are those birds still singing their misplaced songs? The cardinals are building nests here—and things in flower are dogwood, wistaria, magnolia fiscata, cherries,—and phlox and daylilies. I ran out between events and fertilized my camellias. It is raining gently now so that is good.

Love,

Eudora

March 20, 1944

Dear J—

It is about 9 PM—raining—the windows open and the smell of magnolia fuscata comes right in—over the sill—spring night. It is First Day of Spring Eve. How are you? I fertilized the camellias today. After all the blooming was over, Leila came out with an encore of three flowers. They were perfect. Aimee was just like a thundercloud over me the whole time but never stole any though was caught bending over, and Dr. Shands did not dig at my bush. I think with longing of your iris now. Mother says: "It will be a good iris year." Tell me what the iris is like—would it be blooming now? and there was a surprise, you said. I guess it will have to come by word of mouth. The belladonnas look magnificent—they look like Aida. It might be July or August when the flowers come, we might be like Sicily. You would be watching the roses—all are in bud—a Dainty Bess will open up in the morning. I had lots of nice beer yesterday—in the afternoon with AB [Anna Belle] and when I got back two enlisted men from a nearby overseas unit that come over for drinking beer and playing Beethoven were here, and we drank b and played B. [. . .] Diarmuid said that spring had come. Perhaps he knows in some Irish way. He says his tulips will be most beautiful on the 15th of May—so I will try to see them. It will be nice to lie in the Katonah hills and look up at the sky, and there is a place I wanted to take you where there is a mill stream and a little falls, and you can lie and look up at the sky and hear this falls. I did a little work which may not hold up. What do you think of Hubbard's Wells, Allison's Wells, Brown's Wells and all, as a place to make a story about—a kind of merged place—do you think they radiate something?[40]

[. . .] I think what inspired me was that a lady sent me a chocolate layer cake, just as an admirer of the Wide Net—unknown lady from Yazoo. It is fine to get letters so much better from 650.[41] Much love to you. Am trying to see F. Derby and will tomorrow.

Love

E

March 24, 1944
Dear Diarmuid,

Thanks for the British radio thing, which I enjoyed seeing—something else came with it though, that doesn't belong at 1119 Pinehurst. Enclosed, plus something else I got. I read there was snow there—hope it's melted and gone, and spring is cinched. Have the daffodils come up at last? Here it is so beautiful—this morning I was in a little town nearby and we took an early walk and saw the green woods—dogwood, little haws, locusts in bloom, blackberry flowers, wistaria, honeysuckle, wild azaleas—just beautiful. The leaves golden, without any dust on them yet. The cabbages and greens were up. I bought a big shade hat of pink and green straw from the country store to do my work in, I can stay out in the rain in it too. Found Burn Witch Burn on my travel so now I can read. I see the gent has also written a book called Creep Shadow Creep.[42] (I thought of a good detective title, Sleep, Baby Sleep.) The yellow Dutch iris is out here, looking very lovely. I wrote a little on a new story but can't tell if it's good or not—the worst is, it happens in July, and I am so interested in spring.

Love,

Eudora

April 8, 1944
Dear Diarmuid,

(I just saw this was Stratosphere paper—Greetings.[43]) It was nice to get the letters, long or short, and the reason I haven't written any back was I had to swallow some sulfa which drives me crazy in the head. The weekend ideas sound filled with charms and many thanks, I'm sure I can come. I hope Rose hasn't been worrying about some pet weekend scheme and whether I would be taking some bed or not—after all if I don't know what I'm going to do I can sleep in a tree.[44] The other day I wrote to the hotel to see when they had the prospect of a room and the railroad will let me know 30 days early when I can get a seat in a train, and when these two dotted lines meet that will fix the day I depart. It's fantastic about the snow—I had you with daffodils up and almost time to plant the beans. Did you ever get home that night. It's Easter tomorrow—I remember how nice it was last year. I hope the hunt comes off properly in the morning. A little boy here said to his mother, "This year fry 'em, don't dye 'em." The Robbers came safely[45] and thanks—I hope you kept one in the office or home as I think they are so fetching. We have a beautiful open peony today—single white with yellow stamens. The irises are blooming and the air smells so sweet. One of the La. iris is out too. It's grand Tom [Sancton] got some of the gold too. I will write you better later—I am the one who sends awful letters and am sorry. The weeds grow here with a rush practically audible—especially now. I sent you one of A. Merritt's books called The Moon Pool—I just started it but it was so strange I thought I'd better send it right away and get another one to read here.

Love,

Eudora

April 17, 1944

Dear John—

I just today got a long letter you wrote me on March 5—when you had just come back from the front, when Bill Monroe had come in. I guess it was lost and re-photographed. I've been thinking of it all day.

You'd had a cold—I hope it is well now. [. . .] The roses are now just as you might be imagining—so big and deep with scent like a well and so many—all kinds are in bloom now. I am looking at a bowl in the house now, and a little ladybug is riding on the petal of an Editor MacFarland. All around the rose beds we have strawberries and have daily races and fights with the birds to see who gets each berry. Mother indignantly ate a little half-bowl for bkfst this morning. I worked all day Sat. and Sun. in the yard—did belated pruning of the spireas and things, and weeded and carried out stuff by the basketful—and all the time, the roses and irises were smelling to the heavens so I would just drop my digger and breathe, now and then. Is it warm there yet? I moved some Peruvian Squills and white wild spider lilies of La. in together, for next year. The weather was so nice they "didn't look back". The Philippinense (still from Charlie's seed, grandchildren I guess) are full of buds and standing very tall. The camellias are growing well. Leila has new growth the span of your hand on every little twig. I wish you could see. [. . .] I hope you won't be needing to go back to the front soon. I hope your letters come. My love to you. The days are so pretty I wish I could save them for you when it is over. It is 2 o'clock, blue sky with soft clouds, green leaves everywhere now, very cross little robins waiting for me to come out and finish digging where I left off yesterday—they trust me for worms. [. . .] I forgot to tell you the pinks (clove) are wonderful. Keep well—

 Love—

 Eudora-

I am trying to send you a story soon—I am very slow—and house cleaning time—

Anglo-American forces had landed in Anzio, Italy, in January 1944. They were intended to move north towards Rome, but were now suffering heavy casualties. During this period, Robinson was working for General Harold Alexander, commander of Allied Armies in Italy.

April 20, 1944

Dearest John—

 This is just a little note, on kitchen table—Are you all right? I've been thinking of you so much and hope you are fine—It's 10:30 AM—I'm looking out at the drenched garden—many roses and irises, all heavy headed—The peonies closed under the rain—Mother has gone to judge iris live arrangements in the flower show, though—It's been nearly 4 weeks since date of your latest letter and that's not so very long or else terribly long, depending on where you were—I hope maybe tomorrow morning I'll hear—The magnolias are starting to bloom, yesterday I saw a little girl with an obviously stolen first flower running along the street—nose in, eyes out[46]—I "read up" on Alexander—to be sure I had him straight—I hope I hear tomorrow and you are getting along all right—love to you— I did a little hard work this morning on new story—I am making a pot of coffee—the tea kettle is singing—Wish you could have a cup of nice coffee—

 love—Please be well—

 Eudora

April 24, 1944

Dear John—

Three letters—so glad. Everything seems to be all right. [. . .] I had just done the wash—a sunny day—and washed my hair—I had a pompadour of soapsuds on—I should have sung a little Mozart aria—there must be one for getting a letter, if not three, and the post man, a gay blackamoor, could have joined. [. . .] The nice letter on Easter about all the flowers came, and I think I had just written to ask you if you had something in a pot? and it seems it is primroses. They sound like a nice thing to have and very free-blooming. I have tried the yellow ones here but they were never so fine I could have sold them on a street corner, they bloomed just a little. The camellias—how many kinds there must be, or what long seasons of blooms, -so pleased they grow there. It doesn't matter about the names, they sound beautiful. Here it is time for lunch. I can cut up an onion today. Can you imagine no onions? I don't understand it, it's just part of the happenings. But now the heavens have smiled benevolently and we have onions.

—It is a soft warm day here. Everything bending in a little breeze. The iris has been good here though the rain has come down hard on it. I investigated Mrs. Macgowan's—she has some fine and worthy ones but also some fancy kinds—the latest.[47] She is so livid about her labels she won't go out and enjoy the blooms—she told her yard boy to be careful of them so he brought them all to her, carefully laid in a box. Mine—the startlers—I wish they could have come. That a quarantine man could have laid hold of them seems so low a thing to happen to them—I almost wish they had been on the ocean and lost instead, and then they might have floated to some coast and grown there and amazed people—I think they must have been a very beautiful kind. [. . .]

Walter is coming Saturday, with orders to go westward, I fear. It is lucky he can come just now--his baby 6 weeks old. I had a post card from Anna B. from Fla. saying it was fun and they had seen Will [Robinson] go through and drink a glass of milk. I wish you would be on the radio, instead of Lang—nice to hear you, it would be. I don't want to write about the war—I just want it to end. Have not heard about anything yet, though I enclosed stamped airmail envelope![48] I am breathing a knotted hdkf. full of magnolia fuscatas.

My love to you—Yours—

E—

Welty was now planning her next trip to New York, where she hoped to find a job as a writer or journalist that would enable her to travel abroad. Overseas travel was impossible for most civilians.

April 25, 1944
Dear Diarmuid,

[. . .] I do look forward to coming up so. Had hoped to send a story to you but have had much at one time—no maid, or boy to help chop weeds in the yard, all the old dull stuff, and so tired at night. And I only hope the story is better when it's done than it seems to me just now to think of it. How is your spring? Ours is still filled with hail, lightnings and thunder, cyclones and floods. Now and then a jewel-like day shines forth and I run around looking at people's irises. I wonder if you have seen: Prairie Sunset (mauve-gold-pinkish), Great Lakes (clear, live blue, beautiful), Giant Baldwin (an old one that is the purest unadulterated purple I ever saw, with blue beard), Far West (most beautiful subtle subdued color, fawn-pink maybe, with gold beard and astonishing light blue blaze just under it). All these are selfs and have fine form and some are large with falls like the ones you described as bloodhound's ears.[49]

[. . .] Enclosed is some money I owe you, from $70 for two reviews and $50 for a Mag. of Art article, which I might forget in the excitement of coming to NY. It is very dark and rainy. Did I tell you something called a Russian lily, or lillie, ordered from the Farm Bulletin bloomed and is wonderful? I think it *is* a Russian lily. Tulip shaped, with melon-shaped petals, pinkish apricot lightly spotted in center, and dark stamens. From pictures I think it might be L. Dauricum—which does hail from Northeast Asia. It is very glowing and rich and oriental looking.

Love,
Eudora

May 10, 1944
Dearest John—

N.Y.—I just came—Just sitting in my room—349, one window a wall and one a street—Did you ever notice the Bristol was by an Italian restaurant named Vesuvius?[50] Will see about it—I hope you are fine—All the way here it was like going back in time—with the Spring, the chinaberry flowers in Miss then the wild azaleas in N. Georgia, then the iris in Virginia gardens (Va. was beautiful, and in the night those whole valley of moonlight, and the mts.) and up this way dogwood and wisteria and spirea—little new leaves—I miss you being even a little near—I hope to find out something in N.Y. about things—Will see everybody and give them news of you—Will write—The weather is nice and I hear birds and a P-51. I have my beautiful purse and also rosary—Am going to sleep—It is 2:30 PM—

My love to you—

E.

May 23, 1944

Dear John—

So much—all happening where you are—are you all right? Tonight an evening report of an all-out offensive from Anzio[51]—not known if true—I just keep hoping you are if possible still in the town but well and getting along all right—I wish I were nearer than this—you see I would know better—This is Tuesday,—night—I'm back in N.Y. from Katonah—It was beautiful and green—I had a nice time—very full. William was wonderful—while in the middle of spinning a top he suddenly cried "Blue is for boys!" Pammy makes scenes when she has to wear pants and not a dress—[. . .] You would love the country now—it's all green and in flower—and such a late Spring everything is happening at once—azaleas, dogwood, lilac, peonies, tulips and some Rosa hugonis roses—The hills are brilliant—lots of pink dogwood wild there—Walking in the woods you see enormous Jack-in-the-pulpits—It's nice to sleep there—soft smells, lots of mown fields and plowed earth—little birds waking up and singing in the night—Tomorrow Robert van Gelder on the Times is taking me to lunch and I hear is offering me a job here—don't know what[52]—I still feel if I can stay around somehow I might get a chance to go over—Henry [Volkening] who thought he had got Christine Weston (you might remember her) a way to get to India after months, didn't, and now says no hope—Did I tell you I talked to a war correspondent at a cocktail party and he said join the WACS[53]—I was incensed—He had grown a full brown beard but I do not think he leaves this country—he just *can*. [. . .] I look for the picture of your house—and did you put in one of yourself—for you know I would set great store, and feel you were fine, by having it and I think one in the local manner would be nice—one you have to go and have taken—Much love—Everything is covered with mist—windows like the most distant lights—like on an ocean—where are you?

Love to you—

E.

Welty worked as a copy editor and reviewer for the New York Times Book Review *for several months in 1944. She wrote most reviews under her own name, but several reviews of books about the war were published under the pen name "Michael Ravenna."*

The Allies took control of Rome on June 4, 1944. This event was the headline on June 5, but news from Italy would be eclipsed by the Allied invasion of Normandy (D-Day) on June 6.

June 5, 1944

Dear John—

Such tremendous news—such a feeling as you must have. I hope you are fine. Write me all. I think even this town is in a kind of trance of real feeling. If you write anything PRO about this please if you can send to me or tell me how to track down. [. . .] I have to stop now and start my job I guess. I love this day if you are fine and I hope you are. Your balcony sounds nice now. Could those be Lady Banksia roses, the tiny yellow climber? Yesterday I was riding the bus carrying some mock orange branches and the lady next to me admired them, I gave her some, she said she had a window box and a bridge club which was very exclusive but I might come and play. Lots of love

yours,

E—

June 14, 1944

Dear J—riding out in the bus along the river after work—a beautiful sunset—cool winds at last—the sky, palisades and water all one color just now—and a frail line of lights following the shore—I am standing leaning on the wall—a nice evening after a long day—Love to you—

yours,

E

June 28, 1944
Dear John—

[. . .] We move this Saturday and I'm anxious to be in, I will write you what the place is like—neither one of us can remember a thing about it, it was so astonishing to get a place at all, and we think the refrigerator is maybe small.[54] It would be nice if the seeds came and Egyptian things would be growing in all the windows—I'm looking forward to getting some dirt, on the 4th of July—will go to the country and bring the dirt back in a little bucket. I'm anxious to see the little painting on bone—and hope it comes safely. It will be our decoration.[55] [. . .]

Love to you—

E.

Early July 1944
Dear John—

I've been sitting here thinking of that 10-foot fall of pink geranium—your garden does grow well, doesn't it—It sounds beautiful—I think you have the green finger on account of the way the begonias just come up for you—There is no telling what else you might be watering—maybe some amaryllis that comes up and blooms overnight, like the St. James lily—It sounds beautiful to see and I wish I could—the bougainvillea—everything. I'm glad it's the light colored hydrangeas—If you have roses growing I feel better about all—when anything else springs up, let me know—But how could it—do you think there is room? I've wondered if you had to water things much or tend to them or if the rain and sun were always just right—what direction do you face—over the bay? You would be eating your supper out there half the time, it looks like—I wanted to ask you if you saw chicory planted in the kitchen gardens there—it's blooming in the fields now here, and so pretty—in the Italian farm places along the railroad—The moon is full now and comes up so bright that you can see the wild flowers at night walking home from a picnic—

love

—E.

Several of Welty's New York letters use gardening imagery to express her ideas about art and human nature. Although the context of the following letter is unclear, Welty seems to be discussing a work of lit-

erature, perhaps her own story, "The Delta Cousins," that she had sent
to Robinson in late 1943.

Early July 1944
Dear John—

This is from our apt. It is cool (cross ventilation). The moon is coming up—it does right at the end of 10th street, and we can also see the sun going down exactly at the other end. I brought a little mint growing in a pot, along with my baggage, so we will have that right from the first. [. . .]

Yes, I think you have to know how they met—but sometimes it is like a seed, that moment, and sometimes like a spark—combustion, not growth—do you think that is two levels or parts or manifestations of the same thing—or two things? I do think all the growth and expansion must spring from that moment—Maybe one kind of relationship is from the beginning using itself up—and the other kind finds sustenance and food and drink and air to breathe in it—I have a feeling you could always tell a true inception when it happens—and never do anything but cherish it. But I believe the needs of the people involved couldn't determine the whole thing—it could in pattern, maybe, but not in degree, that is unfathomable—for instance, there is no degree in loyalty—or of belief—a plant that you watch grow up from a seed and branch and bud has degrees (maybe it is like this) but when the flower opens full, there is no more thinking of it that way, because you are involved with something fulfilled, even if just in a little flower and one little moment could start something of a magnitude you could not predict even if you knew ahead it would be real and matter a great deal. I believe *two* people always have something infinite between them—with care. The color of a day—one sound—a note—as of a French horn—they stay real as the stars. So do I think so.

Early July 1944
Dear John, a beautiful cool enticing day. Am I a good New Yorker? No. Do I ever get off at the right station on the subway. Not very much, too absentminded and when I do I come up out of the ground in the wrong place. 8th St., which is home, I stop at the right station being in a hurry to get a drink and stretch but it's just as likely I'll come up away over in

Wanamaker's store if I don't look for a banner saying Moe's Clothes, 1 flight up, and take the other way—I say No Moe and go opposite. I hate to get up too, or go to bed either, both essential here. Poor Dolly, I turn off her alarm clock in the mornings—the first thing and I've got it, in my sleep, like slapping a mosquito and Dolly never stirs. It got bad and Dolly put a row of things in my way, between me and the clock on the table, some nail polish, the ink etc. and it slowed my hand. And another thing, I couldn't live for long with a refrigerator and stove in the same piece of furniture. All is very dirty, like a day coach, when we go home at night— poor little plants, I wash their leaves, and think of our hair, getting this.

Another thing is the way they take up garbage. A great big infernal thing, a truck, that eats garbage, grinds it in jaws at the back of the truck (it's marked Danger) comes along and they feed it. You hear bottles and things being ground up—it's like Fe Fi Fo Fum and happens every morning at 7:30 AM, just when I usually have my dreams—*they* all go right in. I never thought they'd do that in the Village. We also have a peeping tom not 10 ft. away across the court. At first we thought it was a *dog*. We have awfully funny knives and forks. The kind there are now have wooden handles which are pretty but the other part turns green—tastes like some kind of grass, vaguely, underneath what you're eating. Sort of mysterious. Interesting for a time but not forever. But nobody ever asks you any questions and that is wonderful—the other night I went to the movies with a suitcase and nobody went through it. The rivers are beautiful—and the ocean and the harbor, and the clouds, and music plays outdoors at night. You can't see the stars well enough to see the constellations except over the river—beautiful then. I never know exactly how the moon is.

July 13, 1944
Dear John—

What fun—your 4th—I'm glad you didn't have on a tie—or if so it was wet—It sounded perfect—it was nice to be written wet plus on 4 dishes of ice cream—such a hot day and I was so dry and hungry—[56]

Excuse me for being so upset over Martha Gellhorn's being there writing her stuff—[57]

Yes I read the Cohn article in Atlantic[58] and thought it pretty balanced. You read aright about Southern troubles brewing—I worry, and wish there were less ignorance plus more knowledge involved (as it's to be wished there were in everything—there in Europe and here—) [. . .] That is why I'm against partition of Germany—as unhealthy and breeding ills—[. . .] You would not dismember a person to keep his character in control—that would at the outset destroy the hope of your work and the chance of its evolution to any good—Suppression and tearing apart never do any good, and make a rigid, inflexible system that when broken, is as if it had never been—[. . .] I still feel that to destroy Germany would destroy something in us too—But to *use* her, to benefit all the ones she has hurt, would show us all—we could learn then as we went—and it would be that much less *waste* in the world—of life and what makes life—Do you think this at all—I am far from everything and mostly just think to myself—and I am no problem solver in my thoughts—instead I have mostly feelings and they are that the life, whatever it is for all of us, will in the end be the little, personal, everyday things—a personal matter, individual—I cherish that still and always—*Moments* will count, still, then—and be magical and colored, good and bad, as some little thing makes it—War and peace do not change that, do they? Not any sheltered thing will seem to have been lost—that is my hope—that days will still be beautiful and nothing between you and the sky like Naples now—[. . .]

Love,
Eudora

July 17, 1944
Dear John,

You would like the medieval gardens growing at the Cloisters,[59] where I went yesterday. Espalier pears, apples, and some kind of plum, and the medlar tree [. . .] and orange trees. The trees would all be along walls or in the middle of the garden, and herbs for the cooking garden all around, and roses, lilies, and spring bulbs for the rest. Stone fountains with jets coming from wild boar's teeth or from the saints. All was in flower—fennel, borage, and the like. Clove pinks and cornflowers. Apples on the walled apple trees, green. I was surprised to see all these things doing so well and in flower, but maybe the warm walls do it. It smelled so delicious. Plenty of mint. There was bulb foliage of Pancratium maritimum, the Mediterranean Lily or sea daffodil, that looked very delicate, and the bluish green that might mean the flower was white or nearly so—do you know it? Inside, the most wonderful thing of all was the series of Unicorn tapestries—5 whole ones, and two fragments—showing the hunt and capture of a Unicorn in a flowery woods. [. . .] The beautiful part is the perfection of all the flower forms, a millefleurs background at times and then in other tapestries a naturalistic treatment, with background of woods (trees growing near each other that really would, oak, walnut, cherry, etc.) and then an orange or plum in a planted place, and near a stream will be irises, columbines, ferns, etc. Each little flower so exact. Hundreds of different kinds. The animals so spirited—the white dogs, the little hindquarters of scampering rabbits, ducks starting up, in the marsh, birds beginning to flush, and most wonderful of all the Unicorn. He has a wonderful scrolled, twisted, towering horn, a little beard, snow white and plumy tail, and soft hairs around his legs and sharp hoofs. He *looks* as if only a virgin could catch him. All around the tapestries, which are as large as the wall of a room, goes a border of twined flowers and fruits and vines—vinca, and blackberry (in flower) [. . .] How are you—I hope everything is all right and the same

    Much love—

    E—

July 18, 1944

Dear John—

My thoughts seem to be more and more in ways I cannot write in— my thoughts are clear but the only words I can find are not—I keep knowing I can't tell you well enough—simply my true vision about any-thing—or the truth *in* it, for that is what I would want to find and it seems now past stories that I would work slowly and hard to write, and past letters that are written fast and without hinderments to you—the 2 ways I could know how to see it and come to this clarity—I never do— It's the truth that comes out of the truth that comes out of the truth, that I look for—If I could just once, you would know it, wouldn't you? I would hope it would be very welcome—well-come to you—not strange—for yours to me hoping the same—I think the boundaries of what we feel change like map boundaries—but it is not that the feeling changes—but that its truth stands still, or gets denied, or expands and grows—when the communicable thing appears—so here and there—anywhere—like lightning bugs all around you, in a field, in the Delta—This isn't much of a letter—

    Much love—

    Eudora

August 5 1944

Dear J—

This is the nicest weekend I ever had—at Katonah—Came out yesterday. The hottest day, you couldn't even *talk*—and here it's cool, leafy—William loves me so, too—every minute, now included—lying across *this*—He has a wide kapok jacket he swims in—a little water rat—so merry—Pammy can swim alone—The pool is so cold in such heat—lovely. We are all sunburned—A picnic last night at Ed and Mary Lou Aswell's—that you'd like—steaks and corn on the cob over charcoal—Moonlight—just 5 people and talk lying down—Later, night. Diarmuid had some *bourbon* tonight —and made juleps—plenty of mint to the nose—we, Rose, D and I, sat on the porch.

Welty continued to work on "The Delta Cousins," which the Atlantic *had rejected in May. Robinson had suggested that in order to learn more about life in the Delta, where Robinson had many relatives, Welty should read a diary that his great-grandmother had kept. In the following letter, Welty's comments suggest that Robinson had sent her a letter from his relative who owned the diary, and that she had agreed to show it to Welty.*

Late August 1944

Dear John—

You know so much and so much more than I and better—yet I know this. I think you were born knowing things. But you see precipices because you love people and suddenly you share their vision, hoping for something (or against)—and I think this meets their moment—and it does something to yours, makes it more pressing, needful—this is real to me inside. Yes—Where are you? Yet I know where to send my love. I do not want pain to hurt you any where, and it does. I want it to be nice for you no matter in the middle of what—some hard, desperate way if necessary—We feel so far ahead of what we know—we try to catch up to our joy and our sorrow—I think (but don't feel sure) that is all our blind moving means—maybe we learn backwards—and feel prophetically—why shouldn't we? Suddenly our hearts are filled—it's time and place that hurt. [. . .] Thanks for letting me read her letter. Shall I keep here. All of them sound so sweet, gentle—Janie, I can see her almost. The ruthlessness of what happens to people makes you want to do everything but write—yet just by holding it intact maybe some of the real thing, that radiance, could be kept by a story. I don't know. If stories could be kept translucent, clear, with no dross of telling—if colors could be filled with their own light, not darkened with the labor of getting them down true. [. . .]—when the war ends, that will be everything—Today they're as near Paris as van Winkle to Jackson[60]—For Christmas do you think? for being home? I hope it.

Love—

Eudora

Allied forces advancing towards Paris had reached the city's suburbs by August 20. On the day Paris was liberated, August 25, Welty wrote Robinson, "It was wonderful about Paris—There were some flags hung out here but it was taken very quietly—All lunch hour I walked along holding my paper, and looking at all of them out on stands and in other people's hands just to see the words again, Paris is Free, which are beautiful—"

September 4, 1944
Labor Day
Dear John—

This is a holiday and I'm glad—as usual—It's a nice day, hazy, half-cloudy—No telling what the news is—I feel we're well into German territory—and that our news doesn't catch up these days [. . .] We're going over to the Van Gelders tonight for dinner—They are the nicest things—real people—Bob is somehow dead set on my staying[61]—but I *must* go plant my bulbs—The other night I dreamed about daffodils—that early spring light, shading the pine tree trunk, and the smell—We're looking forward to Friday—Dolly, Nancy, Alice and I are going to Katonah—Diarmuid and Rose have left on trips, and left us the house—with watermelons—(Are they ripe when they crack around the stem?) I bought a *beautiful Scotch* suit at my lunch hour the other day—Diarmuid who is just like a devil tempting me when he gives me money said "Now go spend this on something pretty to wear" and suddenly I did—I've really come up here, made some money, spent it, and going home—that's my story—and I thought I don't know what was *going* to happen—The other day riding the ferry out to sea, in the waves, I thought this is the nearest—not very far—Did I tell you I could read Cable-ese? I learned out of a detective story and the other day we got a cabled book review from Cairo (C Sulzberger[62]) and I did it into English so nice—It's noon—I think I'll go riding out the river—It's fall like—the air nice—

Love to you—did "Where Angels etc." come?

Eudora

September 8, 1944

Dear J—

Leaving for the country—wish you were. A fine day, blue sky and horse tail clouds. [. . .] Everybody at home is putting up muscadines, and I hope Mother will get back in time, and a man comes along our street, from the river. I wordlessly send her my sugar stamp at such times—she did put up some figs. I hear the ladies in the market bulletin are beginning to spade up looking for their bulbs—I hope they save me some hyacinthus—I think about wiring Terry.[63] Next spring oh for some little parts of the garden solid with those. Did you see belladonnas again? Mine ought to be in the notion of blooming just now. I hear the camellias are setting their buds. I hear the nightblooming cereuses are blooming at home. I'll let you know when I can get a ticket and then write me to Jackson. The letter about Capri, no sign of that, I hope it won't get lost. It's pretty out and cool and maybe we'll have a fire tonight. Are you taking your stove with you, the colonel pleading or not. Must run—Nancy, Alice, Dolly and I are all trying to catch the 5:37.

Love—

E—

September 18, 1944

Dear John,

Here's the letter from my aunt just reaching me and you see she has had a little clue and is hopeful now all is well with them only she still *knows* nothing.[64] [. . .] If you can't find out anything by a letter or call don't be worrying because you see they have this, and I don't want you to worry. Many thanks to you for thinking of it. Mother appreciates it a lot. She is home now and wrote me how each flower was. I'm going on the 10th, on the Southerner. I think I've got hold of some Silver Bells, between Terry and Utica, to plant in the garden—that I wanted you to see. They are hard to get. White, and their petals meet points together over the trumpet—they are very delicate, and nod.

We had a hurricane but in the city you could not hear it howling very well—I was in the Ritz, what a place, during a hurricane! but listened at the cracks, and went out twice and stood on Madison Ave. and it was really wild, but the city no place to feel it. New York of course was just concerned with getting a taxi. Fingers being shaken on every corner, even with people blowing down. And burglar alarms started going off in stores. I tried to phone to see how the Russells were in the woods but the wires still down, and D. was off on an island on the coast painting—he will probably show up tomorrow with a picture all done in dark blue and black, very triumphant. [. . .]

Love to you—

E

September 23, 1944
Dear John,

I'll write to you Vmail for a change—[. . .] How are you? I thought about that place Sunday morning—it stole over me, I was lolling by the East River because I couldn't sleep late—it was a pearly gray morning, the sun not really out, misty and the gray river busy and misty—and all that went opaque, and what was bright and clear was the temple of Apollo, out of your letter, and it had a warm light and smelled sweet on top of that salt air. Like once on a long train trip when I was little and I was given a pear—a warm delicious smelling pear for later, and sat holding it, with all the landscape at the window not nearly as wonderful or real as just to hold the pear. [. . .] I sent you a little Christmas box today, hoping when I tied it up that going over it might pass you coming home. I'll have to make your fruitcake when I have my own stove and Miss. nuts. I hope your airmail letters are all coming. All of them mean a lot but especially those. Take care of yourself. I worry some. What a little note this is. Vmail is hard after a nice time spreading out.

Much love to you—I miss you for the fall you love—

E—

Sept 27 1944
John F. Robinson, 1st Lt. AC
Hq., 416 Night Fighter Squadron[65]
APO 650 c/o Postmaster
New York City
Dear John,

[. . .] The name of your squadron might scare your family a little, just to see—I felt something—it sounds like the heart of things. [. . .] I'm leaving NY Oct. 10 on the Southerner. By the next day I'll be dividing the irises in the yard. I hope you will be fine there. And that it will be over soon. It was good to get the letter and know the what and where and what you think of it. Our air and sun is the kind that shines on haystacks and the air at night is what picnic fires burn in. The sky is high today and there are some sirrius clouds floating very high. Some pigeons on a water tank out my window are shining like rainbows and ruffling themselves.

Love—

E—

October 10, 1944
Dear John—

Just pulling out of NY—I'm by the window—Jersey looks autumnal. [. . .]

I've been saying goodbye a lot—I really hate so to leave—I tell everybody goodbye more than once—The Farleys had a wonderful breakfast Sunday with shad roe and fresh *fish*—where they get these things I don't know—[. . .] I saw Diarmuid last—and will miss him—When I think of him my heart sort of overflows—He is one of the real people—one of the good people—I can never quite understand what he's doing in that city—running a business—and not just sitting on a hill in Ireland, which is his heart. I hope he gets back some day.

[. . .] It will seem strange no longer going to work—through clouds of caramel popcorn [. . .] fighting my last half block to the office through the line going to the morning show at the Paramount—And all the time the sidewalks opening up under my feet for a plumber to come up on an elevator with a little bell ringing that sounds silver—and something—what is it, soot or fine rain, that falls there? You never can tell what kind of day it is at 10 AM. [. . .] Please don't go in any of the good places, where the nicest grapes hang—How *cruel* that is, about the mines—the Germans really think so carefully into other people's carefree ways [. . .] I'm anxious to try now the Delta story—It might turn out to be some long book—It will be nice to see our country again—I will write you how it is looking—If only you could come soon—

Some good bulb work is going to start when I get home—I will let you know how the camellias are—4 fat buds—[. . .]

—It was a lovely summer—Sorry I couldn't get to see you, from there—Sometimes it would almost seem possible—

Love—

E—

October 16, 1944
Jackson
Dear John,

[. . .] I guess my last letter was the one written on the train. Mother and Mittie and Dorothy from Utica met me over there [Meridian, MS]—[. . .] We drove home through the late afternoon, that beautiful October light over those hills near Meridian and the pine woods and cotton patches, and the Pearl River. I went out to see the camellias, took matches—they are all fine. Leila grew what looks about 10 inches on every little twig—a big bush now, you would be pleased to see. Around, the low white rain lilies were blooming. The apple blossom sasanquas that smell like the earth were blooming. A dozen farm bulletins were stacked up in my room and I am about to go over the hyacinthus ladies. It is still warm and sunny here, mild a little like spring—so dry, we have the water running nearly all the day in the shrubbery—to keep the little dogwood tree alive, even. The butterfly lilies were powerful last night. One of those was what you handed me when we started to Mexico.

So I have much to do ahead of me in the yard—pulling out grass and dividing the iris. And I will have to let out the camellia covers—widen the seams and let down the hems. [. . .] I hope the mines are soon out of the grapes. How are the pomegranates? I took some off your tree yesterday morning that dangled right down in my hand. Everybody here is getting along fine and all are well. The days are beautiful. Love and I hope you get some mail soon.

Yours—

Eudora

October 18, 1944

Dear John—

Are you still doing reconnaissance? (if that is what you were doing—) I am terrified of that vulnerable night flying ship—I don't know what your work is, to go, but I wish it would be enough soon—[. . .]

It's a lovely day—I am just now lying on the pine needles in the side yard—it is sunny and sweet smelling—Fall butterflies—A mocking bird and 2 redbirds—Somebody is practicing scales at Belhaven. I hear Mrs. Johnson admonishing Smarty—I'm resting—It's nearly noon—

[. . .] Am working out here—getting all the grass out and watering— The single dahlias are all over the place—those copper colored ones, and deep red, and little chrysanthemums—Butterfly lilies—See if this is sweet or not—I hope the figs get good up there—I hope the trees aren't mined—John—take care—you *have* to be all right—That's all I know but I wish you were here, on this day—so hard—Smelling the sweet air right here in deep breaths—and your eyes on the camellias doing so well—and hear the water running over their roots, the Leila and the Herme—the way it is now—

Are you smoking now? I thought there was cigarette smoke in your letter yesterday—can you get cigarettes?

Love—

E—

Thoughts went out of her head and the landscape filled it. In the Delta, most of the world seemed sky. The clouds were large—larger than horses or houses, larger than boats or churches or gins, larger than anything except the fields the Fairchilds planted. [. . .] The land was perfectly flat and level but it shimmered like the wing of a lighted dragonfly. It seemed strummed, as though it were an instrument and something had touched it. [. . .]

In the Delta the sunsets were reddest light. The sun went down lopsided and wide as a rose on a stem in the west, and the west was a milk-white edge, like the foam of the sea. The sky, the field, the little track, and the bayou, over and over—all that had been bright or dark was now one color. From the warm window sill the endless fields glowed like a hearth in firelight, and Laura, looking out, leaning on her elbows with her head between her hands, felt what an arriver in a land feels—that slow hard pounding in the breast.

—Delta Wedding, 1946

CHAPTER FOUR

October 1944–December 1945

Back in her Jackson garden in October 1944, Welty was still anxious about Robinson, who was volunteering to accompany pilots from his squadron on night missions in northern Italy. The end of the war now seemed much farther off than it had in August when the Allies liberated Paris. The year 1945 brought more of the war's horrors: firebombing in Dresden and Tokyo, concentration camps in Germany, colossal casualties in the Pacific theater. Roosevelt's death on April 12, one day before Welty's thirty-sixth birthday, struck her as "so personal a thing." Although V-E day in May was a relief, the war continued in the Pacific, where Welty's brother Walter was stationed. When the US dropped atomic bombs on Japan, she wrote Robinson, "I only tremble. And you can't even really *tremble* for the whole *universe*" (8.7.45).

Against this backdrop of worry and helplessness, Welty's art had begun to acquire new momentum. Writing about a Delta family was also, for Welty, "so personal a thing," a way to connect with Robinson, who enjoyed reading about his family's home region. The characters in her Delta fiction, unlike their author, showed little concern for events that extended beyond their privileged family, and yet Welty grew fonder of these characters the more she wrote about them; she told Russell, "I am not mad at anybody in the story no matter what they do" (5.25.45). Although she called her work in progress a story, its length was exceeding a story's limits, and it was proving to be more complex and ambitious than any of Welty's previous works. She told Robinson that it "just fascinates me and works me—Enough, though it's like garden work and women's work—never done—" (3.31.45). A synergy among these kinds of work was evident in the letters she wrote that spring. As the months passed and Robinson and her brothers were still not home, flowers and wide horizons continued to appear in Welty's letters as emblems of "the hope that it will end . . . and the world will be gentle again" (2.13.45).

October 20, 1944
Dear John—

Are you all right? This nearly kills me—I didn't know you didn't *need* to go . . . I wish I could think of a way to ask you that would prevail, but do ask you so hard, not to go and be in all the worst danger and it not needed—O God I feel shaky and may be stupid in my head but it sounds wild and crazy and overworked to me and I want you to come out of it—quick—

Do you remember we love you so—I know you do—but I could just *almost* think you don't right now—Could I send you some more picnic lists—call you back—to the earth—I remember I love you and try to think the general will prevail—

Write soon—Don't be in that damned thing—

Love
Eudora

October 23, 1944
Dear John, your nice long letter—mailed the 16th and came in 8 days—so glad you're living in the villa now—and I don't think you'd been up in the air and that was real good to hear—you don't know. Thanks for writing the intelligence officer—maybe he will know something and can tell you—all my aunt has is the telegrams that the boy[1] is a German prisoner. I hope he's still in Yugo so maybe will get free before so long. Mother said thank you a lot—just that you wrote this man makes her feel better. I missed you so yesterday, out in the country—the Delta beautiful and the October day beautiful and we were riding along—all afternoon, and the warm clear light that falls over the fields and lies on the Yazoo—and the little bayous—the sugarcane and the sorghum bright in the fields—cotton very full and the gins running—little fluffs of cotton lining the roads all the way, spilled out of full wagons—the chinaberry trees turning like a fruit, green on one side and bright golden on the other—the maples red and sweetgums red—the Indian mounds. I drew some little things as we flew along and will try to paint them. I saw 2 white herons, one very

close, standing in a lake with cypresses. Haystacks—3 white mules in a little glade—Goldenrod, coreopsis, little asters, bitterweed. Dust rising on the plantation roads. Wagons with chairs, some 6-chair wagons, full. It was about sunset when we got to Sidon—it was that hour when everything chirps and clicks and sings in the grass. We went to the cemetery a little while—the trees all tall and spreading and nothing changed and some pink and white cosmos in bloom and some small red roses. There wouldn't be any sign of the bulbs you planted at this time of year. Cotton wagons going by in the road. We went to see your house and then to that other house that fronts on the bend of the river, and drove up that old road till we came into the highway at I guess Tchula. Here's a leaf that came from Sidon. The river was higher than the Miss. and the Pearl, (why?) and smelled cool and brown you know. The old iron bridge. A long long freight train with leaning caboose, blowing whistle along the railroad, through the sunny fields. You could see the colors of October all in the trees along the ridge in the distance, that comes up from Yazoo. The clouds very full and voluptuous and the sky had that pink haze that comes over the blue in fall afternoons, and some of the clouds were pink or gold on the underside. We would stop for a beer. It was fun in Greenwood, we stayed with Ethel and her new husband who is a cpl. aged about 38 and used to be an English professor—a Yankee, eats 4 kinds of dry cereal all on top of each other with a satisfied mien to begin his day. [. . .] It was a fine time. We came back by Lexington, round the courthouse—I saw the little road where we went that rainy day to hunt for somebody—remember those clear drops falling after the rain where we stood on the porch—ferns. I'm going to see MF in a little while—will indeed take her your congratulations[2]—I think a little bunch of roses? if they look nice enough—we have had some red ones lately. [. . .] The camellias look beautiful. Your flowers sound like fall flowers around the Katonah woods, the little snapdragons I saw. Did the grapes get sweeter. Anna Belle is coming over to eat in a little while with us. Mother is making a pecan pie. It is a beautiful day again. October was never so beautiful and I can think of you in it so easy, just the way you like it—I hope for the day when the river there will carry the snows of the winter down to the Mediterranean the way Forster said in Florence in his story. Keep warm and safe and well—love to you.

Yours—

E—

Late October 1944
Dear Diarmuid,

It sounds beautiful there this week—I hope your cold went away. You did plant some Beershebas, I hope—and the John Evelyns and Silver Stars I remember as being little 35¢ numbers and so lovely. Note any superdupers that come up for you and send me their names. The camellia is not harmed a bit, I'm sure—frost just hurts the open flowers, and it takes a real freeze to get the buds. The new one I was so hopeful of sending you isn't available in the right size for indoors or at all with buds— this is Finlandia, which I've seen in pictures, gorgeous—so after letters back and forth I decided on a Herme, which is the prettiest one I have seen to date in real life. Let me know if it doesn't look as it should when it comes. [. . .] I've been working hard in the garden, pulling out grass etc. and watering all day—we have had a perfect month of clear, radiant days, lovely to see, but dry on the garden. The Delta was full of color—being near rivers hastened that and heightened it—and now color is coming where I live, I wish you could see ours some time because we really have your watercolor sky with the red at the horizon—the Delta had rosy sky halfway up to the zenith—and reflected on the fields. The cotton wagons are hand-painted blue-green. The sugarcane is two shades of green and lovely like bamboo in the breeze. The colored people ride in straight-backed chairs in wagons, some 6-chair wagons went by pulled by snowy white mules, and the Negroes are dressed in every bright color and look pompous. I like that world and would like to go stay in it a while—maybe some very small river town, in one of those houses built on a bend in the river—wonderful gardens reaching away. Shall I buy one of these when I am rich off my writings? Then you all can come down, and stay with me on the Yazoo.

I will write Rosie soon—my brother and his wife have been visiting us since I got home and I haven't had chances to write letters as I wanted. Give my best to Henry too. I hope you are feeling all right by now. Do you grow triteleias (?), spring star-flowers? Mine are coming up—very little bulbs but would do in the grass. Some day lilies are blooming, and the chrysanthemums starting but some kind of bugs are flying over them looking down hard. I can see the memory in their eyes, of how good those chrysanthemums were last year. Happy Hallowe'en—[. . .]

Love,
Eudora

October 25, 1944

Dear J—the day so lovely again—all day I've been outside—doing I don't know what in the yard—Dorothy came and we walked way out the old Canton road—the old Mack Wilson place was just where we stopped in the shade. The soft hay. That old bridge. The baby came over, we put her on a quilt in the side yard—we gave her a rosebud and she put it right in her mouth like a delicate bite—she sits up—she was in a hilarious mood—and when we were all talking, sang like a canary. I tried to make you a painting of the Delta, 2" X 4", but ruined it. [. . .] I wrote my aunt and she will be glad to know you sent a letter about the boy—maybe you will hear news that will tell us if he will be all right where he is. It's night now, clear too, stars, moon over the house —it's 8 o'clock. I wonder what you're doing and hope you're safe and well. I could never hate anything you do—of course it's part of you—I see—I see for ever I think. Just let me know how you are. I hold those flights inside me too, tenderly, no difference. But tell me all the time how you are—you will, won't you? I hope fine tonight and that the whole night goes safely—

much love,

E

November 9, 1944

Dear John, the box has come with everything—the violets from your garden and all—the pods still green to see—and I will plant the seeds to-day—I don't know if I could imagine them first, or see them first—climbing violets—All was safe—the box was a good piece of work—how I wish I could fill it right full of soup and send back to you—strong and built just to fit around your package, still tied up, 2 Stars and Stripes around in the corners—(The little I trusted that man.) I'm looking at the wine glasses—though I'm out in the garden, and put them on a little table—in the light—I love them—come soon and drink—They are lovely and their sound, their little note, is Italian when your finger touches them—I like their red thread—I just came out here with all my seeds, wearing my shoes—it's a fine morning and I am full of visions—of lilies of the field—and the irises, the whole plants you got me—their flowers and all you can still tell about—a kind of fragrance about them it seems as I just take a little whiff—the bulbs so live looking—are 2 of these some kind of ranunculus? It will be wonderful to see—All will be planted as written

[. . .] Just went and brought up a bucket of black dirt—for the seeds. Mother says, "Most of my compost pile has been eaten, by those miserable-old hens"—And sand from the river—Hope this makes garden soil—Our *real* garden soil I would never let a seed of these touch—I'm putting these in labeled pots so I can watch them—Will let you know—

[. . .] Be well and safe and come soon which will be—it will make everything all right here—the way it did always—It's almost too bright to not keep thinking of but I just hope you come an early day and M. E. Skinner's hyacinths turn out every color and flower on the dot for you. There are some early chrysanthemums now—white, and pale pink, and some bronze—and one rose—I can spade in the gloves—[. . .]

Love—

E

On October 31, Russell wrote to thank Welty for sending him pomegranates. "You might when you next write tell me a little more about pomegranates and what one can use them for. Frankly I am disappointed in their appearance. I had imagined that they would be about the size of a grapefruit, sort of salmony in color and glowing with an internal light. It's quite a disappointment to see that they look like apples and not too wonderful at that. But maybe all this will be redeemed if they have some noble use and I look to you to preserve my illusions by sending me at once some recipe for nectar in which these little objects will be involved." In another letter, Russell told Welty how accustomed his children had become to Welty's frequent visits. "William seems to miss you but on several mornings he asks will I bring Nudora back at night and seems disappointed that I can't produce you with as much ease as a packet of matches from my pocket." In this same letter Russell reported selling an essay of his own to the magazine Tomorrow, *and he thanked Welty for the camellia she had sent, noting that it might be two plants growing together (11.9.44).*

November 14, 1944

Dear Diarmuid,

Hooray about Tomorrow[3]—let me know when to look for it. I hope it's soon. [. . .]

Is the camellia split? If it looks split to you, after taking away the sack, don't keep it—I told them particularly you wanted a nicely shaped bush, and nothing straggly. Has it got plenty of buds—only don't count, bad luck. I've been spading today, and rewarded myself with some beer—you spoiled me. I'm enlarging my bulb bed—and have some hyacinths and daffodils coming, I hope. John sent me some seeds and bulbs from Egypt—and some climbing violets from the garden he had in Naples, did you ever hear of such a thing? The irises had flower buds still blue in dried stalks. The seeds are iris Ochrolena [ochroleuca], gladiolus—sword-lily, dark purple; anemone Coronaria, the lily of the field; Adonis Palaestina, an annual; iris sisyrinchium; Ranunculus Asiaticus; Tulipa Montana the famous wild tulip of Palestine; Asphodelus Ramosus, perennial;—all from the shop of card enclosed. Also a packet with 2 seeds, one dark and one light, marked Poison! Gift. I don't know whether I'm supposed to brew it and make a potion and drink it or not. When I have huge flourishing plants of these let me know what you would like to try. I know the pomegranate is not very bright. I've seen brighter and much bigger ones than that (when I was a little girl and lifted them off trees other than in my yard). The best thing to do with them is flavor jelly, like apple or plum—they are wonderfully tart and strong. I will try to do this and you can taste that. In "The Herbalist" it says the flowers and bark and rind are astringent and one thing you can do with them is gargle, when you have sore throat. Or if you just want to "take" it, it says Dose: a teaspoonful of the bark of the root, cut small or granulated to a cup of boiling water. Drink cold one cupful during the day, a large mouthful at a time. I really like the fruit just to eat, plain. But I know, you always did think that Persephone ate this, and it doesn't look equal to that. Did you try to eat it—eat it and then decide. I hope everything is fine—maybe you can paint something in Boston. Have a nice Thanksgiving. When is it? We are having a very gentle little rain.

Love,
Eudora

November 16, 1944
Dear J—

Mother went out to lunch a while ago and I thought now I can just *cry*, in peace by myself, for you. I haven't heard since a letter you wrote 4 weeks ago—and just as I ran upstairs the phone rang and it was Frank[4]—leave, had just flown in—So I had to rejoice with him—Maybe the airmails are just lost, or coming on boats—maybe several will come at one time—I hope you're fine—getting along all right and feel full of health—on your own cooking—I'm anxious to know how it goes—all—with this lone knowledge that you fly, sometimes I think it's just a dream—Not long. Just when I first wake up in the morning—I'll be glad when you are all solidly here, smiling on us—Please send more requests for the soup as they have stamped all the envelopes—Much love to you—I miss you and miss the letters telling how you are—Just hope you are all right and very fit and well—I wish I were where you are and would it be in the kitchen or the sky or where? I always have a dream I could *hand* you something—Have been working right hard in the garden—It rained and is already a little colder today—All well here—

Love to you—

E— Could I meet you.

November 29, 1944

Dear John, a fine long letter got here. All seemed well—of course I was glad there wasn't a good reason for not writing, unless it was coming home. I was just listening for you though. You did get to Florence and on a nice day—I was hoping the sun would shine. And the flowers—a small cape jessamine in bloom, how can I get those flowers straight there—I see them, I think, and then a cape jessamine comes out. [. . .]

The sun just came out—here, the chrysanthemums are blooming, and some Lady Hillington roses—the colors are still pretty—the leaves gone off the tallow trees and they are covered with pearly berries. The other leaves aren't falling at all, and the days are still and everything glows on fair afternoons, the haystacks are all made, some with hats on. The creeks are full now. I know from being out on the old road between the Pocahontas and Canton the other day, the one lined with mock-orange trees. It was lovely and fragrant, some plowing being done, lots of green on the ground still, big old live-oak shade trees. Big fat pigs. A radiant day, the china berries hanging bright, the sycamore leaves and dogwood leaves pure yellow. [. . .]

It's been the 18 months—do they just need you too badly.[5] I wish you could get a rest, in Paris or Jackson (I'd enjoy it more here). I don't know why I thought you were on the way, it was just my interpretation.[6] I wouldn't take my coat to the cleaners for fear it wouldn't be back in time. It would be so fine to see you. I thought I might wander to New York and see you light. Write it plain, when you do come—just say Now.

It will be lovely to have a present from you from Florence, more Southern antique than Florentine,—breakable—you send me so many things, I have so much. I think a violet has sent up a leaf. Will let you know for sure. I put the pots out to catch the rain the last two nights - except the irises that wait till after the rainy season. [. . .]

Much love to you. I sent you some Vmails but hope you get this by air. I know you're working like a demon and hope you get some more little fleet trips in. I hope you keep warm. I wish you could have this nice day, or rather this moment of it with the sun out and a mockingbird is singing. Mother sends love.

Yours,

E

December 15, 1944

Dear John—

A beautiful day, not so cold—went out and lifted the covers off the camellias—showing color. I got your letter Monday written on the 29th—your Thanksgiving dinner sounded special and nice—who's your neighbor that you run over and borrow silver from, the man with the green umbrella? I hope Christmas is nice too—maybe you'll be in Paris for that. It is almost just too much, for everybody else to be ahead of you in getting furloughs. I thought of a petition that all the other men could sign—saying let's draw straws, at least.

I've been pleased beyond words because the beautiful AE painting came.[7] Diarmuid and Rose gave it to me for Christmas—right out of their house—I'm anxious for you to see it, do you remember one of a glade with figures—dark green and light, with lovely groups of girls flung in the grass of [sic] resting. I've just been stretched out looking at it and listening to the Mozart G-Minor—oh lord this world here is very nice and I will be glad when you get back in it. A camellia even blooming in a pot. I had the picture framed the best I could, with a molding frame, standing over them to watch, but hope one day to get a hand carved one. This one is nice—gold, as the light in the picture is, but needs to be a little more subtle. Helen[8] thinks I could rub it, with turquoise paint or something, but I'm scared to start that without her or somebody to say Stop! when it's enough. It is all simply beautiful and radiant.

Well, Christmas can come now—Alphonse is selling his trees on the vacant lot by the old Henry house. This year he has a little similar one helping, maybe Jr. I haven't stopped to see how he talks but he looks studious and polysyllabic too, with very black round face, glasses, and airplane helmet buttoned up. I think he doesn't sell trees but handles the switches of cedar tied together with red ribbon in a V, an apprentice. We will get a tree one day soon and I will see if the little birds still stick on and have their tails.

[. . .] I hope you are having good nights and good luck but I hope all the time you are not working too hard and have some rest. We will be thinking of you as eating off fine cloths and out of grand dishes heaped with beautiful food Christmas day, which I hope will be true. And have a fine Christmas and good things to happen—all you wish, or better, or sooner—I will just gaze at the little wine glasses with Christmas pleasure but wishing for you.

Love
Eudora
Happy New Year

January 1, 1945
Dear Diarmuid—a happy New Year to you. I hope it's a nice day and all the good things begin to happen. Here it's fair, cold, bright blue sky after a big storm in the night—lots of things up but only things blooming 1 daffodil and 1 violet and 2 early camellias named Empress. A little sweetolive tree is filling the air. I cleaned out borders and pruned some things I ought to have pruned before. Buds all over the flowering quince. All yours still slumbers, I know. Did you have a nice Christmas with all the glitter under the tree that you were wrapping up? I guess the day began there at 5 AM with a shout from William—wish I could have seen for a minute. I hope it was marvelous and the turkey was delicious and the day pretty. We had a good day, springlike with sun and clouds both, warm, thunderstorm in the night. Many a hyacinth poked up that day. The picture looked beautiful. Some people came home unexpectedly— lots of eggnog and going from house to house. We had a tree and cut some holly for the mantel and up by the picture and had the Christmas candles lighted, and brought a flowering camellia inside in a pot. We had a turkey too and I *am* glad it's gone now. Today you're supposed to eat blackeyed peas for luck—and for tasting so fine after turkey and cake too, maybe.

Thanks for reading the story so soon and I am glad it does seem all right to you—.[9] What all this Delta stuff will turn into I don't know, but soon I'd like to get to that country and find out. John says he wrote his cousin Nannie Fitz-Gerald again mentioning my visit so maybe she will send me an invitation—I hate to just walk in for she has had troubles. [. . .]

My best to the family and to Henry—and a very happy New Year—
Love, and lots of wishes to you
Eudora
Did some little books ever come for the children—some more silliness to go under the tree?

January 14, 1945
Dear Diarmuid—

Thanks for the letter. I got the one from Rosie and Pammy too. These are the first 4-leaf clovers I ever found, unaided—and you can see it's a spring sign too, to start looking in the grass. They were all in one place. Your own eyes sounded worked too hard and I wish the weekends would go easy on them. Did you finish the Lavin?[10] My eyes are OK, just tired. I heard of an exercise that I'll tell you, for rest, looking at the 4 ceiling corners of the room, round and round, one way then the other. When is your piece about Chandler coming out?—you told me you'd been asked to do it but first didn't think you would.[11] My Jan. issue has never showed up—I hope I didn't miss it? You would never say "novel" to me, I know, and would be my support in what happens to the material—I can't tell what, though. Spring is going to make me wonder and ponder.

Jan. 15—Here's a letter I'd like to know what you think of—haven't answered it. 1946 is like another world to me. I'm not good at history[12]— the other night I told Nash Burger[13] something about the Trace bandits that he doubted—I said I was sure I'd read it somewhere and he said "Yes, you read it in the Robber Bridegroom." It seems bad to put the energy of a whole book into non-fiction, where you have to be settled and 'just.' I don't know what will happen to me even soon. Have you painted any more? You would like the small Algerian irises coming up under the trees that I'm looking at—shining blue—amethyst colored, Iris Stylosa Marginata unless I'm mistaken as is real likely.

Love,
Eudora

What happened about the victrola you told me about? It sounds very fine, like a lucky thing—lucky though expensive. Would it have that FS or FA? that you were speaking of.

Katherine Anne wrote me a note she was bound for Hollywood.

I see Pammy can write. I know she's proud. Will you thank her for me, for the letter? I liked it up-and-down too, the number work.

January 17, 1945

Dear John, after the war—reading—and a little more couldn't you have? Your letters are coming in—I'm glad, I've heard from you *this year* now. I'd been homesick to hear and had spring fever with it, and yesterday went down and spent the day in N.O.—came back and your letter of the 5th had come, and this morning the one of the 2nd. [. . .]

The termite has taken up his bed and gone, I believe—just where, I don't know—yet. I gave him Flit, light and sun, and vetivert roots—surely he staggered. I love that little box, I *can't* part with crumbs, to a termite.[14] It's on the mantel, under Mrs. Komroff's watercolor—you know how their colors together would be. Your seeds that have sprouted without a doubt are Gladiolus, sword lily—Asphodelus Ramosus, perennial pink, blue flower [sic]—Ranunculus Asiaticus L, very showy orange red big flowers—iris sisyrinchium, beautiful lilac flowers—tulipa montana, the famous wild tulip of Palestine, scarlet, white, and red—Anemone Coronaria, the Lily of the Field—and your climbing violets. And the bulbs have a green shoot, as I told you. Some of these I take it will make bulbs after growing this year, and then produce and keep on—of course they might even flower this summer—some will almost for sure, the regular seeds. Some of them are pushing up the little shells of their seeds on their heads, away up, green shoots with little bright red crowns on them.

I see I missed 100 Booth AAA White Leghorn hens, 1½ years old, $1.00 each at my farm. If buyer will write, I will have them caught when he comes. Victor Tidwell, Rt., Batesville. No Rocks. I wanted to see if the man got his wagon out of the yard. He had advertised for 2 issues that he has a wagon in good condition except lacking wheel, and wants to trade for 8 gals. of syrup, you make the exchange. I wonder if anybody's ridden over on horseback carrying the syrup and a wheel, fixed the wagon, and driven it away. There's a rabbit with black ears for sale that knows his name. (It's not told)

I've written your cousin Nancy Fitz-Gerald and hope she will find it all right for me to come in one day. I'm applying for some gas to go on, so I won't be just loose on her, and hope they will consider this part of my work and consider it work—have never applied before. If you like my new story I do feel glad—it means a lot to try to write now—harder than it used to be and somehow it ought to be better work than it naturally would be, or why did I do it. Yet that doesn't *enable* me to write better. It means so much if you don't have a feeling of it's being apart from what matters. Maybe if you weren't kind you would have it, because from where you are I feel that everything must look too small for the eye to see that is not of a certain worth and perhaps of a certain use. I know that I cherish much that is not—life being so personal to me, more than ever now if anything—but it is personal to you too and so I feel proud and in delight if a story pleases you, that's in proportion. You know what I try, which is so comforting—you see how far I can get and where I have to stop and just where that is—a little spot on the wayside—and it's as restful and sleepy as a picnic when you read it and get there too, and you know just where and when and all.

Love,

E—

Reporting on a plant Welty had given him, Russell wrote, "The big camellia is rather a sick looking plant in spite of all the care that has been lavished on it and what I am trying to do is to nurse it through the winter like one would nurse an old man through the winter so that spring and the sun can aid in convalescence" (1.17.45).

January 20, 1945
Dear Diarmuid,

The camellia sounds awful! Did I warn you, I should have, that if it arrived with the ball of earth cracked or disturbed, to send it right back? You read about plants "resenting" being disturbed, or even "highly resenting" but that is pale beside what camellias feel—they all but put an arm out and hit you if the ball is disturbed and if it breaks that is fatal. Fruitlands is supposed to be a good shipper of plants and I'm sure would make one good if it arrived in bad shape. It's just a burden if it's going to do badly. Maybe they're having labor shortages and so on over there too, because Mother gave me a camellia from there for Xmas and it arrived with the bottom of the crate swinging loose and some of the dirt gone as if something—a rat?—had got in—it looks bad, but [. . .] I'd decided it wasn't seriously hurt and didn't report to the nursery. Let me know how it seems to be. The address of the nursery is Fruitlands Nurseries, Augusta, Ga. and I have the shipping slip still somewhere if needed, or rec't or whatever it is. Did the stem seem firm and nothing shake around? I hate for it not even to bloom. Let me know. [. . .]

What did you ever write for Sat. Review? I saw your name in their list of contributors over a period of years, as I was throwing away a stack into the paper drive. Just thought I'd look, and there you were. Write me again about the camellia. And the date you'll be in the Atlantic.

Love,

Eudora

Sometimes I think I'll submit him a little piece on the USO room in the station where I work Sunday nights and yet I guess it's all the same old familiar thing—I get so stirred up, though—the wounded ones who are back—and the men at the prison camp, the things they say. And not being able to really help any of them.[15]

February 7, 1945
Dear J—

I still go ahead not hearing from you but one day maybe the P.O. will catch me up and in the meantime my letters probably sound like one writing blindfolded, on acct. I just wonder how you're doing. [. . .]

It is cold in Jackson but really I am sure it is spring. The trees are red with sap against the sky and the pear tree buds are swelled to the point of one more day before they're flowers—of course it is a very early pear tree. I saw some hasty mocking birds courting out the window a while ago, and plenty of robins and redbirds, that sing right out in the chill, and a frog let go in the lake the other night. The camellias are under cover at this writing, being just at the big fat bud stage with color spilling out when they could be hurt in this cold. Leila is a mid-season bloomer and has not threatened to bloom until the weather is more favorable—one of the things I admire about her. She has nicely held in slim buds now. The bulbs are doing nicely and hyacinths especially.

Didn't get your books sent till yesterday that I may have spoken of, because had to stay in a week with a sprained foot I got from falling down in front of the governor's mansion one pretty springlike day when I wasn't looking and only stepped out yesterday to mail it and drink a couple bottles of beer. This is all the news I know—oh the Vicksburg Barge burned—but went off in glory, they cut it loose and it went down the Mississippi aflame with people gathering from everywhere on the bridge to see. I imagine from everywhere.

Take care of yourself—I hope you do this. I hope you won't mind if I write you dizzy letters about the spring as I am sure to do, when it is so cold there, I am thinking of you but can't help how I love spring in Mississippi.

Love to you

E

February 10, 1945

Dear Diarmuid,

How is everything, are you snowed under and isolated in the country? I hope you all keep warm and don't have any more bad storms, though at least this time you aren't likely to be on a little island with nothing but a pan of watercolors to take shelter under as I was scared of before. The paper makes us all feel so sorry for you as we are having beautiful days. All the spring birds are singing, some at night, and the yellow daffodils are in flower. I'm going to the Delta tomorrow—wrote the lady a little note saying any time this spring she could answer if it was convenient and a letter came back special delivery saying be there in time for Sunday dinner (tomorrow). The OPA gave me some gas to go so I can take the car and that will make me very free and fine.[16] I hope I can read all these old journals and letters aright and see into the way things were and the way they are—will let you know how I got along. It lures me and I wish I could do something—

I forgot to answer about the orange wine—that it is very nice, I think, and that you must have some in your cellar. Hubert Creekmore has you to thank for his job, I imagine, working at Tomorrow[17]—what is Charles Rolo doing there? Mrs. Garrett was down at Duke attending to some little television business, I gather, and more or less hired him by some mental waves, but just so it made a satisfactory interview I guess that was all right. Thanks for what you did for him, he seems pleased with his job. Those little Algerian irises I have been dazzled by are best of all today—so many, and the only things of color under the trees—I bet they would come out of snow and flower.

Love,

Eudora

On Welty's next trip to the Delta, Robinson's cousin Nancy Fitz-Gerald showed Welty a diary kept by Robinson's great-grandmother, Nancy McDougall Robinson, who came to the Delta with her husband in 1832.

February 13, 1945
Dear John—

It was a happy thought to send a Vmail letter to me and it has beat out any others you've sent to me lately, the P.O. has not yielded up any airmails for a while—I hope not to miss any. I was glad to have such a nice long one (of Jan. 26) and feel glad to know you're all feeling hopeful—about the Russians—*when* that could help Italy just in that much, I have been wondering daily, hopeful that it would be soon. Oh the hope that it will end—and knowing that your own life can belong to you again. Very free—and the world will be gentle again—I feel that now the horror is somehow spent, that all people would have it gentle again tonight if only the machinery could be stopped—the wish as passionate as the wish to start it—and hope it will be played out as soon as it can and the end that everybody can see isn't far off now—that it will be a kind of guide, the way lost people finally see a little light in front of them where it's been all the time—do you think it will? I feel very thankful that you are all right. When I think what you do and have done I am almost shy to acknowledge you are safe—I guess it's some kind of ancient instinct. The cherished thing not vaunted—or something. I will keep asking if you are safe and never admit you are, which of course has the truth in it too. I am sorry about the lost crews—

I'm glad the stove works and is warm. When is spring? It must have been the same star and moon—I don't know myself quite know *how*, but wasn't it beautiful.[18] My little trip that you arranged came off fine. I went up Sunday to the cousins and came back this evening—Tues. They were well—[. . .] Mrs. Fitz-Gerald as soon as I came began to show things to me and never did stop—[. . .]—I can't tell you how all she said and did in those diaries moved me—it was a stirring and beautiful kind of experience, that kept me reading without stopping a day, most of a night, all the next day, and when I did fall asleep I seemed not to be forgetting her—not dreaming anything about her, but *thinking* of her through the night.[19] I still do. [. . .]

It rained all that Monday, a dark sky and the bayou very full. You've been to that house even if not to visit them, I guess—the big two story white house, 2 miles this side of Webb across the railroad and facing Cassity [Cassidy] Bayou, with the tens of thousands of bulbs (not blooming yet) and the red and purple magnolias—she has done it over—papered it etc. and a big stove heating the whole upper and lower hall from that side hall. She showed me silver—her watercolors—the portraits of the ones in the diary. There was an old house man named Tiny, that was tiny, and a girl Sadie that would sometimes come up and cook, a few times a week. A little fox terrier named Trumpet. I saw Jerry and Eliz. Falls and their 3 children. Saw the manager, she has an honest one now. We ate so fine—turkey dinner Sunday, and all kinds of treats every meal, and when I left Mrs. Fitz-Gerald pressed on me a big sack of pecans and a doz. fresh eggs and a turkey sandwich in case I got hungry and 3 kinds of cake. I took bites in Sidon, Tchula, and Bentonia. All the way home the frogs were getting very loud and under bridges would deafen your ears. The water very high—bayous on both sides of the road full and only a blue heron and two owls plus little pigs did I see. From Yazoo where the afternoon sun fell behind on the Delta I looked back and saw it blue like the sea, far as could be seen.

Love,
E—

February 20, 1945
Dear John, just had a Vmail letter from you of Jan. 6—just thought I'd answer airmail. It must have started out 3 times—was glad to get it. It said you might be going to Florence for Mardi Gras, which sounded good. Hope you got to. The first flower on the Leila opened today. I've been out looking at it again just now—it is at the back of the bush in the hardest place to see—it means you have to sort of go into the bed on your elbow, full length, and look up—I was willing. It's a beautiful flower and the color is something you just can't keep in your head from year to year—it's a hard one to believe it's so radiant and clear, you just have to be patient and wait for a flower to open and see it again. Birdsfoot violets and blue and white hyacinths are open beside it, and the tulips with fat and pointed buds are coming for the next one (Leila) to open—in 3 or 4 days. I'm so pleased with the way it has done—grown so, and the flowers every single one perfect. This is a fine camellia year and all of them are doing well. Today it's cloudy and warm, faintly drizzling now and then,

and all the flowers look fresh and glow with color. The pear tree is at its height today. Everything smells so good. Birds singing. How I stayed in I don't know, but except for little excursions out in the yard I wrote on a story. It happens just previous to the last one I wrote—on the same afternoon, but in a long context would come before, in the telling. What am I writing? You'll get the new bit when I finish so you can see. Unless I do tear it up altogether tonight for it doesn't do well. [. . .]

Love to you

E.

P.S. Next a.m. Irises opened in a circle around the Leila camellia—just as I'd hoped but had forgotten they might—Look nice—

Glenway Wescott[20] sent me his book which looks so much better than the proofs I reviewed—need to do it over—*so hard* for me.

March 19, 1945

Dear John, your airmail written the 5th and 6th came straight on and it was such a fine long one. Corsica did sound fresh and green and it must be like Mississippi down about Port Gibson—where the trees hang over the road and are like that just now—and it was a little near to it in the flowering trees and the smell in the air surely. I'm glad you get to Rome now and then to see what they have unwrapped and uncovered and when you see the Perseus tell me how beautiful it is.

[. . .] Is it true that bombings and craters have turned up astonishing wildflowers—I read it in some Sunday supplement that you probably couldn't trust—but it seemed that long covered-over seeds of earlier or sport kinds had been brought up to rain and sun by the bombing and were flowering and amazed people.[21] Out of season too I think. I sort of hope the turmoil did not touch them that way though. I hope you get to go back to Corsica another time and be in the cool mts. And feel the sun hot and hear the water rushing over the rocks—it sounded so nice. While I was reading that in your letter a mockingbird was singing in a tree here and went like that.

The garden is all right—General Green is about to get it. We have had rains and the whole place all at once was very lush—the pear tree is in full grown leaf, a billowing tree. The tall iris opening. The things to do now are fertilize the camellias, spray the cape jessamines, and put straw under the strawberries, pull grass, take away the camellia stakes and feed the hyacinths, and miscellaneous things. The little bluets and onion flowers look so pretty in the grass. Just now the last white daffodils are blooming, they were with the latest flower on the Leila, it having a long season of bloom and outlasting the seasons of tulips, hyacinths, and now these. They are named Thalia and are the nodding kind, pure white small trumpets and several to a stalk—unlike any others I have tried. Oh the Blue Wonder Lily is in bud—something I got from Market Bulletin and the lady replied to my question that it had never bloomed and that was why she wondered—will let you know.[22] It is so beautiful in Mississippi—I wish more each spring for you to see, and it is true, the springs have been more beautiful as the time has gone by. This year the cold didn't come back and catch anything, camellias or flowering trees, and all flowered and then the trees stood in bloom for a long time, until the leaves now have come on them. The woods I wish you could see. I don't know whether when you walked up the mt. in Corsica you saw any dogwood trees by the water. The dogwoods on Pearl River, white and pink, and little plum thickets with them are all in the woods, wild azaleas with them, and the whole way to N.O. on the rebel is green.[23] Every day I am torn—work to do inside and outside, and the days never seem long enough. Now the magnolia fiscatas are opening. New leaves on the camellias are opening like fans all over them. Crepe myrtles are all in leaf. Fig trees putting out. The hackberries—so wonderful. It has rained a good bit and the ground too wet and heavy today—I had some more rain lilies to plant. The belladonnas are going to bloom this year I think, an amazing lot of foliage has come up, then doesn't it die down and the flowers rise up naked, July, August? Maybe you can come and see them—? [. . .]

I guess the story is all right so far, it will take much more work. I guess trying to write a novelette, if that is what it is, is all a part of spring energies, but I wish I had a sign to tell me which I had better do that day, write or work the garden. About 100 pages are done—that's the only fact about it I am sure of to tell you. I worry some about how to send it to you but think I will send it in one envelope after the other, instead of in a box like a cake—it will probably weigh more than a cake. The request I would write myself would have to read "Please send me 5 lbs. of your novel," and would he stamp it? If you knew how anxious I am to have you see it—I feel if it gets very bad the portfolio[24] will reject it—shoot it out—like the button marked Reject on the record changer. I wish it would.

It is late at night, the wind is blowing, fresh winds, and it sounds like one drop of rain that just now touched the window. Yes it is raining. Take care of yourself.

Love

Eudora

Just sent you a little homemade stuff—

March 24, 1945

Dear John,

I'll write you a little note early. The sun just came out—it was cloudy early. It's warm and outdoors all green now. A Mermaid rose.

[. . .] The sky has gotten all blue now. I wish the river would go down and take the mosquitoes away so it would be easier to work. I did get the camellias fertilized yesterday and some spireas pruned back, but hope to spray the roses late this evening, and get some other work done before then. The days are full. The housework, there's little to that except the time it takes, the hard part is circumventing Mother—she ought not to do it and knows it but I have to foresee everything she's going to try to do, so she won't beat me—I make her promise for certain things, but forget others—and after I think I'm through and come up, she will sneak down and wash a blanket. I keep my ears open all the time for suspicious sounds—The doctor told her she worries too much, about the war, and all, and has hypertension and should not get fatigued—simple orders but she's so indignant lying down.[25] Walter is getting along all right but I dread when we begin to make landings on the China coast or the Japanese mainland. He is underway now, somewhere. I don't know how far ahead to try to think, about you. [. . .]

I write some afternoons and nights often, on my story, it is astonishing how it grows—I regard it with mixed feelings. So anxious now to finish and then I'll send it to you, somehow, and wait to see what you think. I have had a hard time with the people's names—as usual—the right one will not come to me. I was walking in a field and saw my baby's name—Bluet.[26] The spring is so beautiful—the locust trees are blooming, full of bees. The old fashioned roses are all over the bushes—I do love those, and if I could prevail on Mother we would have those—climbers and pillar roses—so flofferous and beautiful, to me. And they all smell good.

Love,

Eudora

In the woods—all green—the tender green that goes. Haw trees—Blackberry bushes in bloom—They are plowing—My pinks are beginning—

March 31, 1945
Dear John,

The little pitcher and the other little thing (I still think it might be for sugar—pour out of scalloped edge—but I have flowers in it now) came for Easter—[. . .]

Today is lush and wet and all the leaves twice as green, and heavy-headed bushes hanging down and fragrant, and birds loud—The roses have taken on much new growth and are blooming lustily—so sweet—The garden *isn't* wonderful—it needs so much done—the grass so high—I got the hyacinths fertilized for next spring just before the storm broke—a few weeds pulled—But the irises are nice—some that haven't bloomed for 3 years are blooming now. I wish your camellias there were better—no Leilas I know—

The blue wonder lily was a Camassia—spike of small blue star shaped flowers, opening upwards—[27]

Thanks—about aunts and quilts story[28]—I still write as much as I can every day even if I just get to it by a hairs' breath (breadth?)—I jump into it with almost a shout of pleasure—no I don't quite yell—it just fascinates me and works me—Enough, though it's like garden work and women's work—never done—This one I want for you—you know that, but I'm anxious to see how it turns out to be—maybe too many words—about 200 pages now.[29] Every time I hear a whistle I think—maybe it's the end of the war—It seems so near, so hopeful—I hope your Easter is a fine day—So pretty tonight in Jackson—Love—and thanks for the darling things—

Yours,
Eudora

April 3, 1945
Dear Diarmuid,

Late thanks for the check—you will think I don't appreciate Danish underground money—which is just what I do. It's still amazing and sounds a little flighty of the underground.[30] It's good news the spots are vanishing and you and Rose did not get the plague.[31] I hope they never come back or any of their ilk. Was Easter nice? Did something bloom for it? We have had two cyclones since I wrote you last, a lot of trees torn down and flowers crushed, but I've got our yard about cleaned off now. I'd been carrying out big limbs of a tree in the back, where it is woodsy, and all at once looked up and the tree itself was uprooted, just hanging there, in another tree—I ran in the house and called to Mother a tree had fallen. "Just now?" she asked. "No, but I just now saw it." It's iris time here, and irises that haven't bloomed for 3 years are putting up flowers— looks like a good year. The Louisianas are blooming too. A white single peony opened this morning but after about 15 minutes closed again as a rainy wind began coming. I've done some fertilizing of bulbs and spraying of roses and so on, weeded a little, but things are away ahead of me, and nobody will ever come along to cut the grass, it looks like. Rose's knitting inspires me[32] but my story doesn't seem to get any longer, just wider, if that explains it—just now it seems not very good, too, but that may partly be the tedious rewriting and copying that lies ahead—I just don't ever feel there is any time and to tell the truth am tired most of the time—but maybe I can get it done, before the heat comes on. It's already hot in the middle of the day but mornings and evenings are simply beautiful. I would send you some camellia fertilizer to see if your plants wouldn't perk up (how are they?) but can't get the chemicals this year. If you have anything acid in nature you might sprinkle a little on, or any aluminum sulphate will keep the leaves bright and green. We may be able to get that. I've been putting cottonseed meal on ours but that being a very fumey dust, I scarce like to enclose it—it turns you chartreuse yellow—if your secretary were in from christening carriers and chanced to slit the mail open she would be whiffed out flat—of course you probably expect things like that and look out for them.

Love,

Eudora

April 14, 1945

Dear John—how are you? I hope you're getting along all right and the new man is learning and that your work might be a little lighter. How are the eggs? Can you get them any easier. You do so much and it is so long now. Your real job must be getting more and more intensive and must take up all the nights. You do so much—I wish you didn't have to work that hard—and that it would come to the end soon. Have you had good luck—I hope so. Have you got the maps all up and things looking ready for this to finish—I like the fine vine going around, the mosaic. I guess you will be the capt. now—what that matters. Have the nights been nice? Here clear and the stars bright, last night the new moon, so fine a crescent—I was walking up the driveway to Mary Frances and Joe's—the field smelling sweet, and you could almost see things by starlight. Send me a vineyard flower, because I keep wondering what the vines look like in bloom. Or paint it for me.

It's beautiful in Jackson—hot in the middle of the day, but the mornings and evenings fresh, cool—the chinaberry trees at night and the honeysuckle. The iris have passed their peak and the roses are at theirs, I believe—Mother was saying she wished you could see—sure you would admire. I put some polyanthus called Mrs. Finch I think, in the vase you sent me, which look just right. Shell pink as the clusters open. The clove pinks are another thing I love.

So terrible about Roosevelt—so personal a thing—I keep thinking how his death will be a personal thing there, a prop knocked out—[33] [. . .] I hate it for the men so. It's just another thing that *happens* to them tonight. It was always true of course that it will be the men, and the people themselves, their might all together that will somehow push and move the peace into its shape—only I felt that in Roosevelt we had something that would save some suffering and time and would be a force against the powers and big shots and military—I did have faith in him for that, didn't you? Just in his magnitude as a man if nothing else—I felt he had ambition to some extent, but that it was kept subservient, and would be kept subservient. I couldn't sleep last night and couldn't think of anything but the bitterness that will go in hearts kept so far hopeful and young, if we don't do things right, now, in spite of anything even this bad. Do you think when everybody feels this way that it could somehow inflate even politicians to the right size to act? A kind of breath of the world, if that would just make a little man a big one for this moment—[. . .]

I took [Walter's baby daughter, Elizabeth] to see Mrs. Macgowan's irises yesterday and led her around the garden, staggering—Mrs. M. lecturing in front of each iris and the baby reaching lovingly for the stalk with both hands, or backing up her little seat aiming to sit (she is not very good yet) on any bright clump, or giving no uncertain raspberries to the things Mrs. M. declared. Mrs. M. offered the baby one, saying to me at the same time it was a 2nd-rate iris, and the baby pushed it from her, and turned her head away.

[. . .] Have been watering—summer is in. How well everything grows—and so fragrant when you water. Tonight the Boston Symphony will play Daphnis and Chloe. This is a pieced letter—I stop something and run to write you a little. Take care of yourself—love to you—

Yours,

E

April 15, 1945
Dear Diarmuid,

[. . .] You would love this time here, the iris are all at their height. We go from garden to garden. I have a friend who has some Brazilian iris—must go to see it today—he says it is brilliant, not surprising. I think Dymia is fine—Black Wings too—and the Beuchley's Giant and Shining Waters and Great Lakes—also there have been some beautiful white ones around here, that sparkle. Peonies are blooming with them, and of course roses. I guess it is too early for you to be thinking of pinks and such, that we have now.

So terrible about the president—I hate it so for the men (overseas)—wondering what will happen to the peace, just when Roosevelt is needed. All those people that hated him so are probably glad—hard to imagine. I can't think of a worse thing.

Are your daffodils you bought last year coming out fine? [. . .] We need a rain, and I have been watering already. My story languishes for lack of time and also I don't know now how good it is, it seems a lot of words for a simple story.

Love,

Eudora

P. S. [. . .] April 16. Thanks for the contract which came this morning. Glad it is daffodil time at last. What pretty white or pale ones do you recommend that are blooming for you? We had a little sprinkle this morning and all is bright and fragrant. Did you ever smell Confederate Jasmine? Enclosed—

May 1, 1945
Dear John, a letter from you—saying you worked hard—sometimes read in Lycidas—it hurts that you had 8 days from that day still to go, till the "virtual" end. I was glad to have word. How I wait for it now—for you to say you are well and it is over, truly, to hear it from you. It seems to fill the

air, the garden—but still it will feel like hope, until then. I hope you are rested some by the time you get this. I hope you and Paul[34] have met and seen each other to be well, by now. And the ones you have worried for—I hope you can just lie and let peace soak into you like sun. Yesterday when I was writing to you in the park a vast jimson weed in the grass was so shining and tall and green and blowing there in the wind, dancing—it looked beautiful to me—and tears came in my eyes—and last night I dreamed it was on your hill where you could see it (I didn't dream you did, just hope still), only many, it was repeated all along the hill, blowing and bending freely the same, the same beautiful thing, again and again. I'll write Emily—she'll be thinking every minute too. We had written around Easter time. *Don't* be relating yourselves, requisitioning, to any Germans—to cruel men—It makes me want to cry out. I do cry out. C. D. Jones is free—the story in the paper is all we know, I am sending it.[35] Thanks for wishes for Walter—he wrote on the 17th to say he was all right, but he was still there—he enclosed a citation and bronze star in the letter—the thing said it was for shooting down 2 Jap planes under fire in the Philippines invasions. By the way I never read the Bell, should I? Rosie told me there was a man in it that was "so sweet—like John" and knowing this couldn't be likely true it's somehow kept me from reading it.[36] I'm glad you like Fireman Flower too—it seemed a real, passionate talent to me—and those images—the golden cockerel—strong and poetic.[37]

It is a beautiful day. I didn't do a thing—just looked at the garden, and it needs much. Diarmuid wants me to send him some watermelon seeds exactly the kind little black boys steal and eat all alone in a field in the South. Cuban Queen? Black Diamond? I just got the most expensive, Black Diamond, though in the Market Bulletin was a spoonful of Moon and Star that sounded nice to the ear. I was copying some Rilke for you when your letter came and will send it on stopping with the Annunciation though if you think it is beautiful I will finish it. I wish I could see you and know how you are at this moment, from you. The wind is blowing—A.B. [Anna Belle] just phoned that Felice in Vaiden had heard from her husband that he had seen Paul on the night of the 24th before he crossed the Po, and that he was fine then. That is recent and good—I hope soon we know that you are all right and are through with it. Tell me, so that I will know it beyond everything, and say if you are resting and if the nights and days are gentle yet.

Love to you—

E—

May 25, 1945

Dear Diarmuid,

It seems a long time since I wrote you—I've wondered how you are, how the strawberries are doing, if the melons are up, how the anthology is.[38] Have the cool grey days stopped? Here it is suddenly deep summer and very dry—which means the watering must begin. [. . .]

The pomegranate trees are blooming—did I ever tell you, it is the flower that has the color and fire you thought would be in the fruit. Our second crop of strawberries has come in now and we have them every day—so good—are yours? The snail is the enemy. How are your Auratum lilies? Is William going to break any, being so eager again. Why do you suppose we can't have lilies? It isn't lime—because they like acid, don't they? A little thing a foot high comes up and expires. We've never planted anything so carefully either and have made numbers of tries. By following direction we may plant them too deep for the South. Philippinense and Easter lilies are all we can grow in our garden—and I love the speciosum kinds and the little kinds.

My story (first draft) seems truly finished, I think, but I can't seem to ever get to it—to work on or type up. We have no help and my mother has been sick too so there's been a good deal to do just to keep things going. I tried working at night on the story and had to throw most of that away, it was bad. I am so anxious for it to get typed up so I can look at it and see it as a whole—and send it up so you can. For all I know it may be unintelligible (I am almost sure it will seem so to John Woodburn for instance—I am not mad at anybody in the story no matter what they do).

I hope everybody up there is all right. How is Mr. Fowler's son—will he get home.[39] John Robinson is all right but doesn't know what will happen—if things are like the rest of his story in the war he will get sent to the Pacific without any leave, but I hope somewhere a little rest for him—preferably in Jackson. [. . .]

I've been taking up and resetting hyacinths and rain lilies. The daylilies are magnificent now—as tall as my shoulder and very fine. Did yours live through the winter and are they any size at all now. I want to send you a Calypso when the time comes—it is an evening bloomer, so pale it is almost silver, and shines like the new moon, at about that time—and smells sweet.

Love to all of you,

Eudora

June 12, 1945
Dear John,

I hope you're in a good place and the weather the way you like it—I'm hoping you can stay a long enough time to rest without being tired, more than just a week, or 2, if you like it. Are the days fresh and the nights clear and beautiful, and do you smell mimosa trees—when the mimosa is sweet in our yard, I wonder. I hope you know something now—the right news—that you can come and stay—how *can* it be anything else? I wish I could trust them. You have done so much—I know it and it burns inside. Every day is so precious in life—some of these beautiful nights I feel it all night through, each minute mattering so. How precious life is. Here tonight cool, and every now and then a gentle stir of rain in the leaves—very welcome. You can see a few stars—and hear the frogs in the lake. I did some work, enclosed. I feel anxious to get it all done and to you—then you can see if it has been a good or bad try. Sometimes I hit my head. Help me if you can and there is time for it, but your reading it is my help now—it doesn't just go out to the void—you get it. [. . .]

We are having lots of good snapbeans, onions, and home grown tomatoes these days—and our strawberries around the rose garden have been yielding a good second crop. I wanted to put some up, but we're out of sugar. Many Voice of the People letters in the Clarion Ledger[40] about the difficulty of getting sugar to put up things and make cakes for our boys coming home, and the breweries, devil-sent and hell-bent outfits, getting extra sugar in the month of June, and we come up to Jackson to the ration board where they're all sitting there in the shade, and they say come back next Tuesday, and will it do any good? Leviticus, 4–8. *In the shade* got me. [. . .] Take care of yourself and when you find out anything let me know and I hope so hard it is that you are coming and soon and to stay, and all of that, nevermore, and then we can christen the wine glasses, for which I save them. I have been playing Eine Kleine Nachtmusik. The Victrola in a mood of playing out beautiful and full.

Love to you
E—

Both Robinson and Russell received copies of the first installment of Delta Wedding. *Russell wrote, "The carbon arrived safely at noon yesterday and with an inner cheery chuckle I dropped all other matters and settled down to read, finishing it off last night. I can't tell you how good I think this is. . . . I had been afraid secretly that this, your first novel, would be a series of short stories strung together but in fact you seem to have happily fallen into the novel technique as if it was something you had been looking for. . . . I can't find the right words to tell you what a magnificent piece of work this is and how anxiously I'm waiting to see the rest"* (6.19.45). Russell also told Welty that he hoped that Edward Weeks, editor of the Atlantic, would serialize the novel before Harcourt published it later that year.

June 21, 1945
Dear Diarmuid,

I was so glad to get your letter—and to know you think the story is all right—that you think it's good. I value greatly what you say—and felt my spirits rise. Just after sending it I was low about it and was prepared for you to say better abandon it. I only hope the rest seems all right. There are some hard places. If you think when it's all done that there is too heavy a load for too slight a story—that is my worst fear, so I'd like to know your opinion about length then. I don't know about the novel technique! As for Mr. Weeks taking it, that would be nice if he does, but in a way I'd be glad to be relieved of any time pressure if he would put that on me. And just finish it as I could. Of course I realize that sale would be the only money out of the work probably and would do the best I could to meet Atlantic demands as it would be silly not to, but just don't know how well I could. Will wait on that bridge.

I got a book from you—which looks like an interesting one—and I think I'll dive right in. Thanks—it looks like one of those exotic books you know how to run across.

My brother is safe off Okinawa so that is a great thing lifted in our house.

The beans, tomatoes and onions are nice here now (especially one on top of the other on your plate). The flowers are in a lull, with only some day lilies and rain lilies blooming, maybe some phlox coming on. Is your Lilium Auratum making a spectacle of itself about now? The Julia E. Clark lily house I knew, in Oregon, has been taken over by a gent named Romaine B. Ware, who charges outrageous prices and sounds formidable altogether. I sent your name in though for a catalogue, though the new one isn't like the old one, which was a regular lily picture gallery, with descriptions etc. of all.[41] Is it hot enough for the melons?

Thanks again for reading the story and letting me know so soon what you thought of it. I was so anxious. It makes me proud for you to like it.

Love, Eudora

June 24, 1945
Dear John,

I wonder what you know—how I hope it's good, and for soon. Maybe Monday morning a letter saying so—very waitful.

A hot Sunday morning—dense green now—mockingbirds chasing each other. I'm going over to see Will in a little—I wish he could be *here*. If only they would offer to surrender—I would be willing to take anything. Walter writes he is without a ship which sounds bad but he hopes new orders might put a leave in somewhere—we hope—

The garden very dry and I had better water tonight. The belladonna foliage all gone and I am looking for the flowers to come up. I've been lying in bed reading a lily catalogue.

Your vases seem more beautiful than ever. I am so proud of them, to walk in and see them. They are on the mantel now, downstairs, really too heavy for them, those dark bricks, but AE's painting with them—and that's lovely—Do they have a story? How could they fail to, they seem very rich with place, yet so light and lovely.

Yesterday I wildly bought a gold-like dress to wear, in case you come home or anything like that, instead of slacks the porch paint won't come out of etc. The clerk said remember though, if I ever wore it, "our waist could come in tight and we ought to wear green pearls with it"—I hadn't been in the Emporium in a long time, just ran out without looking behind me. I wish I hadn't sent the last bit of story as I've done it almost all over, you'll see it wobbles. I feel by this time that all these people are real beyond what I can say and I have to go more slowly and responsibly for the lightest character than I dreamed when I started and sort of filled up the house. When I sent the section to Weeks I sent it to Diarmuid and he and Rosie both like it which pleases me very much. D. says John Woodburn perplexes him by expressing no desire to read any of it, just wants me to let him know how many pages it will be so they can allot the paper, and I gather it is a great bore. I love all the people in it and don't hate anybody or scorn their ways, that's why. (I believe in the beginning writing, like dancing and music, was a praise of life and nature and I feel in that stream—and the hard work is in making your self fall away wholly—and not partially—sometimes I want to show my own delight.)

The almost full moon was sailing through clouds last night. The 4-oclocks made the streets smell sweet—I picked you some but of course they closed up. Maybe you have them too, like the magnolias and all, just like us—but I wish you had these, these *ones*.

Love—

E—

[*On verso, sketch of zoot-suiters with EW's caption:*] 2 zoots coming up Capitol St. just now—The midriff must be the latest—

Late July 1945

Dear Diarmuid,

I was glad to get your nice long letter—one from Henry too, with the plans for expansion, which I did not think were grand enough, and I didn't think the N. O. branch soon enough. Are you still having the monsoon—we are too, now, only no watermelons growing to profit by it in our garden—we only have a million rainlilies. How are the melons? You will have to have a watermelon party, for which the right name is "a cutting", one fine night, ending with a watermelon fight between the boys and the girls. The lily sounds beautiful—the bulb will probably weigh 10 lbs.[42] I note the catalogue says "Protect from strong winds." How? You yourself will have to go out there and hold your coat. No, I didn't know you liked size so much, but it is probably the influence of the U.S. passing over you. Did you ever grow a Dauricum—it turned out to be something I ordered from a lady who advertised a "Russian Lily", and is early and a beautiful rosy apricot color, pretty loud, but nice. I would love to see your lily garden when it comes up—how I love those flowers, and can't grow them. My ambition would be to try a Szovitsianum—and some of those slender, nodding ones from around Burma that smell spicy, they say. Did they send you an old catalogue with the photographs? Look at Sz. By the way the iris people sent a card your iris would be shipped in late August, is that right or wrong? I have some moreas throwing blooms now and then, pale yellow now. I'm going to dig up all my bulbs as soon as I finish this typing, and ramify them—oh, thanks for the $69.69.

[. . .] I've got back to work now, and hope to finish up soon. We had seven people in our house, including a baby that would type on the story just about as well as I could, now it's quiet. I will surely try to get it to you before September, in case Harcourt would want to give it any paper, does it matter what week in September? I thought of such a good vacation for you, you could go to Tanglewood and paint by day and sit on the hill and listen to Bach and Mozart by night.[43] I heard the broadcast Saturday night from there—Suite in D Major No. 4 by Bach and Mozart's piano concerto in A Maj. played by Brailowsky—you don't like concertos though—but this was magical. You could hear the outdoors around it too—not that studio deadness, just quiet. Wish I could come up in the fall, reward myself for this heavy typing, but it seems to stretch ahead of me so now, and fall seems a long way off—I am hoping the war will be ended by then, but my brother back from the Pacific laughed at me.

Love,

Eudora

August 7, 1945

Dear John—

I *am* glad to have the tomato paste recipe—The sweet red tomatoes of fall are about ready to come in—what a fine day it sounded—I was glad to have the recipe from it—Here is some more story—This part was hard and is very much of a working version as is—but I send.

The baby loves the tin can you sent the sea-gull and bell in, and puts in poker chips and takes out of, the whole time she's here—Yesterday I took her and mother on a real ride, Walter left us some furlough gas, and we went out in the country off the Old Canton Road, old picnic country—fresh and green, big gold and white clouds—yellow flowers—I got "The Nature of the Physical World"[44] off the shelf to look up the atom, but it's too staggering about the bomb, to even think—I only tremble. And you can't even really *tremble* for the whole *universe*—

I will dig tomorrow and not write, but hope to finish soon and you will have all—anxious for that—Tonight canning some pears, our tree laden—Thanks for the Marina di Pisa recipe and to the lady who wrote it down—

Love to you,

E—

Japan did not surrender after the U.S. dropped an atomic bomb on Hiroshima on August 6, so a second bomb was dropped on Nagasaki on August 9. By August 14, Japan had agreed to surrender, although a formal agreement was not signed until September 2.

Earlier that summer, Mississippi's senators had drawn national attention for racist statements they made while filibustering against Truman's Fair Employment Practices Committee. Like most other southern senators, they objected to laws preventing employers from discriminating on the basis of race. Senator James Eastland claimed that African American soldiers had been "an utter and abysmal failure" in the war, and Senator Theodore Bilbo called the committee "a smooth deliberate scheme to integrate the Negro race with the white and foster intermarriage and interbreeding." The filibuster was over by July, but throughout the summer Bilbo, who was up for reelection in 1946, continued to proclaim his belief in white supremacy.

August 23, 1945
Dear John—

I knew you felt that way and it makes me glad for your sake the war's over everywhere now. Surely you'll come soon—surely they will let people who have not done so much do the work from now on and all of you can get back—and out. Mississippi is as bad as those things make you believe and a little worse for the lack of even regret among the people here who could have minded or could start now. Yes, a trance—that is what it must be—if trances are that stubborn. What will happen if we let it keep us—want it to keep us—from seeing things as they really are in Mississippi. I think "when the men come back" many times a day and it gives me both hope and dread—thinking then a little hard-headed sense will be brought to bear, and then aching to think what the men will find if we don't come to. I realize of course, and more from what you just said, that all they've seen too is dependent on the individual—I know not to look for them in numbers to have seen at all what you would see and know anyway, but I can't help but think that regardless and regardless, the *hope* is there—and God knows it ought to be *here*, cherished at home and fed some. I've never been a crusader, being a more shy and private person, but I may be now—the way I speak out, and can't sleep from indignation. It is a fine, cool, gentle evening, it's rained—have been out looking at the camellia buds—firm and growing almost by the day. Goldenrod is everywhere, and it keeps being like fall—on days like this. I picked some little grasses and wild stuff to send you but of course it didn't keep. From some old road out north. Here is all now of the next-to-last chapter. It will need work but that will come when I can see it fresh and more at arm's length—and I wait for what you think—I never wanted to get fancy—did I? [. . .] Tomorrow will finish some urgent garden work, as the rain made the ground so nice, and then will type up the last pages and send. Love to you—

Yours,

E

The following day, Welty wrote Russell, "I started reading [E. M. Forster's] A Passage to India *again—the politics in Mississippi make me so sick I have to get some release and there really isn't any against the rage that comes over me—what is going to happen, with things like this and people like that Bilbo—It's too much for me" (8.24.45). Some "release" came to Welty the following month when she visited New York City and the Russell family, who had asked Welty to be Will Russell's godmother.* Delta Wedding *was now scheduled for a 1946 publication by Harcourt, Brace.*

November 9, 1945

Dear Diarmuid,

Thanks for the check—it is vast. It looks even bigger than it sounded. Now if I can just make it back for H. B. with some eventual sales so they can never feel called on to glare at us about it.[45] The best part is knowing you think the book is a good one so I'm afraid I won't really worry too much about the sales or frowns. Did your girl come in Monday, or not? I hope *somebody* is there by this time. It's nice the picture came out all right and I'll be glad to have them. Some local Episcopalians have raised their eyebrows over my being a godmother, a bishop's daughter cross-examined me. But maybe I will be right for William, who may never accuse me of not being brought up in the church at all, because his heart is tender, and I don't believe he is going to need catechizing from very strict sources anywhere. I've been working in the garden—separating daffodils. John is in this country, have already talked to him and think he's on his way down to Miss. to get separated. My brother in the Pacific has hopes for Christmas—that will be everybody home. [. . .]

Love,

Eudora

Mid-December 1945
Dear Diarmuid,

[. . .] I went down to Louisiana last weekend with the Robinsons, John's family, and drove back with John and his brother who's back from the Pacific. John seems not so rested or well and I hope he will feel better soon—very soon. He has leave accumulated through February of next year, at least. It has been very dark and rainy all day every day. [. . .]

Love,
Eudora

December 30 1945
Sunday
Dear Diarmuid,

I hope the children are better—the paper tells of another cold storm coming down on you—Let me know how everybody is. Don't you and Rosie get flu.

[. . .] I went to the bootlegger's yesterday to get some sherry to go with the Black Bean Soup—[. . .] It was amusing but I've gotten less and less able to bear idiotic doings in Miss. and don't know what will become of us. Bilbo is in Jackson this minute—announcing. I wrote a letter to the paper the other day—it's feeble—I enclose—got some phone calls of approval and 1 anonymous letter saying I was known as a dirty Communist and to keep my mouth shut.[46]

How is your camellia? Mine look fairly well considering the biting cold they endured and ought to open their flowers before long—how I wish you could come down. A little white hyacinth in bloom today out in the falling rain.

I hope all is well up there—and have a Happy New Year and lots of luck and all you'd like to happen I hope it happens then.

Love to all and many wishes—
Eudora

She began to swim in the river, forcing it gently, as she would wish for gentleness to her body. Her breasts around which she felt the water curving were as sensitive at that moment as the tips of wings must feel to birds, or antennae to insects. She felt the sand, grains intricate as little cogged wheels, minute shells of old seas, and the many dark ribbons of grass and mud touch her and leave her, like suggestions and withdrawals of some bondage that might have been dear, now dismembering and losing itself. She moved but like a cloud in skies, aware but only of the nebulous edges of her feeling and the vanishing opacity of her will, the carelessness for the water of the river through which her body had already passed as well as for what was ahead. The bank was all one, where out of the faded September world the little ripening plums started. Memory dappled her like no more than a paler light, which in slight agitations came through leaves, not darkening her for more than an instant. The iron taste of the old river was sweet to her, though. If she opened her eyes she looked at blue-bottles, the skating water-bugs. If she trembled it was at the smoothness of a fish or snake that crossed her knees.

In the middle of the river, whose downstream or upstream could not be told by a current, she lay on her stretched arm, not breathing, floating. Virgie had reached the point where in the next moment she might turn into something without feeling it shock her. She hung suspended in the Big Black River as she would know to hang suspended in felicity. Far to the west, a cloud running fingerlike over the sun made her splash the water. She stood, walked along the soft mud of the bottom and pulled herself out of the water by a willow branch, which like warm rain brushed her back with its leaves.

—"The Wanderers," 1949

CHAPTER FIVE

January 1946–October 1949

By early 1946, many of Welty's wishes during the war years had come true: the war was over and friends and family were safe; John Robinson was out of the army and back in Jackson; *Delta Wedding*, which turned out to be a novel after all, was serialized in the *Atlantic*, then published in book form in April. Robinson's return, however, did not bring the happiness Welty had hoped for. "He has been a little low in his mind," Welty told Russell that winter.[1] In May 1946 Robinson left Jackson to stay with friends in Oxford, Mississippi, the first of many relocations he would make in the late 1940s. During this period, Welty encouraged Robinson to establish himself as a writer and to collaborate with her on new projects. Welty believed that writing would cure Robinson of his discontentment and bring him closer to her. Robinson did produce several short stories, but the couple's artistic and romantic partnership remained more an ideal than a reality.

In her letters to Russell and Robinson in the late '40s, Welty continued to report on plant life, natural scenery, and the seasons, using language that echoed her comments on writing and friendship. Yet the Pinehurst Street garden was not the touchstone for Welty's inner life that it had once been. That garden's limitations were more apparent to Welty, who had grown discouraged after many attempts to amend its Yazoo clay: "After 21 years of feeding the dirt on this place it is still mysteriously like a brickbat," she wrote Robinson (10.23.46).

Her hometown and native state were proving similarly resistant to change in the postwar years. Truman's attempts to improve civil rights for African Americans met with a tremendous white backlash in the South. Mississippi Senator Theodore Bilbo announced publicly during his 1946 campaign that "every red-blooded white man [should] use any means" to prevent African Americans from voting: "And if you don't know what that means, you are just not up on your persuasive measures."[2] Bilbo won the Democratic primary that summer, assuring his victory in the general election in November 1946. That fall, Welty wrote Robinson that working in her garden was often a means of "avoiding people to whom I can't talk" (9.16.46). In the next three years she spent extended periods of time away from home—in San Francisco for over six months in 1946 and '47, in the Northeast for two long summer stays in 1948 and '49.

Meanwhile, Welty was writing the stories that would eventually become *The Golden Apples*. She drafted three separate stories before she realized that characters in one story, set in San Francisco, were from Morgana, the Mississippi town where the other stories were set. More and more interconnections appeared, all the way through Welty's final revisions of the book in early 1949. This was a sign to Welty that the stories were succeeding—that they had taken on their own life, like the plants in her garden. As she told Russell in 1948 after planting camellia seeds, she "always wish[ed] for a magical surprise" (9.48).

January 3, 1946
Dear Diarmuid,

The money came—many thanks. They are paying a lot, aren't they.[3] I'm glad you all seem to be well again—and hope you had a Happy New Year. The packages didn't come in time for Christmas—am so sorry—the mistletoe was late appearing on the scene here and in fact that was all I saw. Are you under a blanket of snow? We had two pretty days—all the bulbs put their noses out of the ground and some white hyacinths opened their flowers even—but now dark and rainy again. I wish spring were soon. The galleys came from Harcourt—no letter accompanying, but I guess they want them done as soon as possible. Bob sent me a book to review called Gumbo Ya-Ya and it looked as if it might have some Digest stuff so am sending on to Rosie in case she hasn't seen it. Louisiana stuff—a little of it goes a long way with me and it seems self-conscious but bit by bit might tickle the palate.

How are you? Write me soon—I feel nervous and bad, really not like any way I ever felt before—don't know what I can do about it but maybe the weather will help if it gets nice and either warm or sunny. Forgive this though.

Love,

Eudora

Russell replied, "I'm worried that you feel badly. Is it just nerves or is the body ailing too? [. . .] you must take care of yourself, Eudora, and I wish you'd write more fully or else I'll have to ask your mother to report on you" (1.7.46). He also told Welty that when he read the first installment of Delta Wedding *in the* Atlantic, *"it seemed so good, so solid, with no waste writing that I felt proud—though why one should feel proud about another's work I don't know."*

Mid-January 1946

Dear Diarmuid,

I'm sorry my letter made you worry—don't, because it was just tension that eventually stops and sleep comes. My health is all right. Thanks for the letter with all the news. I'm glad the children are all right—I got Pammy's fine note—one from Rosie too. Your weather sounds like ours, and here's hoping one day soon the sun will come out over both our roofs. I'm glad the anthology is all done but for the little bit of proofreading. When you get a galley on the finished introduction, could you let me see it then? I look forward to the book and have been thinking it must be coming out before you thought, if the galleys etc. are in so soon? It's cheering that you think the installment on mine sounds all right—I was anxious to know how it would seem but hated to ask anyone to read it *again.* [. . .] How are the camellia buds. They might flower before you think—though they do sound small and late. You would like the camellias that are opening in my garden now—lovely and worth all. White Roman hyacinths now—no daffodils yet. John is interested in camellias and came back from a trip with 10 little rooted cuttings in his car. He has been a little low in his mind and I think they might interest him. All of us need a little sun. It is not fair the way your friends and writers all unload troubles on you of a Monday morning. [. . .] It is raining lightly today but is a little warmer, not so biting—do you see any sign of an early spring? I was wondering if the telephone strike was a bad nuisance there or worse—and only hoped some fine Hollywood deal wasn't threatened just as it was coming through.

Did I ever tell you how much the gold frame from 2nd Ave. becomes the painting? It gleams—and looks the way it should—I believe you would think that this would do. You just couldn't put in the poem (in the anthology) of "with a heart of furious fancies whereof I am commander, with a burning spear and a horse of air through the wilderness I wander"—and the rest, could you? It has been running through my head.[4]

This is enough to write you on some busy day there—thanks for your letter and I hope all is well there.

All of you take care of yourselves—love to you
Eudora

On the book galleys I'm trying to re-write to some extent several scenes with Troy in them—not to make him anything of a buffoon, for fear I'd done that.

You could paint now, with no way to go outside to do work—
E

On January 16 Russell mentioned that Christine Weston's novel "sold for a monstrous sum to the movies." He also reported on his irises, which he thought might benefit from a visit by Welty:

"Perhaps they won't do anything unless you come up to say a magic word over them. I'd like to see this scene with you standing over the plants muttering incantations.

UP BUD
COME FLOWER
SHINE SUN
FALL SHOWER
TIME'S RUN
NOW'S HOUR
yours
Diarmuid"

Late January 1946
Dear Diarmuid,
　　Hooray about the Hollywood sale![5] It was bound to happen but I'm

glad it's really come now—I hope you got a tremendous sum—and that it goes down for *next* year's income tax—

Now what about your trip South? Think on this—What about March or April? Could you? I was glad to get the incantation, which I took out in the yard and tried—we got 2½ days of very springlike weather—Much obliged—A small iris bloomed and 5 camellias, 14 white hyacinths, and 2 snowdrops—I'll use it every 2½ days as that is its power, but the power may be really more, as we have broken 50-year records of bad weather and the opposition may be 10-fold—

[. . .] I hope the Hollywood sales flow along now as if on a feeding belt, and you just yawn—How is the secretary? My best to R., P., W., and H.

Love,
Eudora
P. S. A lady in Memphis wrote me that she liked my story in the Atlantic and she thought I should go on with it.

Early February 1946
Dear Diarmuid,

[. . .] Do you know anything about J. I. Rodale, editor of Organic Gardening?[6] It's like a Movement. He is interested in the compost pile, earthworms as a subsidiary—and maintains a monthly magazine and an organization from Emmaus, Pa. I guess he wrote a book too, Pay Dirt. Anyway you might be interested in him as some sort of character I thought and I'll mail up a copy of the magazine—I take it, and got a lot of material on earthworms too. For Christmas somebody gave me 100 lbs. of commercial fertilizer and now I don't know whether to put it on and murder all my earthworms. [. . .] Is your camellia doing all right? Suppose I send you a little cottonseed meal to spur on the two flowers—this is a warning not to pull open any enclosed envelope and get a coating of yellow flour over you. You would look Fortean[7] to somebody on the street. I feel a little better in my mind most of the time now. It is so cheering about the Hollywood sale and this gives me a glow to think of.

Love to all,
Eudora

February 26, 1946
Dear Diarmuid,

Thanks for the nice long letter but I was sorry about the lumbago—have you got rid of it? I hope so—a painful thing. You mustn't start felling trees right away. Your new garden spot will be fine but I know that burden of more and more added places, we have it too, and still keep on. What will you plant there? I've about fallen back on camellias and bulbs—the c.s take their attention at certain times but at this month of the year when they're all in a burst of glory you feel fired to give them fertilizer and mulch them and everything and think nothing is good enough for them. I've just done this. You should see everything blooming. I ache for your few buds to open when I see my big plant in the yard of the same variety covered with at least 150 open flowers—the least that plant can do up there is to bloom right now and not let those buds fall. I've gone into something new for me—grafting. Have you ever done it, in Ireland? There were two inviting bushes, very unattractive, with fine thick trunks, about 15 years old—bought under incorrect names—so I sawed one off and grafted a fine kind on it. I did that Saturday and felt so awful after sawing down a flowering tree that I couldn't sleep, and Sunday I got John to do the second one. He improved on me, I put only 2 scions of one variety on my rootstock, and he put 5 scions of 2 varieties, a rose and a white—it was a multiple trunk. When they shoot up 36 inches in a year and come out in wild magnificence, then I will write and tell you about it. I wonder how soon you can tell if they take. They are under glass and a piece of burlap now—we read how to do it in a book—which John mistrusts as a method—I should have consulted you. The whole garden is looking nice today and it is a soft spring day with blue and pinkish clouds, leaves on the willow trees, and some redbud I saw has a faint glow. Maybe spring will make your writers write. All I have done is labor in the yard. The pear tree shines over all. How I hope there is not cold again—it was so relentless for a while, clamping down on everything, soul and all, and so black as I have never seen. Do you want any watermelon seed this year? It's available here now. [. . .] I wish you and Rosie were here today and for a supper I'm going to try to cook tomorrow night—except I would have to take the crabmeat out of the salad for you.

Love,
Eudora

March 31, 1946
Dear Diarmuid,

[. . .] We're having summer, and yesterday it was 85, though it will probably freeze next month, but it is green and shady and I've been setting out petunia plants and spraying for aphids—roses blooming—The grafts took. (Camellia) Thanks for the last check. [. . .]

Don't you think it is splendid about the grafts taking? The one we put 5 scions on has new leaves on all five—it will be pink and white flowers, blooming at different times perhaps or maybe together. If I can graft your plants when I come out to see you next I would rather do that than paint—just give me a saw and tell your trees goodbye. My Peruvian scillas are blooming, do you know them? Excuse the looks of this typed with a cut finger in the air.

Love,
Eudora

April 29, 1946
Dear Diarmuid—

Thanks for the letter and I feel cheered you think the book's doing all right so far—somehow I had a feeling you were discouraged about it.[8] Were you about something for the moment—with self-centeredness I thought it was this client's book surely. I hope you're not. Has it rained? We need rain too. It's hot as June, and everything green hanging its head.

It makes me sad not to be leaving on the train tonight so I could be saying hello Wednesday. The nuisance I've got seems to be some sort of virus [. . .]. Is Henry well? Had a dream I was shown "The Gleaners"[9] and as I looked at the painting the gleaners in it turned tail and ran off hopping like jackrabbits, in those same positions, into the deeps of the picture. This was all right, but a voice started explaining—it said "This is infinity, because since the gleaners are in the picture they can never get out of it, no matter how hard they try," and sure enough there they were, sort of treadmilling.

Love
Eudora

To Robinson in Oxford, Mississippi
May 21, 1946
Dear John,

Your letter came, I was glad to have it. [. . .]

The new graft is taking, I will try to keep it cool. Ants and aphids are all over the dirt around it, but have put coffee grounds around to keep them off—made coffee right away. What did you graft on it? The camellias are all right in Jackson after 2 near-cyclones Sun. morning about 3 o'clock and another about 10,—you don't need to worry, because the little new shoots were strong enough and still whole. The Sacco here is sending up a new round of leaves.

It's nice to hear they like the book, when you were so lavish with it, it made me feel responsible and risky in Oxford. There's no news about it, or did I tell you it got panned in the Nation?[10]

I've been reading Faulkner—and how very great he is—you told me he was tremendous but I didn't take it in he was a giant—maybe the giant. "Spotted Horses" I read Sat. night and wished you were reading it along with me— the pages about the horses themselves very marvelous and all of it the very crossgrain and bottom truth about Mississippi—all of it true, compassionate,—funny, beautiful. Have you all his books to lend me soon—some of them to read for the first time, I can't think how I've been that careless. It is his scope that is such a revelation to me, his intensity and fineness I did know.

Charlie's low blue iris is in bloom—I'm waiting on it, then moving it to a better place I've fixed. Some Japanese iris, do you look down on their showiness. All the day lilies, and the one that opens in the evening, Calypso.

[. . .] It is a fine day to work in or out. Is it fine there yet? My energy is all right, truly. How could I be all right in my heart or my mind while not knowing how you felt or doing anything or being anything that would count. It seems a preposterous life to me. Sometimes I feel part of something I don't know all of—or its destination—sometimes left, no part. It is all right the not knowing, but not the not being. So fresh and moist early this morning—sometimes the suspense of life rests like a flying bird not pumping its wings. I felt if we could just ride somewhere, not far, but this morning. [. . .]

Much love,

E

Robinson traveled west, to Jackson, Wyoming, and then to San Francisco, in the summer of 1946. From late June until mid-August, Welty was also away from Jackson, primarily staying in New York.

Welty took a keen interest in Robinson's nascent writing career. In August, she sent a story of Robinson's to William Maxwell, fiction editor at the New Yorker. Welty was already on friendly terms with Maxwell, who had told her in a 1943 letter that he would always be interested in seeing her work. Maxwell accepted Robinson's story, "Room in Algiers," in August.

Welty may have retyped Robinson's New Yorker submission; in an August 21 letter, she told Robinson that "a few paragraphs" were "quietly saved back" in the version she sent to Maxwell. In September Welty shipped her typewriter to Robinson in San Francisco. He kept it the rest of his life; in 1983 he told Welty he was still using "the dear old Royal" to write to her (9.24.83). As Robinson began to send drafts of his own work to Welty, her letters included many more comments on Robinson's writing and on his response to her work, although she continued to report on gardening as well.

September 6, 1946
Dear Diarmuid,

Such a refreshment of cool weather here—I feel full of energy. I hope you are beginning to see out over the pile of mail and stuff that accumulated during your trip. I had a letter from William Maxwell asking if I would let him know if I wrote a story so he could "beard you in your den" and I wrote him it was now—that I hadn't heard from you what you'd done with it yet if anything or even if you liked it, but he might call you. John got a check for $370 for his story—ain't that good? Just sent me a telegram. I hope now he will go on and do some more. For so long I've been trying to get him to, for he is so good, I think, and just now it would be a help to him, maybe to get some things out of the system. How did your garden look? Has your camellia come out all over with buds? Mine here are full up—the size of little nuts. I have to water all day though. Very dry. [. . .]

Give my love to Rosie and the children—hope they are well. Is the little thing on your neck all right?[11]

Love,
Eudora

To Robinson in San Francisco
September 16, 1946
Dear John,

[. . .] It's a cool morning—cloudy, but never has rained except for one little shower early last week. Extremely dry and windy. Your camellias looked not too bad, though they have gone without water badly and watering now may or may not do enough good. The plants themselves, roots, I'm sure aren't hurt. The one that was uprooted and Will "finally put back" looks healthy enough but what do you think should be done, for (it's one of the cuttings) its little ball of roots is still quite separate from the earth around it, and must be subsisting as if in a pot—I hate to touch it when it's had such a hard time already, but feel when the weather is cool it should be maybe lifted out, soaked in water with the ball in a deep bucket to penetrate the root system, and replanted in loosened soil. But I wouldn't touch it without you to say so, and as I say it's getting along somehow. It's so dry to meddle with any of them now. All of them have nice buds and I hope there was water enough for them to stay on. I make allowance for your better soil and cooler place and think they would have got along better for a longer time without attention than some places. Some of the little ones have a touch of scale and I'm trying out Octagon soap on mine, and will wash yours if it looks safe—it wouldn't be good for such little ones if it made the leaves fall off, do you think. Not bad now. No word from Overlook—they have an order I sent in too. Hope they don't come till it is cool and rains some. We haven't any help here inside or outside so I've had busy times and not got to my story, but will in time. Sometimes when I fall in bed dogtired at night I get a frantic feeling about my story and other things—where is my life? but when I can see over the things it's all right. I like the work in the yard, never get tired, and can think out there or maybe it's dreaming. I know it's not my life though. Half of it avoiding people to whom I can't talk. When I get a letter or a story from you things seem different and real. Must go now. Good luck—is it cold and clear there? What can you see out your window? Have you got a good table. Do you sleep all right.

Love,

E

What I started to say just now was, you don't need to study my story or anybody's to see how it is done, when you know you start at the other end. Being good you start with what you must say and then that tells you how. You know. You know. You know.

September 29, 1946
Dear J—

You help greatly—thanks for the letter. I was glad to get it early—was early walking around the yard. Now with this I hope to get the story in a kind of shape today. How much trouble you went to—I didn't want you to. All your news what I most wished—Danke schoen—it was the rhythm in particular I was anxious to have, it had to go with the name of a child. "Beth Olivia, danke schoen"—has it the rhythm and sound to stay in a character's memory a long time?[12] [. . .] My story and yours have titles out of the same forge. I hope each day yours goes to suit you and please you. It sounds imaginative and open to anything. If you find this growing and getting long, all the more natural and good. You wrote very tightly before, which exerted its own power, but your writing if more loosely held in would be different and yet the same thing—a flower more open is expanded but has the same identity and integrity though you can see more into it. [. . .]

A fine morning—soft air, the woods and river on it. I've seen the fields here, asters and goldenrod, a little haze, the sweet smell of grass. You would sniff the fall, and when you saw the sunset you would be sure. I feel well—happy and thankful for much, life does seem to be opening out and once more sweet. There seems to be energy in this air and I feel I might be doing a lot of work as I never did before. Don't let me write *too* much. In the fullness of time, can we work on the play?

Much love
E

September 30, 1946
Dear Diarmuid,

Your letter got missent to Jackson, Michigan and came in its own sweet time. Thank you and Rosie so much, for saying come up for Christmas—the best invitation anybody can give—but I couldn't leave home then. We are very sentimental here and my family would take it hard if anybody went off at that time—Rosie will understand. There's no family I would rather be with around a tree next to my own and maybe it will snow too and look wonderful and different from our Christmas day which is often mild and like a false day out of spring.[13]

How are things? I guess the fall rush is on in your business. I've been working hard on a couple of stories—before the end of the week I hope to have one on the way up. I warn you it will be long and I don't really know any reason for its length. So far it's named "The Golden Apples of the Sun," much too fine for the story and it made me think of somebody in a gorgeous out-of-place hat and beaming out from under the brim. [. . .] We are having wonderful cool weather—it seems summer is over. Blue haze on the fields, and the wonderful fall sunsets. Lots of energy. Love and thanks again for the invitation. I will be up under another sign or day, some equinox or celebration. Is William studying hard in school?

Yours,

Eudora

October 9, 1946
Wednesday again
Dear John—when I got home here had come the camellia dish—! It is the most perfect thing I ever saw—so beautiful—wide—clear—It is a lovely, perfect thing—there never was such a plate for the flowers—to match this, nothing—You were unable to resist it on sight I know—It really takes my breath away—what is it, Swedish? It is all I can do to wait now for the flowers to open—I believe Kellingtonia will be the first—Will see about the stakes now, and covers, to be ready—though I had said I would not cover this year but harden them—(as I say every year). Best of all I believe *you* will see them on the plate, it just seems so, and what a difference that will make—Somehow when I saw the plate I knew you would come home—

Thanks for the beautiful thing—

Love—

E—

October 23, 1946
Dear John,
[. . .] I've been digging up the soil in my border to see why the bulbs were so shy blooming last year, and though I'd replaced every bit of the

clay there with nice, crumbly nourishing humus, where was it? I don't know, but the clay was back again, and the poor bulbs pressed flat like your watch. It is enough to make one pause, but I've made a good mixture again and put bulbs down again, and will see what happens, hoping. After 21 years of feeding the dirt on this place it is still mysteriously like a brickbat. But camellias do all right in it, and Mrs. Barksdale[14] says mine are the finest looking she has seen—they really are *noble*. Leila is bigger around than the arms can reach, and buds like nuts on a little tree. There are two good shy-blooming sasanquas we can saw off and graft on sometime, right big around and grow like smoke. The apple-blossom sasanqua is full of flowers today—I love those. It still hasn't rained, we had two little rains that didn't count last full of the moon, and while I'm anxious about plants in the drouth, still it is so beautiful, every day fine, and so good to garden in—it's irresistible outside in the morning. Spaded up all this A.M. Those belladonna bulbs are the size of watermelons. Giving them good dirt. Make them bigger. Did you ever think anything of writing a little NYer piece about the seed gatherer of Palestine? She seemed delightful—

Sometimes working on a second piece, very different, is a good thing—they both seem to do better right away. But just a thought, and nothing for you to consider if it doesn't come naturally—I was remembering the story you said a few words about, the funny light one too. Just don't worry for any of it, for when you write the writing is beautiful and very alive, and that is the most I can think of for a story to need. I feel confident in my bones—mind and heart, but *bones* are supposed to be where it counts—that it will be good and really signify something to you this time and please you—Luck to it—I hope things now go well—and love to you, very much and good hopes for story and all—

Yours,

E—

November 4, 1946

Dear John,

The big sack [of redwood bark] came, and the stuff inside looks grand—springy with that million-year-old vitality or something, that I hope will be transmitted to our little camellias, for I put a top dressing the way the folder said, on top of all the sunken pots. This was a big trouble to you I know, and it looks as if they wouldn't ship it themselves and you had to lug it to the P.O. Remember to add on all that postage when you pay yourself back, it was about $3! It came fast that way and I was glad. Thanks to you—I didn't know it would be such a bother when I asked if you'd see about it. Hope to work up the rose bed with it— Mother ordered some roses to go right in. Mrs. Barksdale brought another Doctor—beautiful and I'm about to start a rose cutting bed with that—hope for this. It must be potent stuff—dressing for camellias, rose grower, cutting starter, weed killer, bulb feeder, everything—were you impressed when you took it in your fingers?[15] Yours at home—camellias—I haven't been a bit sure of—washed them off, mulched etc. Fri. morning but they're like elephants not forgetting and no water in August still hangs over them—the plants themselves OK I believe but they may lose their greenness and flowers in the meantime. Two or three of the little ones in your higher up row look well though and will be good plants in spite of everything. Now will try redwood and maybe it will do something extra for the big ones, make them all new by spring. Have news, one of the grafts, the one around to the side, is putting out shoots from the scions, new shoots—so I watch it daily and keep it still watered and shaded. Have put fiber on the cuttings I rooted this year, found there were 13 not 10, and all sound looking and nice, so this should invigorate them to some healthy growth by next year. May pot them, with fiber, and start a new camellia cutting bed, worked up with fiber—they say you can try cuttings in November. No telling how many will be growing around here. The Daikagura is about to open a flower today, the first camellia— it may wait until tomorrow. A soft, cloudy, cool day. It is a beautiful glowing bud the size of a plum.

Love—

E

November 10, 1946
Saturday night
Dear John—

The most beautiful night sky—full moon and racing clouds—the clouds pure white and long and traveling fast, north from the southwest—brilliant dark-blue of sky in between—the planets bright and full-looking too, in and out—The air fresh, leaves on the trees stirring, flying—shadows in all kinds of agitation—all bright everywhere—makes you *look back* at it—the world, to come in a house—Those moments when you are without the name of where you are—just on the surface of the world—under that star—I'm hoping you feel fine tonight, have decided about the incidents of the story, and put it from you—Much love—goodnight—It was so urgent and beautiful.

Sunday

[. . .] I do hope now you will be content with this story and put it from you. [. . .] I *know* there is nothing to worry about. Your writing is so tremendous to me, and so great a thing to me, it fills me with great happiness. I want it to make *you* happy, and not anxious—It must, I think, it would make you happy to do a fine thing and you have done it. Just let it flow—just let it be easy when it's easy and strong when it's strong. Trust it. Your writing is full of life—it can accommodate a great deal, my dear, knowledge and certainty and doubt itself included—pain and joy, that too. Writing is a way of knowing and ways to know can be beautiful or ugly—but yours is beautiful and abundant all the way along and I would drop anything at your opening word and come away and listen—each time like new—each word takes hold of me—I knew it would—

Rainy night—I hope you're having a good meeting with the Vardamans[16]—Seeing more of San Francisco—Hope the new story comes in the morning—Will try to send you one soon—Have 2 more in my head—and send you my love and hope the luck is all you hope for or better—A nice rest this weekend to you—

Goodnight and love—

In October, Welty had suggested to Robinson that the two of them should produce their own magazine. "I think it might be quite something," she wrote, but only if the idea appealed to Robinson (10.25.46). Apparently Robinson was interested, and felt ready to ask Russell to become his agent ("So glad you're getting Diarmuid. . . . You do like the magazine idea," she wrote on 11.8.46). Welty's letters from the first week in November suggest that Robinson was discussing the idea with people he knew in California. Later that month, Welty made a trip to New York to investigate possible backers for their venture. She discussed it with Russell, Allen Tate, and editors for magazines owned by Randolph Hearst, and was very optimistic in her reports to Robinson (11.27.46). Ultimately, this funding would not materialize, and the magazine idea would be abandoned.

Welty spent that Thanksgiving with the Russells, who urged her to stay through Christmas, but her plans changed. Robinson invited her to come to San Francisco, and in mid-December she took a train from New York to the West Coast (12.9.46 to Robinson). On Christmas, Welty wrote the Russells to thank them for their gift of a clock: "This morning in the hotel room I have, John and a friend of his and I had our Christmas tree—a real one, with some stuff on it, and some very small presents under the tree as we were poor, and the clock dressed up things and went off, the alarm, as I took it out of the box" (12.25.46).

Welty remained in San Francisco until late March 1947. Her letters to Russell discussed West Coast plants, business (William Maxwell could not persuade the other New Yorker *editors to accept her story "The Whole World Knows"), her work in progress, and Robinson. "I think John feels some better, and is trying to get a good long list of things written," she wrote on January 10, 1947. In February, after the* Atlantic *turned down a story by Robinson, Welty wrote, "John is not in the best of health or spirits. I get worried at times. I'm under no illusion I help him any because that has to come from himself, but it seems hard not to be able. My hope is a story will sell and he will get interested and confident enough to throw himself into writing. The way he feels now, he might just leave S. F. one day, it wouldn't surprise me" (2.9.47). Russell, however, was not convinced that writing would improve things. "If John's mind is uneasy, restless there is no cure except from within" he wrote Welty. "If he wishes to write, really wishes, then that would be good but if it is merely a half-longing, a sort of medicine it doesn't help much" (2.13.47). Meanwhile Welty worked on a new story set in the city she was exploring.*

March 11, 1947
Dear Diarmuid,

This is the most beautiful day you ever saw—it's really springtime, with the grass so slick and green, and all kinds of flowering branches being brought in and sold on the corners, and clear blue sky today—birds, everything. I wish you could look in on it. It sounds so cold and dark there. It doesn't seem right or necessary for people to have to live in the weather of New York. People are out all over the streets today strolling and idling, or they look like it. I have been. As you see, I didn't leave, and I don't know just when I will—I wonder if there can be a real necessity—why should there be? My feeling that worries me is that I left in November for *two weeks*—and though I had no way of knowing I would end up here and like it and have luck with a place to live, it looks sort of underhand or wrong, with my family almost weekly expecting me I think. I feel so well here. And when it's not cold I am so much better in health—have gained weight and sleep pretty well at night. John seemed to be so much better when he was over Sunday that I was very heartened—his look and all seemed different—maybe this makes me feel changed in spirits, for it's bad to see a friend suffer and know you can't really help. I hope he keeps on feeling improved until all is well with him again. How my writing goes out here you will have to judge, 20 pages are typed up but today it looks like about 10 more ahead.[17] I have all the time in the world and a nice quiet room, though expensive for me in a hotel—I bring home a little piece of cake or a cracked crab and eat it in the room sometimes. Your trip to Boston must have been a nice change, though wasn't it cold there? No, I won't be a lawnmower on your new lawn, because remember I was not on the side of cutting down the trees, so that lets me sit in the shade and drink beer.[18] It must afford plenty of snow just now for a tremendous snow man. How are all the healths? I do hope no more colds and flu. Take care of yourselves. Write me when there's free time—I'll let you know if I feel I have to go.

With love,

Eudora.

Did you see the awful quote of a Jackson garden club in N.Y.er?[19] Mother (not *her* club) wrote she was *humiliated*—

P.S. at P.O.—just got Rosie's forwarded letter with the pictures—so pleased to have them—love to all.

March 23, 1947

San Francisco

Dear Diarmuid:

I owe you letters, but I keep thinking I'll have the story typed to the finish to enclose, and it drags out, so I'll send a plain letter. Many thanks for the fine H. B. money—it looked lovely. Thanks also for the other check, for German rights. It's good news the camellia came to its senses—didn't I tell you they were temperamental creatures, prima donnas? I hope it improves in its morals by next year. It really was supposed to bloom when it first started, I believe, and maybe these buds are some that came later and nothing got wrong with them mentally. Did I ever remember to tell you I can't get the camellia you picked out? For the life of me now I can't remember which one it was, but if you remember (or I can look up in letters at home) I can try again now. Varieties are often unavailable before blooming season and then after it growers will sell. I'm not giving you Wolf wolf this time, for I'm going home this Thursday, though I might come back some time, for it's a lovely city. The trouble is I'm paying daily rates at a hotel, which can't continue for ever, and a better place to stay seems not to turn up. I'll get home Sunday night, and I hear it's Spring in Mississippi. The tulip noses sound promising for Katonah too. I'd love to see what you've got hold of in that line. The tulips in florists' shops here are at the top of their magnificence and when you see whole tubs of nodding pure white ones, like wavy trees, it takes your breath away. My story will probably get to you in the week. John's read a version of it, I've done it over a few times, and thinks it's depressing, so I warn you. It is, too, but I hadn't realized anything but the work part of it, until I got to typing it up and can hardly drag through it—sounds worse every minute, doesn't it? I'll be anxious to know what you think of it, for I did a lot of hard work on this baby. [. . .]

Good luck with the long story, though it's a long shot and I fear you will have to work very hard if you sell it. If everything in my new book looks sad so far, I'm going to write some gay ones.

Love,
Eudora

April 6, 1947
Jackson, MS
Dear Diarmuid,

How is spring? Coming along, I hope. My trip home was a nice one. [. . .]

Spring had come here about 3 weeks late, and it has done everything now in the last three days. The trees are coming out—in the woods the dogwood and redbud and yellow Jessamine are everywhere. My garden was in the last flowering of daffodils and camellias—I've been working hard fertilizing them and cleaning out the iris beds. Will send you up some of the camellia fertilizer that you can use at your discretion—it is strong stuff, but the people like Gerbing[20] recommend it. You might blame it with the odd performance of your camellias last year, so do as you think best.

I plan to go down in the deep country soon and ponder on a new story—I wrote part of it but need to see things a bit down there.

Mother told me she hadn't written to acknowledge the various things you sent for her to open, thinking I would, for she told me—so excuse the remiss manners on our part. All came safely. I thought she had reported.

Saw some beautiful white tulips yesterday in somebody's garden—also some beauties in yellow. Are yours looking hopeful? I think they're the finest spring flowers of all, and I'm going to grow them next year—though it means digging them up after flowering, storing, and freezing in the refrigerator for a couple of weeks before planting again. The Dutch iris is blooming now. Our roses look fine and should be in flower before long. I hope your spring doesn't keep you waiting long. Send reports.

Love to all—hope you're all in good health—are you?

Yours,

Eudora

May 12, 1947

Dear John,

A soft spring night and I am wondering how your plans go. It rained about half an hour in the afternoon, gently, and I am glad because we had had dry days with wind. The new growth on the little camellias stood up tall. Today I moved them from their old place which was for wintertime up against the sunny garage wall into the part shade of the big pine tree beyond the Leila, sinking the pots in the earth again.

I went back to work today, some gardening, typing and all, and think I'm about all right again. Went for a short ride about sunset, saw a little rose—begged a cutting. It is a deep velvety red one, so simple it's like a French rose or a Damask one of the old old flowers of this world seems like. Like a red Rosa Mundi. So dark red it's like a dark fruit, a cherry. A little larger in size than a Louis Philippe, and simpler, a coronet of gold stamens within. A climber—did I say. I've been putting white roses in the pewter bowl you gave me—also sometimes those little common primroses—to me beautiful and a flower that should be considered.

[. . .]

Mother dreamed you were coming home on a boat. I'm wondering if you might be giving things a little time—just a little more, so as not to rush yourself—or if you have already gone off into the north and the desert grandness. It is cool and nice tonight—fresh.

Love,

Eudora

May 22, 1947

Dear John,

Blackberry winter we're having—cool and bright today.

Have you written your new story, in part or all? Am anxious for it to come—Have typed 48 pages of G. Apples and it will be about 20 more before I send.

Do you remember "marbelized" pomegranate flowers? Very double like carnations. Just put one in Virgie Rainey's breast.[21] Pomegranates flowering now—They are always too quick in my garden and bloom with the iris, and look harsh, but with the iris gone, they're all right. Mexico has come back to me a lot lately[22]—it's the weather—and smell of cool, and soft rain—perhaps some flowers I've forgotten—not the butterfly lilies, which aren't yet in bloom. Maybe it was going barefooted in the rain across the yard.

What day of the month is this—The way you see it do you think we probably won't meet now for some time?

A baby fox spent the night in our house (Francois). He just crawled in a sack—He didn't even bark—What next? He was gray. Never saw the stars so bright as last night (I was waiting for the little fox to bark). Their colors showed clearly—all the constellations so plain—Down under them the lightning bugs.

[. . .] 2 little seedling camellias are growing under the Sacco—Very pleased—They must be Magnoliaflora seedlings though—finer still—

Can't help but hope things will look up about seeing you before so long. Then who knows, maybe my back wouldn't break any more[23]—How beautiful it is here now—the green still clean, very full leaf every where now—more roses will come in June—Day lilies—an evening blooming one, with petals just the color and substance of the new moon, opens just at that hour—Rain lilies—

Love,

E

In August Welty went to Seattle for the Northwest Pacific Writer's Workshop, where she delivered a lecture on the short story. After a few days in Seattle, she traveled to San Francisco for another extended stay.

August 22, 1947
Dear Diarmuid,

Two nice letters from you in two days—was glad to get. [. . .] John is writing something today in Berkeley, I think—he has come to some clear conclusions about what he wants to do and they are original and good and if only somebody would buy something. I think I'll stay here awhile—would so like to see you, but it's so far just now—I wish you and Rose could come out. It would do you good to get away from the Westchester rites[24] and the rest, however fine it is—there can just be too much of the same thing for anybody to breathe freely. It's nice for old people. Not us. I mean, to keep the same, see the same. I thought of renting a little place (if I can get it) for a few months—settling in with my typewriter—if I can, I really wish you and R. could take off and visit me—think of how nice it would be. As to the next story collection—I'm not sure I want the book to come out yet. Do you understand, for I think the stories in it are all of a certain kind, or of a long, ruminative, etc. turn of thought—and it would be nice to have one or two kinds in a book—do you agree? The longish story I started in Jackson doesn't look so good to me now—I worked on it yesterday—it may or may not turn out—but I want to send you a few others before a book is put together. Let me know your feelings on it. [. . .]

The camellia is certainly an eccentric, like all its family, so the only thing to do is let it alone, I guess. It *should* be setting buds, though. When I left home all mine had little tight hard buds, and one or two crazies had big buds. We had a terrific drouth after I left, the driest summer since 1927 or something, and my mother stayed and valiantly watered things but we don't know. She is now in West Va. and we hear it is stormy and rainy at home.

I guess you saw Bilbo died.[25]

Write me about the new plants. What kinds of azaleas did you order? I love the big loose white flowered ones. I passed through Canby, Ore., on my way down from Seattle and looked out the window for Julia E. Clark's lily farm, but didn't see it. How are yours doing? Can you grow Watsonias there? I was thinking of the new rock garden, and the marshy place—have never seen Watsonias but they sound so beautiful.

[. . .] This hotel is a little one, clean and cheap, that's all, but OK, and right around the corner from Chinatown. The other day I walked around in it and tried on some Chinese clothes—like them. It is a cheap place to eat, fairly. My health is all right, still taking exercises and have had no bad aches.

This is all I know just now—it's too long a letter to come on Monday—but you can read it Tuesday. Write when you can—don't work too hard—you will take some kind of vacation, won't you—maybe ride across the country and come back to San Francisco?

Love
E

P.S. Did Rosie get some chocolates from Chicago, I forgot to put a card and she knows so many people from there she wouldn't know who was putting her and chocolates together. Has Will caught another fish?

To Robinson in Laytonville, CA, from Welty in San Francisco
September 12, 1947
Dear John,

Thanks for the letters—your Monday one just came—Friday afternoon about five o'clock. So you might be gone from Laytonville. It sounds far and high and beautiful, your trip—cold though—(I don't know how warm a sleeping bag is?)—[. . .]

It's good to know you have hold of something you think you might really work with—I hope it's taking its course well—riding with you— that you will feel good about doing it. Oh it *must*, if it has given you that premonition—Then the other things will settle themselves maybe as far as they go—place and all—I hope the work as it gets done is a kind of transparent thing—through which so much—so much will come through of its own power and radiation—I don't know if you feel as I do, but I think some writing can when it's good *of its own* reach a kind of finality, and this is it, and what I hope for yours. Sure it will be labor— and you couldn't ever do it in a rooming house—privacy will mean everything. Do I conflict with it, or could I help you keep it,—can you tell? Can *I*—? I cherish it. It's been beautiful weather, and still is in the middle of the day, but this time of afternoon the fog rolls in—one night I felt I was on an island—I could just see little yellow dull light, one. I hope the sleeping bag *is* warm.

I've walked around these parts—Broadway is up the hill a little and there's all the Bay down under—the ships crossing it and so on. Have been working mostly, have almost done a story, guess I'll finish typing it up tonight—it's called Lake of the Moon—yes, Moon Lake, but I wanted a step back—[. . .] Will you be coming home one day soon? I haven't really cooked much, just the simplest, but I have in mind this cake.

Have a good trip—it is so fine to see the places, and how is it some beautiful spot in a far part of the world makes you see all clear a place at the other end. It will be good to hear everything—the best of luck to the trip and the shape of the work—bring the news—

Love

E

My health has been fairly good, but the beds and the hills of SF keep me exercising like mad to get back at them.

Bring me a little yellow leaf.

You should have the freezer, and make snow ice cream and eat it by Lake Louise.

No news—my story in H Bazaar.[26] The O Henry came out and I went to see if I won any of the prizes but I didn't. Art's book is still not the solid object, that anyone has seen.[27]

Russell and Welty continued to speculate about the stories that were unfolding. Welty wrote that "perhaps the short story I've been working on just lately may be a part of the novel too—hadn't realized that, till yesterday on a cable car. I got the idea and they clanged the bell like mad" (9.2.47). Russell replied, "I begin to suspect that what you really are is a dislocated novelist and that bit by bit as you go on you'll start reintegrating stories. Are you sure that Ida M'Toy, The Sketching Trip and A Visit to Charity aren't really pieces of a novel and how about Old Mr. Granada, The Pageant of Birds and The Wide Net as part of another. Think. At any rate I suspect that we'd better wait the short story collection till the bells have stopped clanging in your mind" (9.5.47). After Welty sent him another story, "Moon Lake," Russell wrote, "I think your sub-conscious must be at work and it must still have quite a lot of work to do [. . .] . But I leave this to you and to the unseen powers in your head. I think it is true that something is

*being worked out and I'm going to be as curious as can be till the task
gets completed" (9.26.47). When he received "Shower of Gold" from
Welty in October, Russell sent her a list of the stories and the characters' ages in each. He wrote, "I can see now in a vague way that your
mind has some pattern it is bent on establishing—not a novel but a
series of stories. And I think you're making all sorts of questions come
to mind" (10.7.47). At almost the same time, Welty wrote Russell from
San Francisco, "I don't know where I'll go from here—I feel not very
good in spirits—maybe better soon" (10.6.47).*

October 10, 1947
Dear Diarmuid,

Thanks for the letters—I've felt cheered to get them. You had the idea
along with me about the interrelated stories—which is cheering too—
and I am glad you like the idea, for it interests me and I think the reason
is that I want to see some of those people again later—or maybe earlier—
and in other places perhaps. So I'll go ahead—In one letter I'd meant to
send you a little time schedule I'd made, but see I didn't, and will here—I
think you have precocious children at home, so you make mine younger
than I did—especially Loch, my Loch couldn't have been as young as
Will, 5, to go down the tree and be interested in the house and all.[28] I had
him 9. Anyway here is the little outline [. . .] .

Thanks—about coming there—yes I know I can anytime and how
nice it would be. The spring would be better, though, when I could see
your azaleas in flower (did they come, or is embargo going to do them
any harm? I hope they aren't balled and Burlaped in some RR station—).
I haven't any warm clothes along with me, and own no warm coat. Thank
you though. Maybe next I can get the stories in this book finished, and
come sailing up in triumph with the little stack. The camellia sounds
in good shape—now I hope it behaves. Since it didn't produce much of
anything last year, this year it ought to have a lot of energy stored up
(they sort of do well alternately, biennially) and shoot the moon this year.
Hope so. [. . .]

Love,
Eudora

Jackson
November 12, 1947
Dear Diarmuid,

Here I am in Mississippi, and thanks for the letters here and I got the two big checks. You are probably having a holiday today and maybe the lilies had come and you got them in the ground. How are the azaleas looking? Yes, if the camellia doesn't act right this year, burn it. It has gone far enough.[29] I came back and looked over some of the antics of mine while I was away, and think the whole tribe should be taught a lesson. Maybe they can hear this low rumble of discontent if we practice it around them, and will heed, fearing the guillotine.

The Italian Wide Net—how much better is the Mediterranean title of Primo Amore—is here and I didn't know I could write so beautifully, I opened the book and loved the way it seemed to sound. So admire myself in other languages. Are the leaves all fallen there? They are still on the trees here, some of them bright and lovely—we had a nice little rain yesterday to break the drouth and today is fine and cold. Nothing is like that Arizona air though and that fine, fine cold, and the yellow aspen trees. The whole state is amazing and beautiful, and I'm trying to track down some books about it—such old country. The Indians there though are starving, truly, it is said. People seem to be investigating, but not doing anything about it yet—

Glad the little brush didn't break and no telling what it will paint. The paper flower I thought was one of those that opens in water, but we are gypped. Excuse it please. The sasanqua camellias are in flower in my yard, at least the pink one is—looks nice. The bulbs are coming up since the rain. Our peonies came from Wayside today.

Love,
Eudora

To Robinson in Berkeley; forwarded to a Los Angeles address
November 13, 1947
Dear John,

How are you today, I wonder? I hope the fever has gone and all is cleared up and you will rout it for good some way. Let me know for I think of you sick in a cold room. Do things about this—What kind of day is it? It's a soft gray day in Mississippi—the trees are colored, quiet colors, leaves on the ground, and piles burning here and there. With one more little rain the spade will go in the ground. There's some work to do, a lot, I suppose. The roses are blooming some, the cuttings have grown up and opened flowers. The reds are so fine. The last butterfly lilies, on the shaggy stalks—with butterflies—the crape myrtle trees with plum–colored leaves, pecans yellow, tallow trees every color and the little berries pearly in their black husks, coming out. These are frosty mornings—the cool feels fresh, nice. Camellias satisfactory. I stood holding the plate—like the White Knight who carried his on horseback, always ready in case of plum cake.[30] I don't think I will cover this year—they must just learn, and take it.

K. Sawada has a splendid flower bud. Oh I would cover that.

[…] I've had out my book on the red figured vases which I lifted from the Times office and have been looking at faces and bodies of recent friends of the Berkeley library etc. Heracles is always just wonderful—big black eyes and as exuberant as all get out. This one I traced (badly) is Perseus cutting off Medusa's head. Since *we* have to look at Medusa, she is pretty,—or is that why? They are all so magnificent and alive that it makes the heart beat fast to see them—I thought that when I stole the book. [. . .] Arizona is a place I feel compelled to go back to—how much of it did you ever see? It's the northern part, the high plateau and aspen tree part, that just held me. It is a beautiful place. I keep thinking of it. When I was there I felt that in such clarity was where we all ought to be. That your sinus would go, and Art's asthma, and not just that, but ailments aside, it was the place. The mountains came up over the horizon when you went a distance, proving the world round for you like ships, you could see clear to the curve of the world. [. . .]

I hope you are well and astir—

much love

Eudora

To Robinson in Los Angeles
November 17, 1947
Dear John,

I'm real glad to hear—and to know your disease is better but the cough at night doesn't sound good. Let me know if it's better. Is "smog" whatever that is any better than the murk of San Francisco—I dread for you to breathe anything with a name like that with that trouble in the respiratory system. Let me know how you feel. It really gets me—the situation. Who would know if you got sick in bed. Would you tell me? For the good it would do—[. . .]

Have worked (manual) all day last 3 days. Just cleaning up leaves, weeds, old branches from the storm etc. and toting in wheelbarrow out to the street. I wish you could see the crape myrtle trees. Flame. The dogwoods are pretty too—and not cut down to decorate Signor Podesta's shop. I think I wrote you your little Sawada has a flower bud—you might not get the letter.

Will you go to a doctor there? [. . .] I feel very troubled about it because it sounded not too far from pneumonia and I don't know how careful you are or can be, in this room, I don't know if it's heated?

Please take care. Write and say how you feel. Things aren't right. Do you think they are?

The weather's been nice—soft rain or soft bright sun—I haven't been happy here but I don't know what I would have been if you hadn't got sick, for all the way home I thought *anyway* you would have your fine, your damn solitude—it's scary for you to be sick down there, the Foffs could have at least talked to you on the telephone in SF and I'd written and asked them how you sounded.

I'll write to this LA address again, if you change let me know where you go. If the smog comes in, you will leave—won't you? I'm glad you left the fog. Remember to see a doctor—take care.

Love
Eudora

December 3, 1947
Dear Diarmuid,

Are you feeling well again? Hope you could eat a fine Thanksgiving dinner, and had a fine weekend with bright weather. I note you went to the office Friday—sad. Thanks for the Swedish cash. Nice manna.

It's lovely here still, the leaves still on the trees for good part, and bright as gold and all the colors. Just a startling fall. I've had a lot of work to do in the yard, since there was nobody to help all summer, and have been cutting away dead stuff and pruning long summer runners on the shrubs, getting up some of the deepest pinestraw and all such rather boring stuff. Winterblooming iris had a flower or two, and the sasanqua camellias are as thickly blooming as azaleas—covered with bees—smelling sweet. The bulbs are up, not high, and all the seedpods around are pretty, berries, etc. Roses fine. I'm trying to set out pansies now. It's wonderful to get away to the woods, though our backyard looks just as brilliant. [. . .]

Mercy, what *do* your children want for Christmas? They have got to an older age. My little niece, aged three, longs for "a little clock"—like the one you and Rosie gave me. [. . .] I haven't given a thought to Christmas, except thinking where to get a little whiskey for the eggnog. Better stir the old brain.

Love,

Eudora

February 8, 1948

Dear Diarmuid,

Where's your coat? Dolly[31] says you're not wearing it *yet*—I'll tell you with frozen fingers (snowing here now) it would warm you and others too if you would. I'm handing you an Overcoat Tract. [. . .]

I've been trying to write ever since Christmas and only do badly. Maybe with spring things will turn out better. Thanks for the Levee contract. Mr. Wasson called me up last night to say they were getting ready to go to press[32] [. . .] .

Is your camellia behaving, it ought to be glad it's left Mississippi, and got a nice home.[33] The plants lived through all the snow and ice storms, many flowers were killed, and maybe the remaining ones were nipped this time—as we had 44 predicted and got 23 in the night—when I woke up they were all stiff as glass, poor things, and some of them with open flowers—a whole week of nice warm gentle rain had passed. Is there any news with you? I think we should all just hibernate, or maybe that's what we're doing. Wish you and Rosie could come down for our spring, if there is a good enough one, it would be sun and green that much earlier. Robins and redbirds are singing all the time already and the crocuses and white hyacinths were in bloom, and one *pink*, but they're every one ice maidens today.

Love—good luck

Eudora

Robinson had left San Francisco in December 1947; Welty told Russell,
"I came back from an overnight trip to New Orleans to find him meet-
ing my train" (12.15.47). By February, Welty was writing to Robinson at
a new address—DeLisle, Mississippi.

February 17, 1948
Dear John,

Good, another letter from De Lisle.[34] Your place sounds delightful now—and you're getting it all fixed up. Name me that camellia better—[. . .]

One freeze after another has hit us, but two soft days now, 72, and I believe things will come out now, the white hyacinths and crocuses already have, now one blue hyacinth, and out on the road there was a green field. I almost can't bear to stay in, but have a deadline to meet, copy for Levee Press, and must type all day today and tomorrow, did that yesterday. To the best of my belief I got the story much better, too. Also shortened it in the process from 46 to about 52 pages.[35] All the time that story was happening to Eugene McLain who had left Battle Hill, Ran's twin, the little sons in Shower of Gold—which cleared everything up—it just came to me in time. Maybe it won't be so bad now as a little book to itself. Another thing I've done was destroy about 60 pages I'd written since Christmas, so I have a clean table, one little corner. But no new story finished like you.[36] Are we letting the Rite wait—or what? [. . .]

Pear trees budding here—the day after my work's finished I'm off to walk around in Jackson Square and the Park, to see there.

Yesterday Diarmuid wrote the snow rose in 8 foot walls on each side of his road—I told him now he knew about the Natchez Trace. Said he's a bit curious about the day when it all melts. His camellia is doing all right.

I feel like burning the Clarion Ledger every morning. Well, I just won't go into it. And the Legislature a disgrace every day, and altogether Mississippi seems to get more hopeless all the time. Jeze! The other day a bill was proposed wherebody (whereby anybody) who didn't like Mississippi could get a free ticket out of it, the state to provide the RR fare and a ten dollar bill to spend when you've got out. Hooray! I'll be the first one—I'll go somewhere nice and be a twenty-minute queen.[37] [. . .]

Good luck—my respects to the Beins[38]—must get to work. D. wrote he was seeing about a sublet for me, and maybe that's what I needed, for somebody just to take me in hand. He urges me to get my book finished soon and I think that's a good idea too. Sansom[39] has a story in Accent, will send if you like, but remember you said you had best keep away from books and stories—Oh, I dreamed that the freeze caused some exotic seed to spring up on the Gulf Coast that had never taken life before (paradox, sounds like), a perfectly wonderful, amazing tree.

    Yours
    Eudora

March 19, 1948

Dear J—to see you was so fine—thanks for our visit—I wish all this around me were DeLisle still, and I would see your evening moth on this windowscreen—and you would be putting in the last stick of wood, chances are, the spring wind rising—that same star and moon, it's just dark. All was good—and wasn't it fair and lovely all the time? I wish it had been that way all the time. To think of leaving, the last night, was the only thing that didn't have any joy about it to me. Days picked out—You had all so nice for us, did too much as always, and to be there was enough. [. . .] We got here about 4:30, plenty of time for Dorothy to catch her bus—for you brought us through that Coast traffic and fog, and caught us up speed—did you get back in time too? It was fine having you come a little way, always that much of the way better. Was your bridge still open? We had a nice ride back and were coming out pink all the way—not tired at all—the spring was rolling backwards as we came north, dogwood folding itself up again—but soon now. The flowers might root—and I would like to bring something to DeLisle too. I like DeLisle and admire its world—and hope it is good to work in for you, if you like, and the weather keeps, and a very splendid story will come—another. It was nice to walk the way we did and come on violets, the black water turkey diving, the big sky and long interesting ways stretching away, the old boat in the trees,—all that and the gracious people,—to be abroad in it or to be still in it or what, couldn't grow old—It was good we could stay as long as we could—I could always have had that same wish to stay longer. It was all lucky. As long as a visit wouldn't interrupt what you came for but could help celebrate it. I think to write a story and then walk in the woods is good, and one thing is working and one is celebrating, but maybe there, of all places, they could be more side by side, two flowers from one stalk in the hand—do you think?

Came home and put the flowers in water, and ate blackeyed peas for supper—after feasts and picnics I guess it was about right. The sun here had brought out the G. Washington suddenlike, and the Sacco, and Leila bearing long loads on every arm, and the Florentine species tulips did open, the ones like golden Turkish slippers—[...]

The wind stirring the trees, that rushing sound. A lovely night. Hope you have a nice weekend—and that the Beins are well, if you see them give my best to them—how is their dog? Ask Charlie about the rose (mermaid). So glad we came—can look forward to another time. I think absence is no *light* thing—yours, to me—ever. It's so good to be over. There was a moment when I touched a post in the sun, on the porch— like "now". You know how real as a warm post it can be to see the brightest and most dancing vision—and how always that post is it—It's always so, when we take a walk in the Mayes Lake parts or your woods, and then it's the way a blue lake flows over some old busy city, beautiful and deep and still holding the city in it but brimming some bigger and older walls still, and reflecting sky, and full of water life, lake life, too—it's the real vision I see with my real eyes, what was there all the time. Restored. And though everything has been all right, I couldn't see the blue lake.

Love, and will write news of All this J and All this J tomorrow—I will mail this tonight if the car comes home—Walter out in it—Take care, all's well I hope, in DeLisle, goodnight—

Yours,

E

April 12, 1948
Dear Diarmuid,

Thanks for the letters—with contract and nice cash, for which thanks too. Here's the signed paper. I'm glad to hear spring really got there—and hope she disposes herself about graciously and stays without any more fidgeting. Any lily signs? Maybe they will decide to bloom somewhat late, so you'll get a sight of them after all, even if you do go away in July.

A letter from Rosie too (I've been away—back to DeLisle again for a shrimp cooking and picnic and all—fine) and will answer right off. Don't

let Eileen be counting on me to live with her—with thanks all the same—
I like Eileen but couldn't take an apt. with anybody and do work.[40] Eileen
won't think this, of course, but it's true and I'm firm. Dolly's asked me
to stay with her which is congenial and all, but I still would have to be
by myself to get anything typed up. Looks now as if I'll content myself
with a brief visit anyway, not a long stay—don't put out any more feelers
about apts. anyway, for it could be trouble to you for nothing. I guess the
fact is I have a case of spring fever as usual, and don't really know what I
will want to do—and always hate, spring or fall, a plan ahead that ties me
down. Mary Lou wrote me about a big apt. that costs very little, only the
owner would share it (a gentleman) except for weekends—which again
would defeat all. I feel I'm being ungracious to people who try to help
me, and am being finicky as everything, but know how I am. It's all part
of a proof that the city is not for me. Why can't people, friends, move
freely and meet by delightful surprise and chance, and not make plans?
A rhetorical question being sent in to New York City. Anyway I'll probably come up in May and then see the look of things and how much I feel
able to do. It will be ever so fine to see you.

[. . .]—Hope all goes well—Will see you before long, no doubt. It's
deep spring here—much work outside to do.

Love,
Eudora

*Welty went to New York in May 1948; for part of that summer, she and
another writer friend, Hildegarde (Hildy) Dolson, house-sat in Westchester County. Welty and Dolson were working on a musical revue
which would eventually be titled* What Year Is This? [41]

*Robinson was now taking graduate classes at UC–Berkeley. He
sent the following letter to Welty in Westchester. No other letters from
Robinson to Welty in this period are extant.*

July 19 1948
Dear E—

Hooray! Looking forward to the show. Success to all. Tried right off to
write a song for it (from the conversation that goes on next door to me.)
[. . .] I wrote some more but shamed to send it, not good. [. . .]

Know you are having a good time with Dolly and all. Your trip must have been wonderful. Would like to just drop and hear and see some of your things for the show. [. . .]

No writing but there's time and DeLisle is going round in my head like a cloud (hanging moss?). Now I must write it down to understand it all. It only occurs to me in little pieces.

Much love. The clock still runs and alarms, the coffee still drips and the poacher does my eggs. [. . .]

I hope you are well and having a good time.

Love, J

Hello to Hildy—

That summer, both Welty and Dolson completed skits for their revue, but Welty's interest in the project seemed to be waning when she returned to Mississippi in September. The following letter was written to Russell from Jackson. Welty was still planning on a collection containing stories about a small town in Mississippi. She did not think this book should be called a novel, but she felt it was more than just a group of separate stories.

Early September 1948

Dear Diarmuid,

Thanks for the letter. Hope all's going well up there—the Sunday Tribune said our storm was going to be an interference over the long holiday, hope it wasn't. We had a day long and night long piece of it, litter to clean up—thank heaven the coast escaped the damage of last summer.

Well, I'm working on a story, just couldn't help it—started coming in my head so fast while I was riding along one day I was writing it with one hand and driving with the other, and I was so glad to see it—hope to send it to you in the week—it may, too, connect too closely with others—and somehow, now, I'm more pleased with the idea of the book of the stories than I was. Maybe prematurely. You might when you see this make a little composition of them all in your head and see how it looks, I mean an over-all picture?

[. . .] Much love to all—I miss you. It's lovely here now—greener than most Septembers, some rain fell in August, and the fall roses are beginning. When Rosie shook her head over me, she may have been right—the ceiling fell. A fact, and means a new roof on our house—about $500—so a trip back looks uncertain especially when I've already pleasured myself the summer long. Will see. (My mother's fixed income won't allow these days for any such things and I can't let her eke out or worry or borrow,— you know.)

Do you suppose I might stand a chance of a Guggenheim if I applied? Would Lambert[42] recommend? Or who—not KAP, she mightn't want to, doesn't write me, and didn't like my last book—wouldn't ask her. Just occurred to me—Remember to bring the little camellia in, or has the time come to give it away. Planted some ripe seeds from mine the other morning—always wish for a magical surprise.

Love,
Eudora

September 23, 1948
Dear John, has school [UC–Berkeley] started, and is it interesting this time? Maybe there is time and good feeling for putting your story down. All the best to it—wishes and love for it. Is it colder now? I hope the fog doesn't come down, at least most of the day. [. . .] A fine cool cloudy morning, quiet, hope for rain. It's been hot and dry again and have watered daily. Many seeds ripening on camellias and I plant—think now of a seedbed and a place to transplant the ones coming up from seed— with some two and three year olds—to watch. They say if you graft them seedlings bloom without having to wait so eternally. Be prepared for a story to come—I'm half through typing, it looks oh, long—I'm writing before I'm tired at end of day. There are several things I wish I could ask you about now, before the final form—but will wait and see if anything seems to you to go too far. It's loosely reined—I think that's right—do you, in this, when you see it? [. . .]

Would like to go on writing to you—have read nothing good lately— the Faulkner never has come—must get to work. I love you, you know it. When I do wrong in it it nearly kills me. Part of me too slow, part too fast, maybe. Wish I could be transformed and made even and bright.

Hope a good day there—
Love,
E

The following day Welty sent Russell and Robinson the story she had been writing, "The Hummingbirds." In 1949, a revised version, entitled "The Wanderers," appeared as the final story in The Golden Apples.

September 30, 1948
Dear J—

Glad for your special—Makes all the difference. And you wrote me soon, knowing how I felt. Good to know you think the work done all right—you were right, it was my utmost just now. Would be glad of things that occurred to you if you would tell me—had some thoughts too—maybe same ones. You put beauty in the stories when they come to you—reading. Are you writing too? I've been having strong feelings you might be busy at something new. Whatever it is, I hope all has been and will be well, and lucky—to please you.

I rode out in the country—it had been a cold damp day—about 5 o'clock the light broke out all over the fields. The gravel roads out Old Canton Road Way—they were a bit muddy, made a little sound riding over—the hills in deep flowers and pink grass, and then the haystacks—bitterweed and goldenrod and coreopsis, the willow trees turning, a persimmon tree hanging full—a fresh wild scent coming out of everything. The fields brighter than the sky, all lovely and slanting and the near trees hanging drops and bright.

Love, and goodnight to you—thanks for reading my story with all your goodness and knowing—and the undeserved praise too I cherish—Who else has you to see, always has? How else could I?

Yours,
E

October 4, 1948
Dear Diarmuid,

Thanks for the letters—felt glad to know you thought the story all right. Hard work on it. For sales, probably too long—but no matter about that. [. . .]

Wish I could have come back up—but plans do you that way. Should never fool with making too many. The house seems fixed up all right now, except for plaster that has to be put back in the ceiling. We get offers of $45,000 etc. for house every now and again—but (a) have nowhere to go—the town is mushrooming with little shingled shacks as everywhere, and all costly whatever is available, and (b) no place to put the money in case we moved into one side of our duplex apt. next door down the street. My mother also is one of the people who would be sacrificing something to uproot herself, at her age. I'm inclined to push the problem off, as I hate and am ignorant of deals, etc. so I guess we'll just stay here a while anyway. I don't like possessions and the only thing I'd really be torn to part with here are all my little camellias. Yet when I see a little new street torn out of some woods I used to know, all lined with close-together tiny houses, I think I would go crazy moving there, if I had to. My true dream is a little place in the country, South, ranch or cabin like, *good soil*, while I'm dreaming, but just a dream.[43][. . .]

Love,

Eudora

PS—A feeling I have about the collection of stories, though, is that a total revelation of all the lives and connections between them isn't necessary or desirable—because it's not a novel—and the revelation is required only insofar as the short story in question requires it. That is, I think it right to leave these people the way they grew to be in the writing of the separate stories—not to add or embellish artificially. In the course of the stories I gradually identified some of the characters as the same people as characters in other stories—and modified and changed as I went—but farther than that I don't want to go with them. Hope you agree with this. E

October 26, 1948

Dear J—

[. . .] It's still aflame here, still the only thing to do is be out in it— would give anything if you could be. There's a sound of hammering somewhere in the distance—do you know, remember how magically those sounds carry on days like these—such a soft echo—the sky all in islands of blue, silver, white, pink—Many yellow butterflies. Smells sweet. Now the gingkho tree turning. But you will see color there if you go just a little north, won't you? Is the sky fine and burning blue now? Hope the sun is warm. When it's beautiful it's so beautiful. Best of wishes for the coming story.

Love to you

E

In November Welty and Robinson, who was still in California, worked together on a screenplay based on her 1942 novella, The Robber

Bridegroom. *In December she was surprised to learn that on January 1, 1949, the* New Yorker *would finally be publishing—and paying for—something she had written: her letter to the magazine criticizing Edmund Wilson's recent article on Faulkner. Later in January, Russell reported that Harcourt wanted the manuscript of her new book no later than the first of March (1.19.49).*

February 2, 1949
Dear Diarmuid,

How are things? I meant to write you before now, and then we had a snowstorm on top of our spring gardens, and I felt out of the writing mood. I do hope the little bulbs you sent will live—I covered them with pinestraw in time, but they were up 4, 5 and 6 inches. Of course the camellia flowers all went, with their buds to come, and the new growth on the roses, which was alarmingly great—and we had little strawberries. Mother's fine lilies she'd planted last fall had some of them come up a foot (the Henryii). The sight of the frozen jonquils and hyacinths fallen in the snow was sad. Snow's still on the ground (the storm Saturday night) so what the damage is fully I don't know yet. Of course it seems petty to feel for your own garden when the West is in the shape it's in. Our pear tree was in flower. Temperature went from 80 to 12. This is Ground Hog day and real bright, so looks like we keep winter on a little longer. Tell me how your potted bulbs are looking. The Roman are my favorite of the hyacinths—so much more graceful than the thick Dutch, aren't they? I hope the camellia went ahead and bloomed. We really had a fine season of flowers before they all got whacked. After all I'm not surprised, shouldn't be, we *always* have this balmy January and then hell to pay.

Am busy getting the stories ready for you. John's helping me type and so is my sister-in-law, and the ones needing revision I'm getting finished more slowly, but will get them in on time. I wouldn't care about a "book this year" at all, but could use the advance. Improving "Moon Lake" a lot I hope—

[. . .] Love to all. Hope everybody's well.
Yours,
Eudora

February 18, 1949
Dear Diarmuid,

[...] Hear it's been 70 up there—must have seemed queer. We're having spring again, but all the good daffodils are blooming lying on their necks, which ain't becoming. My stories lack that long one, Apples, and part of a short one of being done.[44] Mr. Giroux wrote me a letter. He didn't say he was my editor—nobody does—but I think I'll write him anyway and ask if a day or two makes a difference in the deadline. The eyes don't hold up too well and though others offer to type for me, I have to revise, change as I go, proofread etc. so want to finish up myself. I do hope when you see the collection you'll feel pleased at the over-all thing—I wonder myself what it will be like—but as I go it seems to be all right really.

Had a postcard from Rosie inquiring if I was going to England—not this time. Did I tell you, the Cook people offered me a berth in a room for *four*—I declined by return mail. Will wait till I can go a better way, maybe on a slower, cheaper boat, and when maybe a friend will go too, Dolly maybe. Three strange women make me shiver, and there were the same accommodations for coming back. Would also take money—and I didn't want to go to all those writers' conferences to make any—got 6 or 8 of *those* letters again. Would just rather eat cold grits in an attic, that's all. Cold coon and collards. [...]

Yours,
Eudora

Welty completed The Golden Apples *on March 9. After sending the manuscript to Russell, she continued to mull over what she wanted to call the book; although the stories were all connected, she believed the book was too loosely structured to be called a novel. She told Russell she didn't want readers to expect "all ends to be tied, all to be followed up and explained" (3.12.49). She was also anxious to know what Russell thought of the book as a whole. While she was writing Russell the following letter, he telephoned her.*

March 14, 1949
Dear Diarmuid,

Hope the book's read and doesn't press you and you can tell me how the whole is, and that it's turned in and that the fresh pages that reached you today in 2 envelopes didn't simply add to confusion. Now to just sit down and write you a letter.

Hope you're feeling all right. You seemed to be writing away from the office—you know I'm an old detective story reader, and saw the strange typewriter and the handwriting too. Take care of * This is when you called. So fine to talk to you! I felt real set up—a relief and pleasure the book seemed good to you, and glad you were feeling all right, not sniffing or snowbound. Looks like the pages may be late, but hope not too late. Whatever you do about them will be OK with me of course and I hope leaving you with the title choices wasn't a burden and nuisance. Maybe you'll give them a whole set of new titles, all beginning with the same letter or something. It really was interesting, doing the typing up and seeing how all fitted in—surprises all the time, and when that happens it encourages me that the main idea must be safe and in working order, even in spite of me as it were. Hooray that you think it good! It was fine of you to call up indeed.

Your indoor flowers sound consoling. We miss our daffodils this year, no show after the snow caught them in bud. But what a lovely spring it's getting to be—each year I wish this would or could be the place for the spring vacation. (Boston will be springlike later.) The dogwood is beginning to come out, the peach trees beginning—little plum thickets all white in the woods. Yellow knots and fringes coming out over the oak trees. That haze. Dandelions in the grass, onion flowers, bluets. Your bulbs are some of them 7 inches high, I think they're the sparaxis. The bletilla that just came is quiet in its pot, and I will watch out for what happens to all now—I'm looking for mysterious flowers in a month or two.

The camellia must indeed be crowding you by now. And if you're going to give it away give it in time for the new owner to nurse it through the year, not you! Would you like a little one again, different variety? Or are you tired of the care one makes. Maybe come the fall you will feel like looking at a nice young budded one? One of the Japanese kinds, I think of.

Yes, it would be nice to take a little trip—I haven't any plans just now. It's still too cold for my coat. Dolly wrote today that it would about feel good under my coat in May. [. . .]

Still counting on going to the coast this weekend with some girls. We're going to drive down and bask, we think. I would like to stay on a while, send the others back with my car and just stretch out on the sea wall and feel the sun. It will be fine to go having heard from you on the book—I'd thought maybe it would be then.

A shower is stopping outside—cardinals are singing, thrushes. Some are building nests now, so guess it's spring without a doubt. Hope yours comes soon,—winter is too long for anybody.

Love, and thanks again,

Eudora

March 29, 1949

Dear John-

A perfectly beautiful day—I go out in a minute to feed camellias—all have light green crowns on, need feeding. One with the most: Kellingtonia. Are you feeling more ready-like? My lag is on the way out I think. Listen, my dear one, I think that decline and-pause—is a measure of how good we are. Just an observation! If we could have had some lazy picnic or something, it would have got over with ease, who knows. I dreamed about that junction, the one that is like a dream returning when I see it each time I go east, Ooltewah—nothing but a shed, do you know it—in the stretches of Tennessee. The railroads meet there and stretch away in the four points of the compass, and that little gray shed, with Ooltewah on it. The train sits there for a long time—it's usually late afternoon—you can hear the silence all around, no other train comes for ages. I always feel it cross my mind, suppose never—? Not minding at the time, sort of like contemplating the navel. School sounds a little like that just now, too? Don't you have spring vacation? Or do they acknowledge spring in any way in Cal., only you with sweetpeas? I hope the garden has overcome the threats. Always that's the way. You have birds and snails, I have cats just now. They scratch under the camellias day by day—I hate cats anyway. They are also concentrating on some birdnests in our yard. All is green in Mississippi. We had two weeks of tornadoes here and there, Saturday night here was really spectacular—and I wrote you about the tail end of one I was out in in Memphis—all in my new spring hat, appropriate no doubt. I'll tell you what my wish is, without being sure of yours, it's to meet before too long, to do our movie maybe, or something. [...]

Everybody in the world seems to be going to Europe this summer. Did I tell you I had passage, but didn't take it up when the time came, on too big a boat with too many people—anyway I arranged for it at a bad time, I don't like going on a trip that came out of a feeling like that, it might partake. This was to Ireland, England, and Scandinavia. Now I think of warmer countries. And take the car. I don't think I want to be an expatriot [sic], though. I'll wait for interstellar transportation and settle on Vega. Lightyearhouse keeping.

[...] It's about time now—for Bender to unbend and for Gugg. to give out.[45] Be nice if we get our little aprons full. Must go to work outdoors now. It's almost rose time, a Silver Moon yesterday, and the Lady Banksia is blooming all over that old trellis. The dogwood in the country is very pure and lovely. And of course the yellow jasmine. You know.

Love to you,

Eudora

Harcourt Brace paid Welty a five-thousand-dollar advance for her forthcoming book. Welty's 1949 income was significantly higher than in 1948, when she had earned less than three thousand dollars in royalties (DR to EW 1.3.49).

April 3, 1949

Dear Diarmuid,

Thank you for the contracts, that's real gorgeous money, and here's the copy back signed.

Your sparaxis is blooming! if not the ixias—the foliage looks alike but this is the taller. During some tornado like winds and rains and electricity they put up tender green stalks and flower heads. Three flowers are open. A white, funnel-shaped flower (a cloudy day, they might open wider) of 6 petals, about the size of a species tulip, of luminous white outside, and inside splashed with clear bright yellow. The little sheaths of the buds are dark red, and the base of the petals outside greenish. I think I reported the foliage is like species iris. Lovely. I couldn't detect a scent, except a sort of sanitary one, that's why I think they're sparaxis instead of ixioides odorata—they're planted together. Will let you know what next. Wonderful to see strange flowers in bloom, and the only other color I have just now is birdsfoot violet and a species iris, they both look fine with the new exotics.

And they gave me a Guggenheim! Isn't that fine? It's $2500—seems to me that's twice as much as the old one. That plus my advance makes me positively and horridly rich. (Letter said the fellowships not to be told till the 11th—wonder who else got them? I recommended somebody too!) I feel grateful to Mr. Moe this time especially, because I hardly had a project—just said I wanted to feel able to study or think without work for a little so as to do something perhaps very different from before.[46] It was understanding of them, wasn't it?

Mr. Giroux wrote his letter, perhaps after talking to you, and I enclose it and what I wrote back, so as all will be conveyed. I didn't mean to be hard on him, I just can't follow him exactly in his lines of thought and still can't, and didn't want to be ambiguous myself in what *I* thought! It was a matter of honesty to the author of the book, if somebody came up to call stories a novel. If you can wade through the two long letters and let me know your feeling about the titles and subtitles or whatever, I'll feel more settled and happy about things. Don't bother to return Mr. G.'s letter. I don't know if I'll ever be in tune with Mr. G., will you? Where is he from?

Hope you had a fine time in Boston. How did the weather treat you? Hope things are warmer and nicer in NY now—that young daffodil sounds like it. Everything is intensely green here just now—but we've had one near-tornado after another, and today it's dark as dark. I was especially pleased to see the sparaxis, and terribly surprised, as it was one of those sudden bloomers the way tropical things can do you.

Love,
Eudora

April 25, 1949
Dear John—

How are things? I've been so wishing to talk, it's defeated me writing. Not that there's news, or is there? [. . .] How is the little house [in Berkeley]? I wish what you want. Do you still think there's that workable quality in us we could trust to, put to good,—going away isn't all, the truth, of what you think now, is it? It seems wrong to think this yet I want to see the real way it is, not be blind to what you do wish and think. Jackson's not a good place for me to try to understand things—not really making excuses, that's true. The true, fundamental things (to me) I understand, do anywhere, of course, always love to you, but sometimes I can't interpret the world.

We have fine roses now—too—one, the Doctor, is magnificent—a clear fine pink, opening to gold stamens—I love it fullblown, and one that I measured, for purposes of this letter, was 7 inches across at the lower farflung petals, and 5½ inches at the center—and still exquisite and fragile. You know I got one for Faulkner, but just never did take it, the little bush has roses now.[47] In the woods honeysuckle—at night the frogs like silver bells—I used to think that was the sound night made, itself, just the sound of the world at night. The stars, and all the long, winding constellations, far stretched, beautiful lately—have you had clear skies?

[. . .]

Love to you,

E

Welty was in New York from late April to August 1949. On the train ride back to Jackson, she reread The Odyssey, *and she soon began writing another story, "Put Me in the Sky!"* [48] *This story would later be retitled "Circe," the name of its protagonist.*

The Golden Apples *had been published in mid-August. Welty was now making plans for her trip to Europe.*

September 26, 1949

Dear Diarmuid,

[. . .] My ship is supposed to sail on Oct. 14, I guess, and it looks like I'll just get there a little ahead—but do you think I might come out to see you on the Sunday before? I may not be able to get to NY till the Saturday before, on account of the dentist—put off going as usual. If there's a dock strike the boat may not sail anyway—can't tell much by the paper what looms. MJ Ward's review so *low*.[49] Stupid assigning.

Haven't done anything about the little story,but I feel now as if I'd like to send it more or less the way I wrote it to ACCENT, to see what they think—they were nice to me in the beginning and I like the story the way *it* is in the beginning, thorny or not—I'll get it from you or whatever, when I see you.[50]

Hope all well there. Had hoped John was going to be able to go to Italy too, but now—don't know.

Love,

Eudora

To Robinson c/o U.S. Consul, Mexico City
October 12, 1949
NY, Wednesday noon
Dear John, hoping to hear from you soon from Mexico—will be real glad to know everything went off all right. [. . .]

Of course everybody asks about you. And so wish you were here. The boat is in, too, I went and looked at it this morning, with light colored stacks with blue insignia and 3 gold towers on, and lots of little flags fluttering. This time it was a dream that came in the ivory window—do you remember Penelope's dreams, the ones that didn't come true were those that came through the ivory window and the true ones came through the horn.[51] It will be not too long, will it? I don't see how it could be much longer, surely things will break soon—if not one way, another way. I hope it daily. Nightly too. I sure do hope you get some things written down there—that they go the way you want them. Let me know all about Mexico. How Spanish comes back to you and what you read and all. Tell me what flowers are now. Do watch the water and leafy vegetables and stuff—and *them* (alive). The weather must be magnificent—I wonder if Chauvez (?) will be coming down again to conduct and this time you will hear him?[52]

It's been oh so hot here too. A record, it always is. But in the country, where I went Sunday, it was like our falls at home, warm but not hot, cool breezes, soft air, smell of woods and yellow flowers. None of our butterflies we have so many of seem to be flying up here. Do you remember, we had whole clouds. Asters and Goldenrod. The apples are falling, so good and tangy. Took a long walk through woods. Such colors. And the lakes and little streams up there are so clear and skyblue. Rosie had the Merrills (the friends with the Bedford house, and with the stove[53]) and Eileen to dinner Sunday night. The children are fine and D. and Rosie are also looking much better than they were, health improved.

Diarmuid has put away his garden for winter, cut the iris away, re-set his bulbs and put fresh soil in the beds. The last rose.—I took Pammy and Willie some Hallowe'en costumes, witch for P., skeleton for W. Will put his right on and that night came and jumped on me in bed of course. He recited me a long made-up poem which went licketty split—about a puppy. One verse turned out like this, "He saw an old lady, coming his way, bit her in the leg and she cried all day." I bought 5 Halloween costumes from Wanamakers at once—sent some to Elizabeth and Mary Martha,[54]—the witch.

[. . .] I'll write you again before sailing, and to consulate unless hear not—I so want to hear from you—take care of yourself my dear—I hope you are liking it there.

Much love to you,

E

Written while crossing the Atlantic
October 21, 1949
8th day
Dear Diarmuid, here's Portugese stamps—I liked their looks—Thanks for nice wire from the Russells—it set me off right. Also that continental meal—when I get off the boat to try breakfast in Lisbon in the morning, where we put in, I'll see, and let you know. This has been a fine trip—smooth sailing all the way, Mr. Faulkner could have just about made it the whole way in his sailboat of the Mississippi Interior.[55] I've felt fine—all the poor Italians were seasick, though. Beautiful sea and beautiful sky—and the whole half-circuit of the stars. This boat is possibly not for everybody, but suits me just right—I like the people, but have all the peace and privacy I want—With great luck I have the whole cabin to myself, and use the upper berth for a library table and hang my wash out up there. And I have the maid and all to myself. Many funny things happen—I am always interested and amused—On the boat (turistica) Italians, Sicilians, Spaniards, Portugese, 2 Russians, 2 Nigerians (?) (they look more Mississippi to me), Corsican, 1 Pole, and me—My book is in the ship's library, but *I'm* not going to read it. I've learned that Pittura Freschia means Fresh Paint. Hope you've had news about the house and it's good—It's warm here up on deck—

Love to all,

Eudora

*Yet I know they keep something from me, asleep and
awake. There exists a mortal mystery, that, if I knew where
it was, I could crush like an island grape. Only frailty, it
seems, can divine it—and I was not endowed with that
property. They live by frailty! By the moment! I tell myself
that it is only a mystery, and mystery is only uncertainty.
(There is no mystery in magic! Men are swine: let it be
said, and no sooner said than done.) Yet mortals alone can
divine where it lies in each other, can find it and prick it in
all its peril, with an instrument made of air. I swear that
only to possess that one, trifling secret, I would willingly
turn myself into a harmless dove for the rest of eternity!*

　　—"Circe," 1949

*Only for the space of a breath did Gabriella feel she
would rather lie down on that melon cart pulled by a
donkey, that she could see just disappearing around the
corner ahead. Then the melons and the arch of the gate,
the grandmother's folding of the fan and Mama's tears,
the volcano of early morning, and even the long, dangerous voyage behind her—all seemed caught up and held
in something: the golden moment of touch, just given,
just taken, in saying good-by. The moment—bright and
effortless of making, in the end, as a bubble—seemed to go
ahead of them as they walked, to tap without sound across
the dust of the emptying courtyard, and alight in the
grandmother's homely buggy, filling it. The yellow leaves
of the plane trees came down before their feet; and just
beyond the gate the black country horse that would draw
the buggy shivered and tossed his mane, which fell like one
long silver wave as the first of the bells in the still-hidden
heart of Naples began to strike the hour.*

　　—"Going to Naples," 1954

Correspondence from Eudora Welty, Diarmuid Russell, and John Robinson

Eudora Welty Collection
Mississippi Department of Archives and History

All the letters I have quoted or cited from Welty, Robinson, and Russell are listed here in chronological order.

Brackets around a date (e.g., August 18 [1941]) identify information that is not found on the letter itself. Dates enclosed in brackets have been determined from the postmark on the envelope, from internal evidence, and/or from evidence within other letters to and from Welty.

TLS=Typed Letter, Signed; TL=Typed Letter, unsigned
CL=Carbon Letter, unsigned
ALS=Autograph (handwritten) Letter, Signed; AL=Autograph Letter, unsigned
aps=autograph (handwritten) postscript
pp=pages; both sides of page counted if letter is written on both sides

The number of pages is not a consistent indicator of the number of words in a Welty letter, since her handwriting, typewriters, and paper sizes varied. However, because I have included only excerpts from many letters, a page count may have some value to readers who would like an idea of how much of a particular letter has been included.

The page count will also help researchers who wish to locate these letters in the Eudora Welty Collection at the Mississippi Department of Archives and History (MDAH). Since the dates on many letters are missing or incomplete, researchers may have difficulty locating them using only the date I have supplied, which is not always the same date (or "n. d.") that was on the MDAH file folder when I looked at the letters on my visits from 2008 to 2011. The Eudora Welty Collection has grown since Suzanne Marrs's *The Welty Collection* expertly enumerated the collection as it stood in 1988. After Welty's death, MDAH received a large quantity of additional material, including fourteen thousand items of correspondence. Much of this is now open to researchers; Welty family correspondence will become available in 2022. As of 2012, the most complete account of the material currently available in the Eudora Welty Collection is in the MDAH online catalog.

Welty to Russell (EW to DR) May 31 1940 TLS 1 pp

Russell to Welty (DR to EW) June 3 [1940] TLS 1 pp

EW to DR [Early June 1940] TLS aps 1 pp

DR to EW [August 28 1940] TLS 1 pp

DR to EW September 6 [1940] TLS 1 pp

EW to DR [Early September 1940] TLS 3 pp

DR to EW September 10 [1940] TLS 2 pp

EW to DR "Friday" [Probably September 13 1940] TLS 2 pp

DR to EW September 23 [1940] TLS 1 pp

EW to DR [Late September 1940] TLS 2 pp [*This letter is dated September 23, 1940, in Kreyling's* Author and Agent, *but it is later; Welty is replying to a letter from Russell dated and postmarked September 23.*]

DR to EW October 8 1940 TLS 1 pp

EW to DR "Thursday night" [Probably October 10 1940] TLS 1 pp

DR to EW October 29 1940 TLS 1 pp

EW to DR November 5 1940 TLS 1 pp

EW to DR November 12 [1940] TLS 1 pp

DR to EW November 18 1940 TLS 1 pp

EW to DR November 23 1940 TLS 2 pp

DR to EW December 4 1940 TLS 1 pp

EW to DR [Early December 1940] TLS 1 pp

DR to EW [Mid-December 1940] TLS 1 pp

EW to DR [Mid-December 1940] TLS 1 pp, decorated w/watercolor painting by EW

EW to DR December 30 1940 TLS 1 pp

DR to EW January 2 1941 TLS 1 pp

EW to DR January 8 1941 TLS aps 1 pp

EW to DR January 9 1941 TLS 1 pp

DR to EW January 15 1941 TLS 1 pp

EW to DR January 18 1941 TLS 1 pp

DR to EW January 21 1941 TLS 2 pp

DR to EW February 11 1941 TLS aps 2 pp

EW to DR February 14 1941 TLS 2 pp

EW to DR February 21 1941 TLS 2 pp

DR to EW February 24 1941 TLS 1 pp

EW to DR February 26 [1941] TLS 1 pp

DR to EW March 3 1941 TLS aps 2 pp

EW to DR March 8 1941 TLS aps 1 pp

EW to DR March 12 1941 ALS 1 pp

EW to DR March 15 1941 TLS 2 pp

DR to EW March 17 1941 TLS 2 pp

EW to DR March 19 1941 TLS 2 pp

EW to DR "Wednesday" [March 19 1941] TLS 1 pp

EW to DR "Monday" [Probably March 31 1941] TLS 2 pp

DR to EW April 2 1941 TLS 1 pp

EW to DR April 5 1941 TLS 3 pp

EW to DR April 18 1941 TLS 1 pp

DR to EW April 24 1941 TLS 1 pp

EW to DR April 26 1941 TLS aps 1 pp

EW to DR April 30 1941 TLS 2 pp

EW to DR [May 1941] TLS 1 pp, Hotel Bristol stationery

EW to DR [Late May 1941] ALS 2 postcards

EW to DR June 7 1941 ALS 4 pp

DR to EW June 11 1941 TLS 1 pp

EW to DR June 17 1941 TLS aps 2 pp

EW to DR June 26 1941 TLS 2 pp

EW to DR July 14 1941 TLS 1 pp plus 1 pp with drawing of lily

DR to EW July 15 1941 TLS aps 1 pp

EW to DR July 23 1941 TLS 1 pp

EW to DR August 11 1941 TLS 1 pp

EW to DR August 18 [1941] TLS 1 pp

EW to DR August 28 1941 TLS 2 pp

EW to DR September 20 1941 TLS 1 pp

EW to DR September 30 1941 TLS 4 pp

EW to DR October 7 1941 TLS 1 pp

DR to EW October 16 1941 CL 1 pp

EW to DR October 20 [1941] TLS 2 pp

DR to EW November 18 1941 TLS 2 pp

DR to EW November 21 1941 TLS 2 pp

EW to DR November 24 [1941] TLS aps 2 pp

DR to EW December 1 1941 TLS 1 pp

EW to DR December 8 [1941] TLS 2 pp

EW to DR December 12 1941 ALS 2 pp

EW to DR December 23 1941 TLS 4 pp

DR to EW December 26 1941 TLS 2 pp

EW to DR January 7 194[2] TLS 2 pp [*Misdated 1941 by Welty*]

EW to DR January 19 [1942] TLS w/hw PS 1 pp

DR to EW January 20 1942 TLS 1 pp

EW to DR February 4 1942 TLS 2 pp

DR to EW February 6 1942 TLS 1 pp

EW to DR February 9 1942 TLS aps 2 pp

DR to EW February 26 1942 TLS 1 pp

EW to DR March 6 1942 TLS 2 pp

DR to EW March 9 1942 TLS 1 pp

DR to EW March 17 1942 TLS 1 pp

EW to DR "Thursday" [March 19 1942] TLS 2 pp

EW to DR March 23 1942 Western Union Telegram

DR to EW March 23 1942 TLS 1 pp

EW to DR "Friday" [March 27 1942] TLS 3 pp

EW to DR "Easter" [April 5 1942] TLS 2 pp

EW to DR [April 20 1942] TLS 2 pp [*Dated "Monday" on page 1, "Later" on page 2*] [*Dated April 23, 1942, by Kreyling in* Author and Agent, *but the letter replies to DR's 4.17.42 letter, and the Monday following 4.17.42 is 4.20.42.*]

EW to DR [Late April 1942] TLS 1 pp [*Replies to DR's letter of April 23 1942*]

EW to DR May 4 1942 TLS 1 pp

EW to DR June 8 [1942] TLS 3 pp

DR to EW June 8 1942 TLS 1 pp

EW to DR June 12 1942 TLS 2 pp

EW to DR June 20 1942 TLS 1 pp and 1 pp drawing of flower, labeled by EW

EW to DR June 26 1942 TLS 2 pp

EW to DR July 13 [1942] TLS 1 pp

DR to EW July 15 1942 TLS 1 pp

Welty to Robinson (EW to JR) "Thursday" [July 1942] TLS 4 pp

EW to DR August 8 1942 TLS 1 pp

EW to DR August 13 1942 TLS 1 pp w/encl clipping

DR to EW August 17 1942 TLS 1 pp

EW to DR "Monday" [August 31 1942] TLS 1 [*Marrs, in* Eudora Welty, *identifies this as "late August" (588). EW seems to be responding to a letter from DR dated August 26 1942.*]

EW to JR [September 12 1942] TLS 6 pp

EW to DR September 14 1942 TLS 1 pp

EW to DR September 28 [1942] TLS 1 pp

EW to DR "Hallowe'en"[October 31 1942] TLS 1 pp

EW to DR November 6 1942 TLS aps 2 pp

DR to EW November 10 1942 TLS 1 pp

EW to DR [Mid-November, 12 or 13, 1942] TLS 2 pp *["Philadelphia Inquirer" in DR's handwriting is penciled in top right. Letter responds to DR's November 10 1942 letter.]*

EW to JR [November 13 1942] TLS 6 pp

EW to DR November 22 1942 TLS 2 pp

DR to EW November 25 1942 TLS 2 pp

EW to DR November 25 1942 TLS 1 pp

EW to DR December 4 1942 TLS 1 pp

EW to DR December 16 1942 TLS 2 pp

EW to DR December 26 1942 TLS 2 pp

DR to EW February 9 1943 TLS 1 pp

EW to DR February 15 1943 TLS 1 pp

DR to EW March 15 1943 TLS 1 pp

EW to DR March 19 1943 TLS 1 pp

EW to DR May 5 1943 TLS aps 2 pp

EW to JR "Monday" [May 11 1943] TLS 2 pp *[Later in the letter: "Tuesday morning"]*

EW to DR May 15 1943 TLS and handwritten note 2pp

DR to EW May 18 1943 TLS 1 pp

DR to EW May 25 1943 TLS 1 pp

EW to DR June 1 1943 TLS 1 pp

EW to DR June 9 1943 TLS 1 pp

DR to EW June 10 1943 TLS 1 pp

EW to JR "Tuesday" [June 23 1943] TLS 1 pp w/encl photo

EW to DR June 23 1943 TLS 1 pp

DR to EW "June" [July] 2 1943 TLS 1 pp

EW to DR July 8 1943 TLS 1 pp aps

EW to JR July 9 [1943] ALS 4 pp

EW to DR July 12 1943 TLS 1 pp

EW to JR July 19 [1943] TLS V-mail 1 pp

EW to JR July 28 [1943] TLS V-mail 1 pp

EW to DR August 6 [1943] TLS aps 1 pp

JR to EW August 8 [1943] TLS 4 pp [Typed in all uppercase]

EW to DR August 18 [1943] TLS 1 pp

DR to EW August 20 1943 TLS 2 pp

EW to JR August 21 [1943] TLS 1 pp V-mail [Typed in all uppercase]

EW to JR August 26 1943 TLS 1 pp V-mail

EW to DR August 28 [1943] TLS aps 1 pp

EW to JR September 1 1943 ALS 4 pp w encl *[4 pp made from one sheet folded into 4 sections; encl.* Market Bulletin *clippings and sketch of "Phantom" in a "Napoleon hat"]*

EW to JR September 12 1943 TLS 1 pp V-mail

EW to DR September 13 1943 TLS aps 1 pp

EW to JR September 17 [1943], also dated September 21 [1943] TLS aps 2 pp

EW to DR September 21 [1943] TLS 1 pp

EW to JR September 24 1943 TLS 1 pp V-mail

EW to DR September 27 [1943] TLS 1 pp

EW to JR September 28 [1943] ALS 2 pp

DR to EW October 14 1943 TLS 1 pp

EW to DR October 18 [1943] TLS 1 pp

EW to JR October 25 [1943] TLS 1 pp V-mail

EW to JR October 29 [1943] ALS 6 pp

EW to DR November 1 [1943] TLS 1 pp

EW to DR "Guy Fawkes Day" [November 5 1943] TLS 1 pp V-mail

EW to JR "Wed." [November 10 1943] TLS 2 pp

DR to EW November 10 1943 TLS 1 pp

EW to DR November 13 [1943] TLS aps 1 pp

EW to JR "Thanksgiving—morning" [November 25 1943] TLS aps 1 pp V-mail

EW to JR November 26 [1943] ALS 6 pp

EW to JR December 7 [1943] TLS 1 pp V-mail

DR to EW December 7 1943 TLS 1 pp

EW to DR December 10 1943 TLS 2 pp

DR to EW December 13 1943 TLS 1 pp

EW to JR December 15 [1943] TLS 1 pp V-mail

EW to JR "Christmas" [December 25 1943] ALS 1 pp V-mail

EW to DR January 13 1944 TLS aps and drawing 2 pp

DR to EW January 14 1944 TLS 1 pp

EW to JR "Friday" [January 21 1944] ALS 2 pp w/numerous handmade valentines

EW to JR January 23 [1944] TLS 1 pp V-mail

EW to JR February 8 [1944] ALS 2 pp V-mail

EW to JR February 12 [1944] TLS w/drawing of pear tree 1 pp V- mail

EW to JR February 17 [1944] TLS 2 pp V-mail

EW to JR February 28 [1944] TLS 1 pp V-mail

EW to DR February 29 [1944] TLS 1 pp [*MDAH dated this as 1945, but leap year is 1944, not 1945*]

EW to JR March 3 [1944] TLS 1 pp V-mail

EW to DR March 6 [1944] TLS 2 pp

EW to JR March 13 [1944] TLS 1 pp V-mail

EW to JR March 18 [1944] TLS 1 pp V-mail

EW to DR March 18 [1944] TLS 1 pp

EW to JR March 20 [1944] TLS 2 pp V-mail

EW to DR March 24 [1944] TLS 1 pp

DR to EW April 4 1944 TLS 1 pp

EW to DR April 8 [1944] TLS 1 pp

EW to JR April 17 [1944] TLS aps 1 pp V-mail

EW to JR April 20 [1944] ALS 1 pp V-mail

EW to JR April 24 [1944] TLS 1 pp V-mail

EW to DR April 25 [1944] TLS 2 pp

EW to JR May 10 [1944] ALS 1 pp

EW to JR May 23 [1944] ALS 3 pp V-mail

EW to JR June 5 [1944] TLS 1 pp V-mail

EW to JR June 14 [1944] TL [poetry quotations] 3 pp ALS on last page

EW to JR June 28 [1944] TLS 1 pp V-mail

EW to JR July 5 [1944] TLS 1 pp V-mail

EW to JR [Early July 1944] AL and TL 6 pp w encl

    Letters in envelope postmarked July 8 1944:

    AL 2 pp, *NY Times Book Review* stationery

    TL 4 pp, small squares of scrap paper

    [*Typed letter notes full moon (July 6 1944).*]

    Encl: Welty's review of S. J. Perelman's *Crazy Like a Fox*

EW to JR [Early July 1944] 4 pp TL and AL [*Typed (1–2) and handwritten (3–4) on small lined notebook paper, 4 pp, unsigned. June 28 letter had said they would move to apartment "this Saturday"—July 1. This letter "is from our apartment." It may have been enclosed in the same July 8 1944 envelope with other early July letters.*]

EW to JR July 11 [1944] TLS 1 pp V-mail

EW to JR [July 13 1944] ALS 8 pp

EW to JR July 17 [1944] TLS 2 pp

EW to JR July 18 [1944] ALS 1 pp V-mail

EW to JR August 5 [1944] ALS 1pp V-mail

EW to JR [Late] August [1944] TLS 2 pp V-mail

EW to JR August 25 [1944] ALS 3 pp

EW to JR "Labor Day" [September 4 1944] ALS 2 pp V-mail

EW to JR [September 8 1944] TLS 2 pp [torn scrap of paper]

EW to JR "Mon." [September] 18 [1944] TLS 1 pp

EW to JR September 23 [1944] TLS 1 pp V-mail

EW to JR September 27 [1944] TLS 1 pp V-mail

EW to JR October 10 [1944] ALS 8 pp

EW to JR October 16 [1944] TLS 2 pp

Ew to JR October 18 [1944] ALS 2 pp

EW to JR [October 20 1944] ALS 2 pp

EW to JR October 23 [1944] TLS 2 pp

EW to DR [Late October 1944] TLS 2 pp

EW to JR October 25 [1944] TLS 1 pp

DR to EW October 31 1944 TLS 2 pp

DR to EW November 9 1944 TLS 1 pp

EW to JR November 9 [1944] ALS 8 pp

EW to DR November 14 [1944] TLS 3 pp [*filed at MDAH as November 14 (1945)*]

EW to JR November 16 [1944] ALS 1 pp V-mail

EW to JR November 17 [1944] TLS 1 pp V-mail

DR to EW November 17 1944 TLS 1 pp

EW to JR [November 29 1944] TLS 4 pp

EW to JR December 4 [1944] TLS 2 pp and encl. card, handwritten front and back

EW to JR December 15 [1944] TLS aps 2 pp

EW to DR December 19 [1944] TLS 1 pp

EW to DR January 1 [1945] TLS aps 2 pp

EW to JR January 8 [1945] TLS 2 pp

EW to DR January 14 [1945] TLS 2 pp

EW to JR January 17 [1945] TLS 4 pp

DR to EW January 17 1945 TLS 1 pp

DR to EW January 17 1945 TLS aps 2 pp

EW to DR January 20 [1945] TLS 2 pp

EW to JR February 7 [1945] TLS 2 pp

EW to DR February 10 [1945] TLS 2 pp

EW to JR February 13 [1945] TLS 2 pp V-mail

EW to JR February 14 [1945] TLS 2 pp

EW to JR February 20 [1945] TLS aps 2 pp

EW to JR March 9 [1945] ALS 4 pp

EW to JR March 19 [1945] TLS aps 3 pp

EW to JR March 24 [1945] TLS aps 2 pp

DR to EW March 27 1945 TLS 1 pp

DR to EW March 28 1945 TLS 1 pp

EW to JR March 31 [1945] ALS 6 pp

EW to DR April 3 [1945] TLS 2 pp

EW to JR [April 14 1945] TLS, last page handwritten; encl. pressed flower; 6 pp

EW to DR "Sunday" [April 15 1945] TLS 2 pp

EW to JR May 1 [1945] TLS 1 pp

EW to DR May 25 [1945] TLS 4 pp

EW to JR June 12 [1945] TLS aps 2 pp

DR to EW June 19 1945 TLS 1 pp

EW to DR June 21 [1945] TLS 1 pp

EW to JR June 24 [1945] TLS on first page w/sketch on verso, 2 pp

DR to EW July 20 1945 TLS 2 pp

EW to DR [Late July 1945] TLS 2 pp [*Reply to DR to EW 7.20.45*]

EW to JR August 7 [1945] ALS 2 pp

EW to JR August 23 [1945] TLS 2 pp

EW to DR August 24 [1945] TLS 1 pp

EW to DR November 9 [1945] TLS 1 pp

EW to DR [Mid-December 1945] TLS 1 pp [*Written between 12/11 and 12/19*]

EW to DR "Sunday" [December 30 1945] TLS 3 pp

DR to EW January 2 1946 TLS 1 pp

EW to DR January 3 [1946] TLS 1 pp

DR to EW January 7 1946 TLS 1 pp

EW to DR [Mid-January 1946] TLS 2 pp [*EW's personal stationery; in reply to DR to EW January 7 1946*]

DR to EW January 16 1946 TLS 2 pp

EW to DR [Late January 1946] ALS 2 pp [*In reply to DR to EW January 16 1946*]

EW to DR [Early February 1946] TLS 2 pp [*EW's personal stationery; DR to EW February 11 1946 seems to respond to this letter*]

EW to DR [February] 26 [1946] TLS aps 2 pp [*EW dates this January 26, which is incorrect; she responds to information in February 11 and February 21 letters from DR*]

EW to DR March 31 [1946] TLS 2 pp

EW to DR April 29 [1946] TLS 2 pp

DR to EW May 10 1946 TLS 1 pp

DR to EW May 14 1946 TLS 1 pp

EW to JR "Tuesday" [May 21 1946] TLS 2 pp

EW to JR "Sat." [August] 17 [1946] TLS aps 2 pp

EW to JR "Wed. AM" [August 21 1946] TLS aps 2 pp

EW to DR "Wed. AM" August 21 1946 TLS aps 2 pp

EW to DR September 6 1946 TLS aps 2 pp

EW to JR "Monday" [September 16 1946] TLS 2 pp

EW to JR "Sunday morning" [September 29 1946] TLS aps 2 pp

EW to DR September 30 [1946] TLS aps 2 pp

EW to JR [October 8 1946] TLS 2 pp

EW to JR "Wednesday again" [October 9 1946] ALS 2 pp

EW to JR "Monday" [October 14 1946] TLS aps 2 pp

DR to EW October 14 1946 ALS 2 pp

EW to JR [October 18 1946] ALS 12 pp, w/encl [*EW enclosed DR's letter of October 14*]

EW to JR "Wednesday" [October 23 1946] TLS aps 6 pp

EW to JR "Thursday night" [October 25 1946] ALS 5 pp

EW to JR "Sunday" [October 28 1946] ALS 8 pp

EW to JR "Monday" [November 4 1946] TLS 2 pp

EW to JR "Thursday" [November 7 1946] TLS 3 pp

EW to JR "Friday" [November 8 1946] TLS aps 2 pp

EW to JR "Saturday night" [November 10 1946] AL 1st page, TL 2nd page, AL 3rd page. [*Begun November 9; EW dates typed portion of letter "Sunday." No signature on any pages.*]

EW to JR "Wed. AM early" [November 27 1946] ALS 3 pp

EW to JR "Monday" [December 9 1946] ALS 2 pp

EW to DR December 25 [1946] ALS 4 pp

EW to DR January 10 1947 ALS 3 pp

EW to DR February 9 1947 TLS 2 pp

DR to EW February 13 1947 TLS 1 pp

EW to DR March 11 [1947] TLS aps 1 pp

EW to DR March 23 1947 TLS 2 pp

EW to DR April 6 1947 TLS 2 pp

EW to JR "Monday night" [May 12 1947] TLS 2 pp

EW to JR "Thurs. AM" [May 22 1947] ALS 2 pp

EW to DR August 22 [1947] TLS 4 pp

EW to DR September 2 [1947] TLS 2 pp

DR to EW September 5 1947 TLS aps 1 pp

EW to JR [September 12 1947] TLS 2 pp

DR to EW September 26 1947 TLS 1 pp

EW to DR October 6 1947 TLS aps 1 pp

DR to EW October 7 1947 TLS 1 pp

EW to DR October 10 1947 TLS 2 pp

DR to EW November 7 1947 TLS 1 pp

EW to DR November 12 [1947] TLS 2 pp

EW to JR "Thursday" [November 13 1947] TLS 2 pp

EW to JR "Monday" [November 17 1947] TLS 2 pp

EW to DR December 3 [1947] TLS 2 pp

EW to DR December 15 [1947] TLS 1 pp

EW to DR February 8 1948 TLS 2 pp

EW to JR "Tuesday" [February 17 1948] TLS aps 3 pp

EW to DR February 18 [1948] TLS 2 pp

DR to EW February 20 1948 TLS 2 pp

EW to JR "Thursday" [March 19 1948] TLS 3 pp [*completed March 18, mailed March 19*]

EW to DR April 12 [1948] TLS aps 2 pp

JR to EW "Monday" [July 19 1948] TLS aps 1 pp

EW to DR [Early September 1948] TLS 4 pp

EW to JR "Thursday morning" [September 23 1948] TLS 2 pp

EW to JR "Wednesday" [September 30 1948] TLS 1 pp (*Written evening of September 29, mailed September 30*)

EW to DR October 4 1948 TLS 2 pp

EW to JR "Tuesday" [October 26 1948] TLS 4 pp [*This letter is not filed with an envelope at MDAH. An envelope postmarked October 26 1948 has been filed separately, unassigned to any letter. That envelope is the right size for this "Tuesday" letter, and October 26 fell on a Tuesday in 1948.*]

DR to EW January 3 1949 TLS 1 pp

DR to EW January 19 1949 TLS 2 pp

EW to DR February 2 [1949] TLS aps 2 pp

EW to DR February 18 [1949] TLS 2 pp

EW to DR March 12 [1949] TLS 2 pp

EW to DR March 14 [1949] TLS 4 pp

EW to JR [March 29 1949] TLS 2 pp

EW to DR April 3 [1949] TLS 2 pp

EW to JR [April 25 1949] TLS 4 pp

EW to DR September 26 1949 TLS 1 pp

EW to JR "Wednesday" [October 12 1949] TLS 3 pp

EW to DR "8th day" [October 21 1949] ALS 3 pp [*Written on the eighth day of EW's journey, which began October 14*]

JR to EW September 24 [1983] TLS aps 2 pp

NOTES

Introduction

1. See the appendix for more detail on each letter cited or included in this book.

2. *One Writer's Beginnings*, Welty's 1984 memoir (*Stories, Essays, and Memoir*, 943).

3. The Welty-Maxwell correspondence is now available in *What There Is to Say We Have Said* (2011), edited by Suzanne Marrs.

4. Michael Robinson, quoted in Ruth Laney's January 2012 article, "Man of Letters," in *Country Roads* magazine.

5. Patti Carr Black, personal interview, August 5, 2011; Suzanne Marrs, personal interview, August 6, 2011.

6. Welty made this comment to Millar in a letter dated May 18, 1973, quoted in Suzanne Marrs's *Eudora Welty: A Biography*, 391.

7. These quotations appear in Marrs's biography, pages 358 (Millar to Welty, 4.20.71) and 470 (Welty to Millar, 3.16.82).

Chapter 1

1. These publishers were Reynal and Hitchcock, Houghton Mifflin, Alfred A. Knopf, Harcourt Brace, G. P. Putnam's Sons, and Doubleday, Doran (Marrs, *The Welty Collection*, 162–167).

2. Bracketed ellipses indicate that a portion of a letter has been omitted. The appendix, which lists in chronological order each letter cited in this book, indicates the number of pages of each letter.

3. This letter's precise date could not be determined. I have been able to date most of Welty's undated or incompletely dated letters through postmarks or other evidence (Russell's letters to Welty, for example, almost always bear a complete date).

4. Russell had written Welty he thought the story, "Clytie," was good but somewhat more obscure than her other stories (6.3.40).

5. Ford Madox Ford (1873–1939), editor and author of fiction, literary criticism, and biography. Of his many novels, the best known today is *The Good Soldier* (1915). Ford learned of Welty's stories from Katherine Anne Porter (1890–1980). She was a well-known southern fiction writer, having published *Flowering Judas and Other Stories* in 1936 and *Pale Horse, Pale*

Rider in 1939. Porter was married to Albert Erskine, the managing editor of *The Southern Review*, when she met Welty in 1939.

6. Russell had written to Welty about Johnny Appleseed, whom he had heard of only recently, as a possible subject for a children's book (8.28.40). At least four plays about John Chapman, the man who called himself Johnny Appleseed, were published from the 1920s to 1930. Welty may also have read Vachel Lindsay's *Johnny Appleseed and Other Poems*, published in several editions beginning in 1929.

7. Seed and nursery catalogue from Robert Wayman of New York.

8. Edward Lear (1812–1888) was the author and illustrator of Nonsense Books, limericks, "The Owl and the Pussycat," and "The Jumblies" and was a great favorite of Welty and her brothers in their childhood. A recipe for "Gosky Patties" appears in Lear's "Nonsense Cookery" (*Nonsense Books*, 137).

9. Cleanth Brooks (1906–1994) was an editor, with Robert Penn Warren, of *The Southern Review*. By July 1940 they had published six of Welty's stories and rejected a similar number; they returned "Powerhouse" to her on September 18. In 1943 when Brooks and Warren published the first edition of *Understanding Fiction*, an influential college textbook, they included two Welty stories, "Old Mr. Marblehall" and "A Piece of News."

10. Edward Loomis Davenport Seymour, *The Garden Encyclopedia* (New York: W. H. Wise & Co, 1936).

11. The Book of Kells, a ninth-century illuminated manuscript of the four Gospels, has been on display since the mid-nineteenth century in the Old Library of Trinity College, Dublin.

12. Katherine Anne Porter; Welty and Russell often referred to her by initials.

13. Kreyling, *Author and Agent*, 54.

14. In January 1940, before Russell had become Welty's agent, James Laughlin had accepted "Keela, the Outcast Indian Maiden" for publication in the annual *New Directions in Prose and Poetry*.

15. From Blake's *The Four Zoas: Night the Eighth*.

16. The Russells' second child, Will, was born on January 28, 1941.

17. This photograph has not been identified.

18. Vaughn's Seed Store, of Chicago and New York, sold an array of seeds, bulbs, and plants.

19. Robert O. Rubel, Jr., who operated Longview Nursery in Crichton, Alabama, collected and republished books on camellia culture and wrote his own, *Camellia Culture Under Glass*, in 1936.

20. This photograph was later published by Doubleday in a booklet publicizing *A Curtain of Green*.

21. Henry Miller (1891–1980) was the author of *Tropic of Cancer* (1934) and other works reflecting the bohemian experiences of American expatriates like himself in Paris. Miller's 1941 tour of the United States furnished material for a book of essays on American culture (*The Air-*

Conditioned Nightmare, 1945). Years later, Welty recalled how "my beloved editor, John Woodburn, who was a big tease," had suggested to Miller that he visit Welty during his 1941 travels. During Miller's Jackson stopover, Welty and her friends took Miller out to eat in Jackson and drove him around the picturesque countryside, but did not invite him to the Welty home, since Welty's mother considered Miller's work less than respectable (*Eudora Welty: Photographs*, xxii).

22. Katherine Anne Porter had recommended that Welty be invited for a sojourn at Yaddo, an artist's colony in Saratoga Springs, New York.

23. John Slocum, the junior member of the Russell and Volkening firm, had been drafted.

24. Russell had written Welty, "Someone told me that you live in monastic solitude and that you are locked in your room [. . .] . I know I'd sleep and the end of the Yaddo holiday would see me emerging from the room like a bear from hibernation except that I would be fat and sleek" (4.2.41).

25. On April 26, Welty said of the story, "I'm glad you think Asphodel is good—I thought it was either good or terrible and sat up nights having debates with myself."

26. Russell had reported, "I think the iris you sent and the birds feet violets have been blasted out of existence by the winter" (4.24.41).

27. At Breadloaf in 1940, Welty had met novelist Carson McCullers (1917–1967), whose behavior, including loud professions of love for Katherine Anne Porter, had caused Welty to dislike her. By the time of McCullers's 1941 stay at Yaddo, she had published *The Heart Is a Lonely Hunter* (1940) and *Reflections in a Golden Eye* (1941); her best-known book, *A Member of the Wedding*, was published in 1947.

28. Russell had reported, "The gladiolus are now over the 100 mark and maybe in four or five years or so will produce flowers. There's nothing like a long range view" (6.11.41).

29. This sculptor was José de Creeft. In 1944 Welty wrote a short essay on de Creeft's work for *The Magazine of Art*; it is reprinted in *Occasions: Selected Writings*.

30. Russell answered Welty's question in his next letter: "The lily is an excellent drawing of the Canada Lily which is now out everywhere. It has a good many other names also but the Latin name is Lilium Canadensis" (7.15.41). Russell was very knowledgeable about wildflowers and wished there were better information available about American varieties. In the fifties and early sixties, Russell was instrumental in raising funds for the New York Botanical Garden's production of H. W. Rickett's *Wild Flowers of the United States* (Rickett, "Foreword," v), a 1966 publication the *New Yorker* called "The Million-Dollar Book" (White 221).

31. "The Key" was published in the August 1941 issue of *Harper's Bazaar*.

32. Malaria was still fairly common in the early twentieth century in Mississippi, despite efforts to eradicate it. Welty reported periodic bouts with the disease, which was treatable but could recur; some strains of malaria remained dormant for months or years in a previously infected patient.

33. The *Junior League Magazine* published "Women! Make Turban in Own Home!" in November 1941. The piece is reprinted in *Occasions: Selected Writings*.

34. From *The Candle of Vision* (1918), the autobiography of Diarmuid Russell's father, George William Russell, "A.E." (1867–1935). A poet, playwright, and mystic, A.E. was a major figure in the Irish literary renaissance, a movement that sought to revive ancient Irish folklore and traditions and to create new works that would promote Irish nationalism.

35. Cornelia Otis Skinner (1901–1979), actress, playwright, radio personality, and author of *Our Hearts Were Young and Gay* (1942) and other humorous books.

36. This may have been the same picture that appears in *Eudora Welty: Photographs*, of a woman pointing at a tomato-shaped structure advertising the town of Crystal Springs, Mississippi, "The Tomatropolis." This is Photograph 73; Welty's editor later identified the woman as Jackson artist Helen Jay Lotterhos (Cole, 30).

37. Marrs, *Eudora Welty*, 84.

38. The Houyhnhnms, from Part IV of *Gulliver's Travels*, are well-spoken horses whose advanced civilization avoids wars. Earlier that month, Russell had sent Welty a book of essays by Alfred Richard Orage (1873–1934), editor of *New Age* and *New English Weekly* (11.18.41).

39. Welty's essay, "Ida M'Toy," was about a Jackson midwife and secondhand clothes dealer whose self-assurance, verve, and eccentricity fascinated Welty. *Accent* published the essay in summer 1942; it was reprinted in *The Eye of the Story*.

40. After fertilizing his garden, Russell wrote, he had manure to spare, so he fertilized his grass as well; "next year I expect to have a lawn such as only gods can sit on and not feel embarrassed" (12.1.41).

41. L. H. Myer's *The Root and the Flower*, published in the 1930s, was a series of novels set in sixteenth-century India.

42. Welty took good care of these sketches. Today they are on view at the Welty House, in person and via the online virtual tour at http://mdah.state.ms.us/welty/mantel.html.

43. Three days later, Russell wrote, "The camellia came safely as I wrote you and is being cherished and if the plant has any affection it will do something wonderful so that I can write down to you that the flowers never fade and smile when I come into the room in the morning" (12.26.41).

44. In his 1943 book on camellias, grower Gustav Gerbing said of the Eleanor of Fairoaks variety, "If you own one, you are indeed fortunate" (66).

Chapter 2

1. Russell replied, "You didn't say what the good news was that made you lay down the digger and go to work on THE WINDS and as Mary Lou never told me I can only guess that

they have said they will take it with a few changes" (1.20.42). Mary Lou Aswell, fiction editor at *Harper's Bazaar*, had responded to the story more enthusiastically than Russell, who admitted to Welty that he was somewhat confused by it.

2. The present-day garden of the Eudora Welty House contains forty-one camellia shrubs that were cultivated by the Weltys (EW House website).

3. In northern Mississippi.

4. Writing that Welty's "extravagant flowers arrived in good condition and were lovely," Russell added that another friend had told him that "the classic way to send them was to cut little pieces of potato and insert the stems in them and that they used to keep quite fresh this way, even in the old days when they were sent by parcel post" (3.17.42).

5. Guggenheim Fellowships, established in 1925, supported academic or creative work. Recipients needed to demonstrate promise of continued success, but the award carried no other conditions. In 1942 the award was twelve hundred dollars.

6. Henry Volkening, Russell's partner at the agency, and John Woodburn, Welty's editor at Doubleday, Doran.

7. Middle English, from the General Prologue to the *Canterbury Tales*; Chaucer writes that the month of April is when people long to go on pilgrimages.

8. The seedpods of the beggar-lice plant are covered with stiff hairs that cause the pods to stick, Velcro-like, to passersby.

9. The *Atlantic* had accepted "Livvie Is Back," later titled "Livvie."

10. Tires were the first item to be rationed by the Office of Price Administration, in late December 1941. In May 1941, gasoline rationing began (Schneider and Schneider, 55).

11. Welty enclosed a letter from J. F. Henry, sent to her care of *Harper's*, where "The Wide Net" had been published in May 1942.

12. Oakhurst Gardens of Arcadia, California, advertised "Out of the Ordinary Bulbs."

13. Russell had written that cutworms "seem to find good eating in my garden" (6. 8. 42).

14. Welty had become friends with Edna Frederikson (1904–1998) in 1941 at Yaddo. Frederikson published short stories and poems in little magazines, and in 1971 published a novel, *Three Parts Earth*.

15. The Leila camellia is also known as "Catherine Cathcart."

16. This structure had been built by Welty's brothers as a teenage lair; in the thirties, Welty and her friends sometimes used it as a gathering place. A reconstructed version of the little house now stands in its place, behind the garden in the backyard of the Welty House.

17. Junior Commandoes were the invention of Harold Gray, who portrayed them in his *Little Orphan Annie* comics. Gray, like many creators of comics, encouraged readers to support the government's efforts to collect scrap paper, rubber, and metal to support wartime production needs and offset domestic shortages.

18. Charlie Bein, a friend from New Orleans.

19. Fannye Cook, a boarder at the Weltys' home, was a conservationist, biologist, and the founder and director of the Mississippi Museum of Natural Science.

20. On March 9, 1942, Russell had reported on his gardening to Welty, "It delights my heart to be able to do this for it is something which has no connection with the war but is part of something older and more important."

21. The campus of Belhaven College, across the street from the Welty home, was visible from the front windows. Welty wrote later that her story "June Recital" was partly inspired by the piano playing she could hear from Belhaven's practice rooms as she wrote in her upstairs bedroom (*Occasions*, 315).

22. As Welty's agent, Russell received 10 percent of her earnings.

23. "The Winds" appeared in the August 1942 *Harper's Bazaar*.

24. Aimee Shands, a high school friend of Welty's, had been part of a group of classmates who attended Columbia University along with Welty in 1930–31. By now Aimee was evidently a more active member of Jackson's Junior League than Welty, who had described herself to Russell as "a member in bad standing of the J. L." (7.23.41). Aimee's father was Dr. Shands, the neighbor who provided gas-heated winter covers for his camellias.

25. Robinson was working in the U.S. Army Air Corps Intelligence.

26. This article, "AE (George William Russell)," appeared in the February 1943 issue of the *Atlantic Monthly*.

27. Welty is quoting from a letter about beer seed that she received from another *Market Bulletin* reader and then forwarded to Russell (8.13.42).

28. Russell had written that he was about to be "citizenized" (11.10.42).

29. Seta Alexander Sancton, one of Welty's Jackson friends. She had married a writer, Tom Sancton, who for a time was Russell's client.

30. Elizabeth Lawrence, *Gardening for Love: The Market Bulletins*, 41.

31. Welty wrote Robinson in 1945 that "the Blue Wonder lily is in bud—something I got from Market Bulletin and the lady replied to my question that it had never bloomed and that was why she wondered" (3.19.45).

32. Mr. Aswell was married to Mary Lou Aswell, fiction editor of *Harper's Bazaar*. Russell had written Welty, "I got so mad last Saturday. We went down to Ed Aswell's for dinner and he had a bud on his camellia, the little one you gave me and which I passed on to him when I got the big plant last Christmas. The annoying thing too is that his cam. hasn't grown very much but my one has innumerable shoots and ought to be treble the size next year, all the leaves large and green and glossy. The gardenia also looks in wonderful shape. It lost a few leaves when I brought it in for the winter but all the other leaves are rich green and not yellow as they have been in the past. Maybe my cam. will do wonders next year and that I will look forward to" (11.25.42).

33. William Maxwell was a fiction editor at the *New Yorker*; he became a close friend of

Welty's. Her reply to the letter she mentions here, followed by fifty years' correspondence between Maxwell and Welty, can be found in *What There Is to Say We Have Said*, edited by Suzanne Marrs.

34. S. S. Berry was a company that advertised "Daffodils and Irises for Your Garden."

35. Russell had reported, "They are the only plants we have ever found that grow in deep shade—white flowers and deep green foliage without ever getting lanky" (2.9.43).

36. The Office of War Information (OWI), established in June 1942, produced propaganda in support of the U.S. war effort. It urged women to join the workforce as a (temporary) patriotic duty, and encouraged writers and publishers to produce work with patriotic themes.

37. An example that confirms Welty's view of this kind of writing is an excerpt from a newsletter she wrote in May 1944, reprinted in *Occasions* (130–131).

38. Russell had written to suggest a date for her visit, informing her that she would be receiving about two hundred dollars in royalties soon (3.15.43).

39. In Welty's story "The Wanderers," she describes Virgie Rainey walking to her house after getting off the train from Memphis: "in that interim between train and home, she walked and ran looking about her in a kind of glory, by the back way" (546).

40. Paintings by Henri Rousseau (1844–1910), such as *Equatorial Jungle*, featured stylized wildlife and lush, oversized vegetation.

41. Welty described this soldier forty years later in part III of *One Writer's Beginnings* (*Stories, Essays, and Memoir*, 941).

42. Rodney, MS, was once a river town; after the Mississippi River changed course in the late nineteenth century, most of its inhabitants left. Rodney was the setting for Welty's "At the Landing" and was one of the towns described in her article "Some Notes on River Country," *Harper's Bazaar*, February 1944.

43. Russell replied, "Are they seeds? for they look so transparent and gummy that I doubt their growing and as for the liquid they might produce I am full of suspicion—would be less suspicious if I could gather them from my own plant but as it is I can't quite imagine how they are produced and I'm full of scientific scepticism" (5.18.43).

44. In chapter I of Welty's 1946 novel *Delta Wedding*, India Fairchild calls "Greenie!" on Laura McRaven, who admits that the two girls are still joined in Greenie. "'All right,' Laura said. 'Owe you something.' She stooped and put a pinch of grass in her shoe" (*Complete Novels*, 98).

45. Russell had written that a plant "grows in Africa which is so sour that after a taste lemons seem unbearably sweet. It is mentioned in Fairchild's book about plant exploring" (5.25.43).

46. "Don't worry about that story for for what it is it succeeds," was Russell's reply. "The Purple Hat" had been sold to England as well as to *Harper's Bazaar* (6.10.43).

47. In May Russell wrote that he had planted vegetables beside a spotting post (5.18.43). Elsewhere he wrote of being on night duty at the spotting post with other volunteers. The U.S. Army Air Forces enrolled civilian volunteers in the Ground Observer Corps, which watched for enemy planes.

48. Dorothy Dix was the pen name of a syndicated advice columnist, Elizabeth Meriwether Gilmer (1870–1951).

49. In chapter V of *Delta Wedding*, Troy advises Robbie, "A wet leaf on the head prevents the sunstroke" (239).

50. On July 2, Russell had reported that something was still eating his vegetables, "a spirit animal" that he hoped to "exorcise."

51. This was likely the same Mrs. Fox who traded a jar of pickled peaches with Welty in 1940 when Welty wanted some to send to Russell. At the time, Welty wrote Russell that Mrs. Fox should have been ashamed to have traded a jar containing smashed pickles, and that in retaliation, Welty had put a label with Mrs. Fox's name on the jar, sent it to Russell, then told Mrs. Fox that it had been sent to New York with her name on it (9.13.40).

52. Mary Lou Aswell, editor at *Harper's Bazaar*, who was editing Welty's essay "Some Notes on River Country."

53. Marrs, *Eudora Welty*, 45.

54. Dorothy Simmons, a long-time friend from Jackson who now lived in Utica, MS.

55. Russell had written, "One [melon] is a sort of a mystery. It was given to me as a honeydew but of all the seeds planted only one is a honeydew and the others are quite different. [. . .] Perhaps it is a cross and out of that will come some delectable flavor that will enchant mankind for evermore" (8.20.43).

Chapter 3

1. Judge G. Garland Lyell was the father of Welty's friend Frank Lyell.

2. Warner (1898–1978), a British writer of fiction and poetry, published *A Garland of Straw and Other Stories* in 1943.

3. Welty's 1942 novella, *The Robber Bridegroom*.

4. On 9/10 Welty wrote, "It is nice to hear about the belladonna amaryllis—I hope none of them or the roses were hurt by the bomb in the garden."

5. The "bulb author" was probably Allen H. Wood, Jr., whose *Bulbs for Your Garden* (Boston: Houghton Mifflin, 1936) is among the books in the Welty House. Wood uses the same terminology to describe the varieties of *Amaryllis belladonna*, and says they must be kept "in a cool cellar until March" (30–31). Welty's description of the sea-daffodil seems to come from Elizabeth Lawrence's *A Southern Garden* (135).

6. Harcourt Brace, the publisher of Welty's *The Wide Net and Other Stories*, which came out in September 1943. *A Curtain of Green* and *The Robber Bridegroom* had been published by Doubleday, Doran and edited by John Woodburn. Welty switched publishers when Woodburn left Doubleday for Harcourt Brace.

7. Martha Foley was editor of Houghton Mifflin's annual collection, *The Best Short Stories*, from 1942 to 1976.

8. Whit Burnett was editor of *Story* magazine and former husband of Martha Foley, with whom he had founded the magazine in 1931. He had written Welty requesting to include her story "A Still Moment" in an anthology he was preparing.

9. According to the September 27, 1943, *Time* review, "These eight stories about the South present as perplexing and exasperating a mixture of good and bad as U.S. writing can show. [. . .] These flashing, strange stories of Miss Welty's are about as human as a fish."

10. Diana Trilling's review appeared in the October 2, 1943, issue of *Nation*.

11. Pamela Travers, Russell's client and friend, the author of the Mary Poppins books.

12. Russell's landlady, Charlotte Fowler, had praised one of his paintings so much that he felt obliged to give it to her, even though "I do so few good ones I would have liked to have kept it," he told Welty (10.14.43).

13. Welty's friend Dorothy Simmons lived in Utica, MS, about forty miles from Jackson.

14. "The Delta Cousins."

15. Florence Lehman (1884–1961) was the aunt of Welty's and Robinson's Jackson-born friend Lehman Engel (1910–1982), a composer and conductor for theatre, film, and television.

16. Renowned Italian conductor Arturo Toscanini (1867–1957) was director of the NBC Symphony from 1937 to 1954.

17. Willie Belle was the Russells' housekeeper.

18. Russell said of the story, "The Delta Cousins," that "every individual section seems good and yet as a whole it doesn't quite have the effect it ought to have" (11.10.43).

19. Mary Frances and Joe Skinner, fellow Jacksonians and friends of Welty and Robinson.

20. French for "but."

21. Robinson, who was stationed in Algiers, had just moved to a new address, having been billeted for a time in the home of an Algierian landlady who grew increasingly hostile towards Robinson for using the electricity, taking baths, or sitting on her furniture. After the war Robinson wrote an account of this experience, "Room in Algiers," that appeared in the *New Yorker* on October 19, 1946.

22. Welty had received a leather portfolio, bulbs, and other gifts from Robinson on November 26.

23. Both the Russell children were in bed with the flu and, in Russell's words, "had to be amused and read to and wanted all sorts of things every few moments" (12.7.43).

24. "As the catterpiller [*sic*] chooses the fairest leaves to lay her eggs on, so the priest lays his curse on the fairest joys," wrote William Blake in "Proverbs of Hell."

25. *Indigo* (1943) was by Christine Weston, one of Russell's clients.

26. *Farewell, My Lovely* (1940) and *The Lady in the Lake* (1943) were crime-detective novels by Raymond Chandler.

27. Raymond, MS, is about sixteen miles west of Jackson. Terry, MS, is sixteen miles south.

28. This was another of the presents Welty had received from Robinson on November 26.

29. Russell had written on December 13, "My head is stupid today on account of having tried some new kind of liquor last night—prepared old-fashioneds that you just pour out of a bottle. I warn you against them."

30. French—"for the spring."

31. Helen Jay Lotterhos, a Jackson painter.

32. Dr. Harley Shands, a prominent surgeon, was the father of Aimee Shands Welty's class-mate and Junior League stalwart. Welty described Dr. Shands's elaborate camellia-warming devices in an earlier letter to Russell (1.7.42). Other letters periodically record Welty's belief that Dr. Shands and Aimee were not above stealing camellia cuttings from the Weltys' yard.

33. The Jitney Jungle No. 14, a grocery store a few blocks from Welty's home.

34. *Left Hand, Right Hand!*, Sitwell's autobiography, was serialized in the *Atlantic* begin-ning in January 1944.

35. British publisher.

36. Welty and Robinson, along with Robinson's sister Anna Belle and brother Will, took a trip to Mexico in the summer of 1937 (Marrs, *Eudora Welty*, 56).

37. Edward Weeks, editor of the *Atlantic*, was considering Welty's story "The Delta Cous-ins."

38. Mittie Creekmore Welty was Walter's wife and the sister of Robinson's and Welty's friend and classmate Hubert Creekmore. Walter and Mittie's baby, Elizabeth, was the elder of Welty's nieces.

39. The wartime paper shortage made it difficult for magazines to publish works as long as "The Delta Cousins." Weeks had agreed to publish the story if Welty would cut three to four thousand words, but because the publication date was six months away, Welty now had more time to decide what to cut. She hoped to complete another story by that time, so that Weeks could have a choice of which to publish (Kreyling, 107).

40. Welty was writing "A Sketching Trip," set in Fergusson's Wells, a fictional town in the Mississippi Delta.

41. APO 650 was Robinson's new military address.

42. These science fiction novels were by Abraham P. Merritt (1916).

43. Stratosphere was a brand of writing paper. In his April 4 letter, Russell said he had writ-ten Welty "the worst kind of letters for some weeks—short, terse, uninformative and devoid of any lustre." He theorized that lack of exercise and variety caused his dullness, just as the moon-dwellers in H. G. Wells's *The First Men in the Moon* had become distorted from overspecializa-tion. This may explain Welty's parenthetical "Greetings" from the stratosphere.

44. Russell said Rose was "holding off on all invitations" in hopes that Welty would visit them in May (4.4.44).

45. English editions of *The Robber Bridegroom*.

46. In "June Recital," Virgie brings Miss Eckhart "a magnolia bloom which she had stolen" (*Stories, Essays, and Memoir*, 350).

47. Mrs. Macgowan was an active member of the Jackson Garden Club, according to Chestina Welty's history of that organization (MDAH).

48. In February 1943 Welty told Russell of writing to inquire about OWI (Office of War Information) jobs (2.15.43).

49. Selfs are flowers that have only one color.

50. The legendary volcano Vesuvius, which destroyed Pompeii and Herculaneum in AD 79, had just erupted in March 1944, damaging Allied aircraft in a nearby airfield.

51. This was the Allies' fourth attempt to break through German lines south of Rome.

52. Robert Van Gelder, editor of the *New York Times Book Review*, who had already published several book reviews by Welty.

53. WACS were Women's Army Corps (WAC), originally the Women's Army Auxiliary Corps (WAAC).

54. Welty had found a sublet to share with Dolly Wells, a friend from Jackson, at 25 E. 10th Street, just below the apartment of Robinson's friends Alice and Nancy Farley.

55. Robinson apparently told Welty that he had gotten her several presents, including a painting on bone, on his recent trip to Egypt. These gifts arrived in Jackson in November 1944.

56. Welty wrote to Robinson on July 5 to describe how she spent the July 4 holiday: "I went to a 'picnic'—from which I stood a little aback." At this very formal party, Welty "felt so homesick—all the men had on their ties. It was such a beautiful day too" (7.5.44).

57. Gellhorn, a pioneering female journalist as well as a fiction writer, was covering the war for *Collier's* magazine. In a previous letter Welty had told Robinson that "it burns me up that that phoney can get over there" (7.11.44).

58. "How the South Feels," by Mississippian David L. Cohn, had been in the January 1944 *Atlantic Monthly*. Cohn wrote that "Southern paternalism towards the Negro" was being replaced by more overt hostility between blacks and whites, and that "the Negro question is insoluble, as are all complex social questions" (49).

59. The Cloisters, both a garden and a museum, is part of the Metropolitan Museum of Art. The collection features works from medieval Europe, including the Unicorn Tapestries Welty describes.

60. Van Winkle, MS, is five miles from Jackson.

61. Robert Van Gelder, editor of the *New York Times Book Review*.

62. Cyrus "Cy" Sulzberger, foreign affairs correspondent for the *New York Times*.

63. Terry, MS, where Welty sometimes got bulbs, is sixteen miles south of Jackson.

64. Robinson was seeking information about a cousin of Welty's who had been reported missing in action.

65. Before this letter, Welty had been writing to Robinson at "H.Q, 62 Fighter Wing."

Chapter 4

1. Welty's cousin.

2. Congratulations were for Joe and Mary Frances Skinner's new baby, Mary Martha.

3. This essay must have been "The Literature of Utility," *Tomorrow* IV (March 1945): 34–35. Welty's "At the Landing" had appeared in the magazine in 1943.

4. Frank Lyell, a close friend of Welty and Robinson.

5. Servicemen were normally eligible for a leave every eighteen months, unless their work was deemed too important for them to be spared.

6. On November 17, Welty had written, "I think of the last sentence in the last letter, that you might get here to see the bulbs, and hope it is true and will be soon."

7. After Welty asked Russell to look at a gallery in New York that had advertised A.E. paintings for sale, Russell told her that the painting was not really worth buying and that he would give Welty an A.E. painting that was in his home for her Christmas present (11.17.44). Robinson could have seen this painting when he visited Welty and the Russells in the spring of 1943.

8. Welty's friend Helen Jay Lotterhos was a painter.

9. "A Little Triumph," which Welty later revised and incorporated into *Delta Wedding*. She sent the story to Russell and the carbon to Robinson on December 19.

10. Mary Lavin, an Irish writer of short stories and novels, was a client of Russell's. In November 1944, the *Atlantic* began serializing her novel *Gabriel Galloway*.

11. Russell's article, "Raymond Chandler and the Future of Whodunits," appeared in the June 17, 1945, issue of the *New York Times*.

12. Welty had been asked to write a nonfiction book on the Natchez Trace.

13. Nash Burger, a friend of Welty's from Jackson, who worked from 1945 to 1974 for the *New York Times Book Review*.

14. A wooden box in which Robinson had shipped Welty's presents, which had arrived in November, also contained a live termite. Flit was an insecticide. Prior to her extermination campaign, Welty sent Robinson a poem in the voice of this insect, known as Choo Choo, lamenting, "I want to have Christmas on the Isle of Capri" (12.4.44).

15. Welty told Robinson on January 8, "I failed to get a sick marine a ticket to Chicago hospital where his folks could come to see him because the Red Cross wouldn't accept his little pieces of paper as proof and his hands trembling to go through his paper suitcase of clothes looking for what would convince them."

16. The U.S. Office of Price Administration had been rationing gas since 1942. Citizens who demonstrated that they needed the gasoline for their work were eligible for more than the standard amount, which was three gallons a week in 1945 (Schneider and Schneider, 79).

17. *Tomorrow* was a small magazine published and edited by Eileen Garrett, a well-known medium; it published Welty's "At the Landing" and Russell's essay "The Literature of Utility." Hubert Creekmore, Welty's friend and the brother of her sister-in-law Mittie, was an editor,

translator, and author of three collections of poetry and three novels. His final book was *Daffodils Are Dangerous: The Poisonous Plants in Your Garden* (1966).

18. Welty wrote Russell about "the moon and star" that were visible on December 18, 1944. "So beautiful—we were phoning each other all over Jackson" (12.19.44).

19. Welty wrote Robinson a few days later, "She was a beautiful person—I cannot forget her ever—her China roses in the wilderness" (2.14.45).

20. Glenway Wescott, novelist and poet from Wisconsin. Welty reviewed his novel *Household in Athens* for the *New York Times Book Review* in March.

21. Rosebay willow herb, known as fireweed in the U.S., germinates very rapidly after exposure to heat and light—conditions created when bombs destroyed trees and buildings and the seeds of these plants had room to grow. The purple-flowering willow herb was the most common of the flowers that grew profusely in London bomb craters. A 1943 *New York Times* article, "Strange Plants Bloom in London Where Nazi Bombs Leveled the City," reported that these flowers were widely rumored to have sprung from centuries-old seeds, but that English botanists had found only willow herb and other common plants growing in bomb craters.

22. Welty had discussed this bulb, which was advertised for sale in the *Mississippi Market Bulletin*, in letters during the summer of 1942 (see chapter 2).

23. The Rebel was the train that ran from Jackson to New Orleans.

24. Robinson had sent Welty a leather portfolio in 1943.

25. Chestina Welty's high blood pressure was undoubtedly worsened by her anxiety. According to Welty's biographer and friend, Suzanne Marrs, Chestina sometimes listened to the radio all night to keep up with war news (Marrs, *Eudora Welty*, 120).

26. Bluet was the youngest member of the Fairchild family in Welty's "Delta story."

27. In 1942 Welty had told Russell she was "furious" to learn that this bulb was not expected to bloom for four more years (11.25.42); apparently it bloomed a year ahead of schedule, in 1945. Welty had corresponded with Elizabeth Lawrence about a "blue wonder lily," although she seems not to have told Lawrence that when this bulb bloomed, it had proved to be a Camassia. Years later, Lawrence discussed Welty's "wonder lily" in her gardening column; she wrote that another gardener had helped Lawrence identify this plant as a seven-year hyacinthus (*Through the Garden Gate*, 189).

28. On March 9, Welty asked Robinson for permission to use this anecdote.

29. Apparently the manuscript had doubled in size since March 19, when she told Robinson she had written "about 100 pages."

30. Denmark was occupied by Germany but had an extensive network of resistance. Russell's letter of March 28, 1945, explained that the Office of War Information had helped the Danish underground arrange to publish Welty's work.

31. The Russell children were recovering from the chicken pox, which they had caught from Pamela Travers's son Camillus when he stayed with them.

32. Noting that Welty seemed to think her Delta story might "go on forever," Russell told her how Rose had begun knitting without knowing how to stop, so that her work grew from a pot holder to a muffler to a fifteen-foot length she had to abandon. Russell predicted that "next you'll write that you are on page 917 and that the girl has just had her second child. You will, in fact, be engaged in a life work and in the year 2067, a few years after you are dead some literary executor will be working through some 27,000 pages of ms. and year after year for some 70 or 80 years a book by you will appear"(3.27.45). This book of letters is one in that series.

33. Franklin Delano Roosevelt, who had been president since 1933, died on April 12, 1945.

34. Paul was the husband of Robinson's sister Anna Belle; their wedding had occurred on the weekend that Pearl Harbor was attacked.

35. In 1944, after Jackson resident C. D. Jones was reported missing in action, Welty, who knew Jones's family, had asked Robinson to make inquiries, and Robinson had verified that Jones was still alive (Marrs, *Eudora Welty*, 108).

36. Welty may be talking about Hemingway's *For Whom the Bell Tolls*, which was on the best seller list in 1940 and 1941 and was made into a film in 1943.

37. *Fireman Flower* was a 1944 collection of short stories by William Sansom, reviewed by Welty in May 1945 in *Tomorrow* (reprinted in *Occasions*, 66–67).

38. Russell was editing *The Portable Irish Reader* (Viking, 1946).

39. Mr. Fowler was Russell's landlord.

40. The Jackson *Clarion-Ledger* published letters to the editor under the title "Voice of the People."

41. Katharine S. White mentioned Ware in "A Romp in the Catalogues" in her gardening column in the *New Yorker* on March 1, 1958, calling his "the most attractive catalogue I have seen" for lily bulbs (*Onward and Upward*, 13).

42. Russell had written, "I'm going to try one of the giganticum himalaicum or whatever it is called that grows 12 feet high. [. . .] I have wanted one of those giganticum lilies ever since I was born in Dublin" (7.20.45).

43. Tanglewood Music Center, the Lenox, Massachussetts, summer home of the Boston Symphony Orchestra, holds a summer music festival featuring open-air concerts.

44. Arthur Stanley Eddington, *The Nature of the Physical World*, 1928.

45. Harcourt Brace paid Welty an advance of five thousand dollars. By May 1946 *Delta Wedding* was in its third printing, earning back the advance (DR to EW 5.10.46).

46. Bilbo was announcing his run for a third term in the U.S. Senate. Welty's letter to the editor appeared in the Jackson *Clarion-Ledger* on December 28, 1945. In it she denounced the recent visit of the virulently anti-Semitic Gerald L.K. Smith and the newspaper's treatment of him as a legitimate politician. She also predicted Bilbo's ouster in the next election, "God willing." Russell wrote back to Welty, "Good for you and the letter. But this sort of stuff will probably have the Klan out for your blood. I must say Mississippi has a few people it ought to be apologetic about" (1.2.46).

Chapter 5

1. Undated letter from mid-January 1946.

2. The *New York Times* reported this comment in a June 30, 1946, article written by Hodding Carter, a Greenville, MS, newpaper editor who was also a friend of Welty and Robinson.

3. The *Atlantic*'s first payment was one thousand dollars.

4. The lines Welty recalled in this letter are from the anonymous "Tom O'Bedlam's Song." The poem had been quoted in Isaac Disraeli's *Curiosities of Literature* (1834) and cited by several fiction writers, including Edgar Allan Poe, Walter de la Mare, and John Galsworthy. Bedlam was a mental hospital in London; perhaps the name O'Bedlam made Welty think this verse was eligible to be included in the *Portable Irish Reader* that Russell was completing.

Welty's 1946 experience of lines of verse "running through my head" prefigures a character's experience in a story she did not yet know she was going to write, "June Recital." Throughout that story, the protagonist, Cassie, remembers stray lines from "The Song of Wandering Aengus," a Yeats poem.

5. Christine Weston's novel, *The Dark Woods*, was sold to Twentieth Century Fox and cast (Otto Preminger was to direct, Maureen O'Hara and Tyrone Power to star) but never produced.

6. J. I. Rodale (1891–1971), who began publishing his magazine *Organic Gardening* in 1942. His 1943 book *Compost and How to Make It* is among the books at the Eudora Welty House.

7. Charles Hoy Fort (1874–1932) collected and published accounts of UFOs, teleportations, poltergeists, and other events that he said could not be explained by modern science.

8. Two weeks later, Russell wrote Welty that the book had made the *Herald-Tribune* Best Seller List (5.14.46).

9. *The Gleaners* (1857), a painting by Jean-François Millet, portrays three stooping women gathering wheat that harvesters left behind.

10. Diana Trilling, "Fiction in Review," *Nation*, May 11, 1946.

11. A lump on Russell's neck was later biopsied and found to be noncancerous, as Welty reported to Robinson in October (10.18.46).

12. This story, originally called "The Golden Apples," became "June Recital." Its piano teacher is called Miss Eckhart and the girl is Virgie Rainey, so Miss Eckhart's phrase became "Virgie Rainey, *danke schoen.*"

13. Welty wrote Robinson in California on 10.8.46, "This has been one of those times I've been unnerved lately—Rosie inviting me to Katonah for Christmas—I'm no good at times. I thought if you were at Box 706 [California] for Christmas I would just turn my face to the wall." On 10.14.46 she wrote, "Of course don't think of Christmas now if you don't want to—no need—you know. I must have told you before how forehanded Rosie is with plans. Part of it's childlike eagerness to see what others are going to do. I shouldn't have let it stir me so, in October."

14. Mrs. Barksdale, a long-time member and past president of the Jackson Garden Club, also wrote a gardening column, according to a history of the club written by Chestina Welty.

15. A few days later, Welty added, "How wonderful the stuff you got for me. So glad to have it. Suppose it lightens and freshens all this clay—be a difference in my life" (11.7.46).

16. Vardamans may have been Robinson's relatives. His late step-grandfather was the Mississippi politician James K. Vardaman (1861–1930).

17. This story, "Dowdie's Guilt," eventually became "Music from Spain."

18. During Welty's last stay at Katonah, she had witnessed the Russells' cutting of numerous trees.

19. This quote was in the March 1, 1947, *New Yorker*. An item on page 87 quoted a *Jackson Daily News* report of the meeting of the Flower Lovers' Garden Club. Members voted to write a resolution protesting the U.S. Senate's refusal to seat Senator-elect Theodore Bilbo and commending Bilbo for "upholding the traditions of the South." The article then noted that the meeting's main program was a talk on spring flowers, "placing particular emphasis on color." The *New Yorker*'s comment on this report was, "Well, naturally."

20. Gustav Gerbing, a Florida camellia grower and author of *Camellias* (1943).

21. In "June Recital," as this story was eventually to be called, this flower indicates Virgie's self-assurance, even vanity, about her piano playing. Virgie is practicing on her teacher's piano when Miss Eckhart's elderly mother appears in the studio and screams, *"Danke schoen, danke schoen, danke schoen!"* The narrator observed, "Virgie, of course, kept on practicing—it was a Schumann 'forest piece.' She had a pomegranate flower (the marbleized kind, from the Moodys') stuck in her breast-pin, and it did not even move" (*Stories, Essays, and Memoir*, 369).

22. Welty had taken a road trip to Mexico in 1937 with Robinson, his sister Anna Belle, and his brother Will.

23. Welty's letters in the forties report recurring problems with back pain.

24. Katonah, New York, was in Westchester County, where most residents were very well off.

25. Shortly after his election, Bilbo had been diagnosed with cancer of the jaw and throat. In January 1947, he had postponed an operation in order to be sworn in for his new Senate term. Opposition to Bilbo had increased considerably in late 1946, what with his calls for violence against black voters, admission of his Klan membership, and new evidence that he took bribes in exchange for wartime construction contracts; two Senate committees conducted investigations of Bilbo and a third recommended that he not be sworn in for his new term. On January 3, 1947, Bilbo was not sworn in like other senators-elect, but his credentials were tacitly accepted. He and his staff were put on the Senate payroll, and Bilbo left Washington the next day for further cancer treatment. He died on August 21, 1947.

26. "The Golden Apples," published in the September 1947 issue of *Harper's Bazaar*, was later retitled "June Recital."

27. Art Foff and his wife, Toni, were friends Robinson and Welty had made in San Francisco. Foff, a client of Russell's, was awaiting the appearance of his 1947 novel, *Glorious in Another Day.*

28. Loch is the younger brother of Cassie Morrison, the protagonist of "June Recital." Welty's narration alternates between these two characters' points of view: Cassie daydreams in her room while Loch, in his room, observes the house next door through his telescope.

29. Russell had written that "the camellia looks fine. I hope it isn't planning any more elusive tricks. I just detest its practice of getting three-quarters open and then getting no further and after a while dropping off. Tantalizing and irritating" (11.7.47).

30. In chapter 8 of *Alice through the Looking Glass*, when the White Knight sets out into the woods with Alice, he brings along a plum-cake dish, explaining that "it will come in handy if we find any plum-cake." Welty's "holding the plate" probably refers to her hopes of finding a blossom on a fall-blooming camellia; in fall 1946, Robinson had sent Welty a plate made to hold camellia flowers (10.9.46).

31. Welty's friend Dolly (Rosa) Wells, with whom she had shared an apartment during her 1944 sojourn in New York, still lived in the city.

32. Levee Press, in Greenwood, Mississippi, was publishing Welty's story set in San Francisco, "Music from Spain," as a small book.

33. Later that month, Russell wrote, "The camellia has five flowers on it now, blooming its head off, God Bless It. I think it saw the three feet of snow outside and thought if it didn't do something I'd throw it out" (2.20.48).

34. DeLisle is just north of Pass Christian and Bay St. Louis on the Gulf Coast.

35. It's unclear if Welty had intended to type "shortened it from 52 to about 46," or if she was ironically reporting that this story had gotten longer with revision, as many of her works did.

36. A new story, "Sir Rabbit," was not long in coming. Welty wrote Russell the next day, "I felt cheered by your letter and maybe that's why at 11 o'clock last night I began writing a new story and finished it up right then in bed. I'd already typed solidly all day getting Music from S. ready for Levee (wrote the whole damn thing just about over—but really I think *this* time I got it right—and the key is, you'd never guess, the little man in it is from Battle Hill and who he is is one of the McLain twins—don't faint. Cleared everything up)" (2.18.48). Robinson's story, "Rite of Spring," was eventually published in *Horizon* in November 1948 under the title ". . . All This Juice and All This Joy."

37. Many white southerners were bitterly opposing Truman's stance on civil rights. In December 1946 he created a Commission on Civil Rights, partly in response to numerous instances of violence against African Americans, including ex-servicemen (Leuchtenburg, 166). In October 1947 the commission released its report, documenting widespread racial discrimination and proposing federal measures to guarantee voting rights, enforce laws against lynching, and end discrimination in education, housing, and employment. On February 2, 1948, Truman urged Congress to enact some of these recommendations. On February 12, Mississippi

legislators unanimously approved a resolution inviting "all true white Jeffersonian Democrats" to join them in opposing Truman's civil rights proposals; this event made the front page of the next day's *New York Times*.

38. Emily and Charlie Bein, Robinson's friends from New Orleans.

39. William Sansom, whose earlier book, *Fireman Flower*, Welty had reviewed.

40. Eileen McGrath, from Mt. Kisco, New York, whom Welty had met through the Russells and who was now in medical school.

41. A sketch Welty wrote for this revue, "Bye-Bye, Brevoort, " was first performed in Massachusetts in summer 1949 (Gordon, 48–52).

42. Lambert Davis, an editor at Harcourt Brace.

43. Welty continued to explore possible alternatives to Pinehurst Street in Jackson. In 1950, after returning from her travels in Europe, Welty looked for a property in rural Mississippi, hoping to renovate or build (a plan her mother opposed). She was particularly interested in a house for sale in Learned, Mississippi, but its owner would not sell to an unmarried woman (Marrs, *Eudora Welty*, 191).

44. The "long one" had been called "The Golden Apples," but Welty decided to use that title for her book, so she retitled the story "June Recital."

45. Robinson had applied for an Albert Bender Grant and Welty had applied for a Guggenheim.

46. Henry Allen Moe (1894–1975) was the chief administrator for the Guggenheim Foundation from 1925 to 1963.

47. Welty and Robinson had met Faulkner at a party in Oxford, Mississippi, in May 1948; Faulkner, who admired Welty's work, had then invited them to dinner the following evening.

48. Marrs, *Eudora Welty*, 173.

49. Mary Jane Ward's unfavorable review of Fritz Peters's book, *The World Next Door*, appeared in the *New York Times* on September 18, 1949. Welty favorably reviewed the book on the same day in the *New York Times Book Review*. Peters was briefly married to Welty's friend Mary Lou Aswell, fiction editor of *Harper's Bazaar*.

50. "Put Me in the Sky!" was published in *Accent* later that year; Welty revised the story and retitled it "Circe" when it appeared in *The Bride of the Innisfallen and Other Stories* (1955).

51. This comes from Book 19 of *The Odyssey*. Welty's "dream that came in the ivory window" was probably her hope of making this trip with Robinson.

52. Carlos Antonio de Padua Chávez y Ramírez was a composer and the conductor of the Mexican Symphonic Orchestra.

53. Welty and Hildy Dolson had house-sat in the Merrills' home in summer 1948.

54. Wanamaker's, a large department store in Philadelphia, also had a branch in New York City. Elizabeth was Welty's niece, and Mary Martha was the daughter of Jackson friends Joe and Mary Frances Skinner.

55. In August 1949, Faulkner had taken Welty and Robinson sailing.

BIBLIOGRAPHY

N. B. This list includes the most recent editions of Welty's published work. For a detailed publication history of individual works, readers should consult Noel Polk's *Eudora Welty: A Bibliography of Her Work*; updates appear in the *Eudora Welty Review*.

A.E. (George William Russell). *The Candle of Vision.* London: Macmillan and Company, 1918. Print.

Barilleaux, Rene Paul, ed. *Passionate Observer: Eudora Welty Among Artists of the Thirties.* Jackson: Mississippi Museum of Art, 2002. Print.

Black, Patti Carr. Personal interview. 4 Aug. 2011.

Blake, William. *The Poems and Prophecies of William Blake.* Ed. Max Plowman. London: J. M. Dent & Sons, 1927. Print.

Carter, Hodding. "'The Man' From Misssississippi—Bilbo." *New York Times* 30 June 1946: 12+. *ProQuest Historical Newspapers: The New York Times (1851–2008).* Web. 26 Feb. 2012.

"Catherine Cathcart." *Web Camellia Register.* International Camellia Society, 27 June 2011. Web. 7 Mar. 2012.

Cohn, David L. "How the South Feels." *Atlantic Monthly* 87 (January 1944): 47–51. Print.

Cole, Hunter. "On the Publishing of *Photographs.*" In *Eudora Welty and the Poetics of the Body,* ed. Geraldine Chouard and Daniele Pitavy-Souques. Rennes: Presses Universitaires de Rennes, 2005. 25–32. Print.

Eudora Welty House Accession Register: Books. Jackson, MS: Eudora Welty House, 12 Aug. 2011. Print.

"The Eudora Welty House Garden." *The Eudora Welty House.* 2006. Web. 2 Feb. 2012.

Galey, Forrest. "Eudora Welty Collection at Mississippi Department of Archives and History." *Eudora Welty Review* 3 (2011): 190–198. Print.

Gerbing, Gustav. *Camellias.* Fernandina, FL: G. G. Gerbing, 1943. Print.

Gordon, Leslie H. "Eudora Welty's Theatrical Sketches of 1948: Summer Division or Lost Potential? 'Bye-Bye, Brevoort' and Other Sketches." Thesis. Georgia State University, 2010. Paper 102, Digital Archive @ Georgia State University. Web. 24 Feb. 2012.

Green, A. Wigfall. *The Man: Bilbo.* Baton Rouge: Louisiana State University Press, 1963. Print.

Kreyling, Michael. *Author and Agent: Eudora Welty and Diarmuid Russell.* New York: Farrar, Straus, Giroux, 1991. Print.

Laney, Ruth. "Man of Letters." *Country Roads.* Jan. 2012. Web. 28 Jan. 2012.

Lawrence, Elizabeth. *Gardening for Love: The Market Bulletins.* Ed. Allen Lacy. Durham, NC: Duke University Press, 1987. Print.

———. *A Southern Garden: A Handbook for the Middle South*. Chapel Hill: University of North Carolina Press, 1942. Print.

———. *Through the Garden Gate*. Ed. Bill Neal. Chapel Hill: University of North Carolina Press, 1990. Print.

Lear, Edward. *Nonsense Books*. 1888. Boston: Little, Brown, and Company, 1917. Print.

Leuchtenburg, William E. *The White House Looks South: Franklin D. Roosevelt, Harry S. Truman, Lyndon B. Johnson*. Baton Rouge: Louisiana State University Press, 2005. Print.

Marrs, Suzanne. *Eudora Welty: A Biography*. New York: Harcourt, 2005. Print.

———. *One Writer's Imagination: The Fiction of Eudora Welty*. Baton Rouge: Louisiana State University Press, 2002. Print.

———. Personal interview. 5 Aug. 2011.

———. *The Welty Collection: A Guide to the Eudora Welty Manuscripts and Documents at the Mississippi Department of Archives and History*. Jackson: University Press of Mississippi, 1988. Print.

Marrs, Suzanne, and Harriet Pollack, eds. *Eudora Welty and Politics: Did the Writer Crusade?* Baton Rouge: Louisiana State University Press, 2001. Print.

McLemore, Richard Aubrey, ed. *A History of Mississippi*, vol. 2. Hattiesburg: University and College Press of Mississippi, 1973. Print.

Middleton, Drew. "Allied Airmen Severely Lash Sicily; Raid Gerbini 20 Times in One Day." *New York Times* 9 July 1943: 1. *ProQuest Historical Newspapers: The New York Times (1851–2008)*. Web. 4 Feb. 2012.

Mississippi Department of Archives and History Online Catalog. Mississippi Department of Archives and History, Archives and Records Services Division. Web.

"Negro Troops Fail, Eastland Asserts: Mississippi Senator, Carrying On FEPC Filibuster, Quotes New York Times." *New York Times* 30 June 1945: 9. *ProQuest Historical Newspapers: The New York Times (1851–2008)*. Web. 4 Feb. 2012.

"Our Tanks Smash Into Suburbs of Paris, Vatican Paper Reports City Liberated." *New York Times* 20 Aug. 1944: 1. *ProQuest Historical Newspapers: The New York Times (1851–2008)*. Web. 12 Feb. 2012.

Polk, Noel. *Eudora Welty: A Bibliography of Her Work*. Jackson: University Press of Mississippi, 1994. Print.

Pollack, Harriet. "Reading John Robinson." *Mississippi Quarterly* 56.2 (2003): 175–208. Print.

Popham, John M. "4,000 In Mississippi Want Truman Out: They Call on 'All True, White Jeffersonian Democrats.'" *New York Times* 13 Feb. 1948: 1. *ProQuest Historical Newspapers: The New York Times (1851–2008)*. Web. 4 Feb. 2012.

Prenshaw, Peggy Whitman, ed. *Conversations with Eudora Welty*. Jackson: University Press of Mississippi, 1984. Print.

———. *More Conversations with Eudora Welty*. Jackson: University Press of Mississippi, 1996. Print.

Rickett, Harold William. *Wild Flowers of the United States: The Northeastern States*, vol. 1. Ed. William C. Steere et al. New York: McGraw-Hill Book Company, 1966. Print.

Robinson, John F. Letters to Eudora Welty. Welty (Eudora Alice) Collection. Mississippi Department of Archives and History, Jackson, Mississippi.

———. "Room in Algiers." *New Yorker* (19 Oct. 1946): 82+. Print.

Robinson, Michael G. "John Fraiser Robinson." Message to the author. 12 Aug. 2011. E-mail.

Russell, Diarmuid. "AE (George William Russell)." *Atlantic Monthly* 171 (February 1943): 51–57. Print.

———. Letters to Eudora Welty. Welty (Eudora Alice) Collection. Mississippi Department of Archives and History, Jackson, Mississippi.

———. "The Literature of Utility." *Tomorrow* IV (March 1945): 34–35. Print.

———. "Raymond Chandler and the Future of Whodunits." *New York Times*, 17 June 1945: BR4. *ProQuest Historical Newspapers: The New York Times (1851–2007)*. Web. 15 Aug. 2011.

Schneider, Carl J., and Dorothy Schneider. *An Eyewitness History: World War II*. New York: Facts on File, 2003. Print.

"Sense and Sensibility." *Time* 42 (27 Sept. 1943): 100–101. Print.

Serpas, Geary. "Antique (Pre-1900) Camellias." Chart. *White and Antique Varieties—Complete Sizing List*. American Camellia Society, Feb. 2011. Web. 7 Mar. 2012.

Seymour, Edward Loomis Davenport. *The Garden Encyclopedia*. New York: W. H. Wise & Co., 1939. Print.

"SICILY BASES RAIDED AROUND THE CLOCK: North Africa and Middle East Planes Encounter Few Enemy Interceptors." *New York Times* 8 July 1943: 1. *ProQuest Historical Newspapers: The New York Times (1851–2008)*. Web. 7 Feb. 2012.

"Strange Plants Bloom in London Where Nazi Bombs Leveled City: Public Imagination Traces Growth to 18th Century—Science Sees Influence of Birds, Wind, and Dobbin's Feedbag." *New York Times* 28 July 1943: 12. *ProQuest Historical Newspapers: The New York Times (1851–2008)*. Web. 30 Dec. 2011.

Swearingen, Bethany C. *Eudora Welty: A Critical Bibliography, 1936–1958*. Jackson: University Press of Mississippi, 1984. Print.

Trilling, Diana. "Fiction in Review." *The Nation*, 152 (2 Oct. 1943): 386–387. Print.

Unrue, Darlene Harbour. *Katherine Anne Porter: The Life of an Artist*. Jackson: University Press of Mississippi, 2005. Print.

"Victory Mail Online Exhibit." *Smithsonian National Postal Museum*. Smithsonian Institution, 2008. Web. 05 Mar. 2012.

Weill, Susan. *In a Madhouse's Din: Civil Rights Coverage by Mississippi's Daily Press, 1948–1968*. Westport, CT: Praeger, 2002. Print.

Welty, Chestina. "History of the Jackson Garden Club, Jackson, Mississippi, 1931–1953." Welty (Eudora Alice) Collection, Mississippi Department of Archives and History, Jackson, Mississippi. Print.

Welty, Eudora. *The Complete Novels.* New York: Library of America, 1998. Print.

———. "Department of Amplification." *New Yorker,* January 1, 1949. Print.

———. *Early Escapades.* Ed. Patti Carr Black. Jackson: University Press of Mississippi, 2005. Print.

———. *Eudora.* Selected and edited by Patti Carr Black. Jackson: Mississippi Department of Archives and History, 1984. Print.

———. *Eudora Welty as Photographer.* Ed. Pearl Amelia McHaney, with contributions by Sandra S. Phillips and Deborah Willis. Jackson: University Press of Mississippi, 2009. Print.

———. *The Eye of the Story: Selected Essays and Reviews.* New York: Random House, 1978. Print.

———. "José de Creeft." *The Magazine of Art* 37 (February 1944): 42-47. Print. Rpt. in *Occasions.*

———. Letters to John Robinson and Diarmuid Russell. Welty (Eudora Alice) Collection. Mississippi Department of Archives and History, Jackson, Mississippi.

———. *Occasions: Selected Writings.* Ed. Pearl Amelia McHaney. Jackson: University Press of Mississippi, 2009. Print.

———. *One Time, One Place.* New York: Random House, 1971. Print.

———. *Photographs.* Jackson: University Press of Mississippi, 1989. Print.

———. *Stories, Essays, and Memoir.* New York: Library of America, 1998. Print.

———. "Women! Make Turban In Own Home!" *Junior League Magazine* XXVIII (November 1941): 20–21, 62. Print. Rpt. in *Occasions.*

———. *A Writer's Eye: Collected Book Reviews.* Ed. Pearl Amelia McHaney. Jackson: University Press of Mississippi, 1994. Print.

Welty, Eudora, and William Maxwell. *What There Is to Say We Have Said: The Correspondence of Eudora Welty and William Maxwell.* Ed. Suzanne Marrs. Boston: Houghton Mifflin Harcourt, 2011. Print.

Welty Family Photographs and Family Photo Album. Welty (Eudora Alice) Collection. Mississippi Department of Archives and History, Jackson, Mississippi.

Welty Family Photographs. Personal Collection of Mary Alice Welty White and Elizabeth Welty Thompson.

White, Katharine Sergeant Angell. *Onward and Upward in the Garden.* New York: Farrar, Straus, Giroux, 1979. Print.

White, Mary Alice Welty. Personal interview. 3 Aug. 2011.

Wood, Allen H. *Bulbs for Your Garden.* Boston: Houghton Mifflin, 1936. Print.

INDEX

Iris, 15, 18, 25, 26, 27, 56, 85–86, 98, 110, 119, 123, 126, 127, 128, 129, 149, 162, 165, 167, 174, 184, 185, 188, 208; African, 105; Algerian (*stylosa marginata*), 78, 79, 89, 155, 159; Beuchley's Giant, 168; Black Wings, 168; Brazilian, 168; dream of, 57; Dutch, 53, 121, 122, 124, 199; Dymia, 168; Far West, 128; Giant Baldwin, 128; Great Lakes, 128, 168; Japanese, 84; Louisiana, 86, 125, 166; native, 42; Pluie d'or, 61; Prairie Sunset, 128; Shining Waters, 168

Italian Campaign: Anzio, Italy, 126, 129; Robinson's night fighter missions, 140, 142, 146, 149; Rome taken by Allies, 130; Sicily invasion, 86–87, 90, 93

Italy: art in, 11; Corsica, 162, 163; Florence, 152; gardens, 99–100; Perseus statue in, 162; Rome, 162

Ixias, 33, 221

Ixioides odorata, 222

Jacaranda, 62

Jack-in-the-pulpit, 129

Jackson, Mississippi
bootlegger, 19
Canton Road, 149, 152, 175, 215
Emporium, 173
garden clubs, 29, 88, 197, 248n47, 253n14, 253n19
Jitney Jungle, 117
Junior League, 31, 35, 241n33, 243n24
military bases, 35, 36
military planes, 35, 85
movie theaters, 14, 85
Night-Blooming Cereus Club, 91
post office, 53
residents: children, 22, 66, 68, 70, 85,

100, 125, 126; Christmas tree salesman (Alphonse), 16, 153–54; Mrs. Fox, 9, 88, 98; Mrs. Lester Franklin, 74; Florence Lehman, 106, 107; Frank Lyell, xxviii, 75, 151, 245n1; Judge G. Garland Lyell, 98; Mrs. MacGowan, 127, 167, 248n47; Seta Alexander Sancton, 74, 117; Sassafras seller, 50; Aimee Shands, 70, 100, 115, 123, 243n24, 247n32; Aunt Alma Shands, 118; Dr. Harley Shands, 48, 117, 118, 123, 247n32 (see also Robinson, John Fraiser)
storms, 13, 52–53, 86, 107, 128, 166, 188, 220–22 Jackson *Clarion-Ledger*, 209; letters to, 171, 178, 251n46

Japanese beetles, 68

Jasmine (jessamine): Cape Jessamine, 8, 29, 152, 162; Confederate Jessamine, 25, 168; night-blooming, 72; yellow, 24, 115, 119, 198, 221

Jeep, 88, 89, 92–93

Jimson weed, 169

Jitney Jungle, 117

John Lane (publisher), 119

Johnny Appleseed, 6, 42, 44–45, 239n6

Jones, C. D., 138–39, 146, 149, 169

Jonquil, 6, 51, 106, 114, 217

July 4th, 131, 133

Junior Commandoes, 66, 68

Junior League, 31, 35, 241n33, 243n24

Kangaroo Paw, 64

Katonah, New York, 123; improvements to, 53, 103, 112, 186; visits by Welty, 5, 11, 28, 31–32, 39, 61, 72, 79–80, 123, 195–96, 224–25

Lady slipper, 83

Ladybug, 125